Nationalism, Imperialism and Identity in
Late Victorian Culture

Nationalism, Imperialism and Identity in Late Victorian Culture

Civil and Military Worlds

Steve Attridge

palgrave
macmillan

First published 2003 by
PALGRAVE MACMILLAN
Houndmills, Basingstoke, Hampshire RC21 6XS and
175 Fifth Avenue, New York, N.Y. 10010
Companies and representatives throughout the world

PALGRAVE MACMILLAN is the global academic imprint of the Palgrave Macmillan division of St. Martin's Press, LLC and of Palgrave Macmillan Ltd. Macmillan® is a registered trademark in the United States, United Kingdom and other countries. Palgrave is a registered trademark in the European Union and other countries.

ISBN 0–333–80251–9

This book is printed on paper suitable for recycling and made from fully managed and sustained forest sources.

A catalogue record for this book is available from the British Library.

Library of Congress Cataloging-in-Publication Data
Attridge, Steve.
   Nationalism, imperialism, and identity in late Victorian culture: civil and military worlds/Steve Attridge.
      p.cm.
   Includes bibliographical references and index.
   ISBN 0–333–80251–9 (cloth)
      1. Great Britain – History, Military – 19th century. 2. South African War, 1899–1902 – Foreign public opinion, British. 3. National characteristics, British – History – 19th century. 4. Popular culture – Great Britain – History – 19th century. 5. Nationalism – Great Britain – History – 19th century. 6. South African War, 1899–1902 – Literature and the war. 7. Great Britain – History – Victoria, 1837–1901. 8. Imperialism – History – 19th century. 9. Soldiers in literature. I. Title.
DA68.A88 2002
320.54'0941'09034—dc21   2002028677

10   9   8   7   6   5   4   3   2   1
12   11   10   09   08   07   06   05   04   03

Printed and bound in Great Britain by
Antony Rowe Ltd, Chippenham and Eastbourne

For my parents and my son Jake

Contents

List of Illustrations

Preface

This book offers an account of the re-fashioning of ideas about national character in late Victorian culture, with a wide reference to literature and popular culture around the time of the Boer War (1899–1902), and a particular scrutiny of images of the soldier. In specific images, narratives and motifs, the book highlights dynamic tensions between the external boundaries of empire and those of civil society, and between class antagonisms and national projections. I show how the trauma of the Boer War for British political culture may be explored in changing representations of the soldier. These changes cannot be theorized adequately in terms of an intensification of patriotism, the development of nationalism or the crisis of imperialism. A pervasive approach, often drawing on the work of Edward Said, has as its central premise that imperial polity imposes a discourse of domination on its recalcitrant Other. This approach will be found to lack the conceptual nuances needed to address the different forms of representation examined in the book, and observes that the idea of discourse theory to explain all forms and ideas is a brittle orthodoxy that asserts without detailed explanation. These different forms represent a range of responses to the repercussion of the war on the relation between the external boundaries of Empire and the shifting internal boundaries between state and civil society, civilian and military identities, class antagonisms and national projections. Changes in the image of the soldier bear the irresistible politicization as well as the burdens of the attempted pacification of those related internal and external boundaries. New sources and materials are introduced here.

I would like to thank Professor John Stokes and Professor Fred Inglis for their patience and constructive criticisms, and for their friendship.

STEVE ATTRIDGE

Introduction

For England, the Boer War (1899–1902) was a pendulum that swung not only between centuries, but between national assurance and introspection, between Victorian certainties and the doubts and vicissitudes of modernity, between a national character that knew exactly who it was and one which was confused. Even the War Office took up arms against itself. The 'Africans' versus the 'Indians', so named because of their military backgrounds, was a vituperative and often underhand war itself. The Africans comprised Garnet Wolseley, Commander-in-Chief Major-General Sir John Ardagh, General Sir Redvers Buller; the Indians included Lord Roberts, Major-General Sir Penn Symons and Lieutenant-General Sir George White. Wolseley wanted army reform but met with resistance from an administrative machinery locked in a time warp. Where was the problem? For nearly fifty years Britain had waged war on a shoestring, bullets against spears, soldiers against mostly disunited African and Indian tribesmen. The stuff of legend was satisfied in occasional heroic sieges, as in the battle of Rorke's Drift, but always the main British Army would arrive to slaughter the enemy.

Little strategic thinking was needed, so when the Boer War began on 11 October 1899, it was assumed by everyone (except Buller) that it would be business as usual. Send in an advanced force that would do whatever heroics were necessary, then the main body of troops would arrive, steamroller any Boer resistance, and everyone could come home. It would be short but not too troublesome. The Secretary of State for War, the Marquis of Lansdowne, sided with the 'Indians'. Parliament gave no coherent lead: 'So far as British politicians were concerned, it might be said that the greater the inefficiency of the army (except on military parades and annual military tournaments) the greater the contentment.'[1] Poor sister to the navy, the army was short on supplies, artillery, manpower and ideas. It was a small-war army that had no idea it was about to embark on a big war.

When war began, with the Orange Free State joining the Transvaal against the British, the Boers had field artillery, thousands of rapid-fire Mauser rifles, and 'Long Tom' cannons. The veld was home; they knew the terrain well, of course, which Sir George White (an 'Indian') definitely did not when he led the initial force of 15 000 men. He ignored Buller's advice, to entrench forces and not venture too far into Northern Natal, and was caught out by a Boer invasion.

At first the Boers had considerable success. British forces were sealed off and besieged in Mafeking and Ladysmith. A British expectation that set-piece battles would determine the outcome was wholly misplaced. The Boers simply didn't fight like that. Kitchener thought it outrageous when he arrived. Why wouldn't they stand still and allow themselves to be shot, like poorly armed tribesmen?

> The Boers are not like the Sudanese who stood up to a fair fight. They are always running away on their little ponies... there are a good many foreigners among the Boers but they are easily shot as they do not slink about like the Boers themselves.[2]

Clearly, tactical withdrawals and aggressive defence were ideas wholly alien to the British military mind. The trench became a new weapon. The Boers dug in, either literally or by using the terrain, and tempted the British into the open. Mounted infantry conducted quick attacks and counter-attacks. The British forces were slow and cumbersome. Officers needed wagons for their champagne, regimental uniforms, portable baths, well-stocked kitchens, gramophones and occasionally, pianos.[3] Consequently they could never travel far from a railway line. The Boers knew this from the outset and began train and line wrecking to cut off supplies.

The structure of Thomas Pakenham's seminal book, *The Boer War*, itself suggests the main phases of the war: Part 2 is called 'Buller's Reverse', Part 3 is 'Roberts's Advance', and Part 4 'Kitchener's Peace', though each title I take to be ambiguous. Buller is not, Pakenham argues, the hapless figure many thought him to be, Roberts's advance was often a counterproductive steamrollering, and Kitchener's peace extended the 'scorched earth' policy of burning houses and farms, and dumping civilians in concentration camps.[4]

The war is a story of reversals, miscalculations, pyrrhic victories and betrayals – mostly of the British by the British. The best generals of the war were exclusively Boer: De Wet, De La Rey, Botha and Smuts himself perhaps. The storming of Spion Kop had echoes of the Charge of the Light Brigade during the Crimean War; the reversals at Colenso, the death rate from disease, all contributed to what some, such as Wolseley, knew – the British army was a dinosaur and the world had changed. A culture of blame festered through the upper echelons of the army. Roberts starved Buller of troops when he needed them in Natal, then had him sacked and made the whipping boy for military failures.[5] It was, as one of Roberts's old soldiers said, 'the worst run war ever – no transport, no grub, nothing'.[6]

The Boers never had more than 40000 men in the field. The British numbered 450000 at the height of the war; 7792 British were killed in action and 13250 from disease. The Boers lost 6000 men, while 26370 women and children died in concentration camps. The official figure of 14154 blacks dying in camps is now known to be wrong. It was over 20000 – they were incarcerated because the British feared they might help the Boers and because a cheap labour force would be needed once the gold mines in Witwatersrand were reopened. Such was Africa at the turn of the century.[7]

A mountain of print and pictures such as the world had never seen accompanied the war. Unsurprisingly many of them were concerned with soldiers and this book is about them – not the real flesh and blood characters with names and addresses and graves, but the representations of them, whether for political and polemical purposes, or to entertain, enthral, shock or persuade. The ghosts of the real are somewhere behind them, but this is a study of texts and images, not a history. The images say something about the history, about what a people thought of themselves, or wished to think of themselves, and it is part of my purpose to suggest that behind and alongside the bluster of imperialist language, and sometimes pulsing at the heart of it, is anxiety and introspection. During 1890–1900 the empire swelled (in Africa control was secured of Rhodesia, Nigeria, Uganda, Kenya, Nyasaland, the Sudan, the Orange Free State and the Transvaal) but newspapers still expressed fears of putrefaction from within, of imperial and national collapse. There were invasion scares, as in, for example, Erskine Childer's *The Riddle of the Sands*. England's cities were often compared to jungles, full of malcontents and ill-bred roughs. Britain no longer had enough ships to be strong everywhere and the army was in a far worse state. There were Russian forces at the Afghan border. The Boer War was going badly and international opinion was not with the British – France and Germany were particularly hostile, and even at home there were voices speaking out against it. The war eventually cost £20 000 000. The British were not invincible. Britain was, of course, still a powerful nation, *the* most powerful nation, but what exactly did that now mean?

The common claim in late Victorian England that the British nation was the apotheosis of unity, became, for many, an imperative during the Boer War. The idea of the nation as both a recognizable unity of peoples and as a unifying principle epitomized the fully developed Western nation-state, in which nationality and state were conflated: a people with a cultural and historical identity in a permanent territory which harboured the traces of ancestral lines, and in which the state, as an instrument of law and material distribution, was also assumed to be an instrument of the nation. Persuasively conceptualized, the nation-state could appear to transcend social classes, remain impervious to the different and conflicting interests of society and signify what Hannah Arendt, in her discussion of nationalism in *The Origins of Totalitarianism*, calls 'the true and only representative of the nation as a whole'.[8]

The development of the nation-state was partly articulated and engendered by what Benedict Anderson calls 'print capitalism', a period when writing meets technology and creates a new political impetus in the speed of distribution and sheer mass of print. When, as Anderson argues in *Imagined Communities*, the three cultural conceptions of a sacerdotal script language, absolute belief in divinely sanctioned monarchs, and a temporal conflation of cosmology and history, lost their absolute ontological grip on a people's thinking, nothing was perhaps more precipitous than 'print capitalism' in the search of 'rapidly growing numbers of people to think about themselves, and to relate themselves to others, in new ways'.[9] At such a moment, he writes: 'the convergence of capitalism and print technology on the fatal diversity of human languages created the possibility of a new form of imagined community which in its basic morphology set the stage for the modern nation'.[10]

The nation is to a great extent what its members imagine it to be. In this context, the images, forms and representations I analyse here suggest that 'imagining the nation' primarily reveals the act of imagining itself, rather than any innate properties of the nation; also that this imagining of the nation is ambiguously placed in its attempt to overcome the discrepancies between ideals of the nation and social and political actualities.

It is in the alchemy of assumptions, beliefs and theories concerning the imagined community of nation that phantasmagoria were made. I show how, in a wide range of sources, the soldier is variously cast as a metaphor for the nation, as epitomizing both the best and worst of the nation, as Romantic hero and as urban malcontent. Different kinds of certainties, uncertainties and ambiguities inform images of the soldier at a time when the army was very much in the public mind.

Terms such as nation-state, nationalism, imperialism and patriotism must be distinguished from each other, if they are not to be conflated to the point of collapse. It is difficult, for example, to see exactly why the three volumes of *Patriotism: The Making and Unmaking of British National Identity*, edited by Raphael Samuel, are so called. I assume that the title offers a self-explanatory definition of patriotism, but the Preface shifts its own rhetorical ground, so that in one paragraph 'patriotic sentiments' elapse into 'national identity', 'nationalism' and 'national appeal'.[11] Similarly, in John MacKenzie's *Propaganda and Empire: The Manipulation of British Public Opinion 1880–1960*, sentences such as 'Hugh Cunningham sees the 1870s as the vital decade in the wedding of patriotism to the new nationalist, imperialist, and royalist ideology, in the new romantic treatment of the Indian Empire, and the famous outburst of jingoism of 1878' are offered as if the terms used are easily identifiable and more easily distinguished.[12]

I take imperialism to mean a political system involving the governing of colonies from an imperial centre, either directly or indirectly, which also has economic aims in the investment and control of markets in those colonies. Imperialism often assumes a mission, a civilizing role, either real or imagined. In the 1890s the word was adopted by advocates, led by Chamberlain, to promote the British Empire at the expense of home development, the supporters of which were decried as 'Little Englanders'. Yet the empire was a protean and sometimes arbitrary vessel, acknowledging and discarding nationalities, customs and allegiances according to the moment, and in an alchemy of convenience, economy, sentiment, blood and profit. Its loyalties could be confusing, even to itself, and its policies convoluted and contradictory.[13] Nationalism emanates from a sense of belonging to a common race, language and history, invariably defined by territory. The ideology attached to this exalts the nation-state as the pinnacle of political organization and demands loyalty from its citizens. In trying to differentiate nationalism and patriotism Grainger says in his book, *Patriotisms*:

> Rather than distinguish patriotism from nationalism it might be better to differentiate between kinds of patriotisms and to think of nationalism as an historical category, patriotism as its latest locus or 'form', and to have recourse to Carlton Hayes's conclusion that nationalism is a critical fusion of patriotism and national consciousness.[14]

Given that there was not universal support for the Boer War, the term 'patriot' begins the century ambiguously. One could be for England in principle and patria but against its activities abroad. It is interesting to note that in *The New Fontana Dictionary of Modern Thought* the word 'patriotism' does not even warrant an entry, whereas 'nationalism' and 'imperialism' are perceived as culturally active terms, suggesting that for some, patriotism has no currency in twentieth century thinking.[15] Of course, these terms are notoriously slippery and Janus-faced, and can often only be contextually defined, as evinced in works such as *The Imperialist Imagination* (ed. S. Friedrichsmeyer), S. Smith's *British Imperialism*, T. Lloyd's *Empire* and R. Griffiths's *Patriotism Perverted*.[16]

Clearly royalty held a powerful imaginative hold over the machinery of the British Empire. By the time of the Boer War the monarch in England had passed from absolute constitutional power to national symbol. The political powers of the monarchy were circumscribed in what was now a limited, constitutional nation-state, but Victoria was still both national myth and Empress of India, both mother to the nation and imperial icon. In such a political climate in which both the monarch and the nation had become part of a symbolic order, with the national flag as a valuable 'commercial asset', as Cecil Rhodes was later to say,[17] there was a precarious balance between nation and state. The liberal individualism of British political life fostered the illusion that the state ruled over what Arendt calls 'mere individuals, when in reality it ruled over classes, and which saw in the state a kind of supreme individual before which all others had to bow'.[18] It was in this fundamental contradiction between nation and state that nationalism became a bond between individuals and the state, between a centralized state and an atomized society. Once the idea of 'the nation' is distinguished from the constitutional binding of the 'nation-state', its complex and conceptually difficult nature is revealed.

Taking his cue from Ernest Gellner's book *Thought and Change*, that the nation proper can only come into being once it has been imagined, Anderson writes that the nation is 'an imagined political community – and imagined as both inherently limited and sovereign'.[19] He offers an analysis of the cenotaphs and tombs of Unknown Soldiers as potent emblems of modernity, evocations of the timeless and eternal, potent precisely because of the absence of real mortal remains, but therefore 'saturated with ghostly national imaginings'. The lack of specific identity is, he argues, a sign of the imaginative potency of these tactile symbols for the observer: 'What else could they be but Germans, Americans, Argentinians ...?'[20] The soldier is an archetype, symbolizing race and nation.

As Hobsbawm has argued, in *Nations and Nationalism since 1870*, 'race' and 'nation' became conflated in popular usage, so that the idea of nation as racially determined, itself a precursor to the belief in racial hierarchies, led inevitably to warring nations.[21] 'Patriotism', with its connotations of identification with more or less liberal constitutional arrangements yet its fervent displays which exceed any such limited measure, can be seen as symbol and symptom of this fundamental slide from nation-state to nationalism. British patriotism at the turn of the century is protean, and the varied uses of the term in contemporary sources embrace heritage, race, 'blood and soil' identifications and local and national custom. It is an associative term, politically embedded in the growth of the nation-state, both assertive and uncertain in its harnessing of the imperial to the domestic.

It is in the context and consequences of Cecil Rhodes dictum, 'expansion is everything'[22] that we can see empire exposing the contradiction of the nation-state and as requiring a form of nationalism which leads indissolubly to imperialist designs. Surplus capital reached the borders of the nation and needed further outlets and further labour; if accumulation were to be realized, it had to travel. Arendt argues, as did J.A. Hobson and Lenin, that this economic impetus redefined the relationship of the bourgeoisie to the body politic; for the bourgeoisie entered the political sphere by default:

> The bourgeoisie turned to politics out of economic necessity; for it did not want to give up the capitalist system whose inherent law is constant economic growth, it had to impose this law upon its home governments and to proclaim expansion to be an ultimate political goal of foreign policy.[23]

The concept of expansion in this context is politically cloaked, originating 'in the realm of business speculation... characteristic of the nineteenth century'.[24] However, economic expansion, which, theoretically, is only limited by the globe itself, is based on the unlimited productivity of man, whereas constant political expansion has no such energizing resource and carries the seeds of its own collapse: 'the nation state is least suited to unlimited growth because the genuine consent at its base cannot be stretched indefinitely, and is only rarely, and with difficulty, won from conquered peoples'.[25] Furthermore, the intrinsic instability of imperial conquest, even when justified by the export of the Revolution, had been demonstrated within Europe itself by the reverses of the French Revolutionary armies: 'The inner contradiction between the

nation's body politic and conquest as a political device had been obvious since the failure of the Napoleonic dream'.[26]

Cecil Rhodes was nothing if not a dreamer and if he had not invented
himself, others would have, because he both articulated and represented
what the conflation of economic expansion and political goals were
fuelled by: the adoption of a very particular kind of patriotism where
ostensible support for constitutional ideals thinly disguises economic
interests and racially defined political hegemony. Rhodes statement
that the national flag was a good 'commercial asset'[27] epitomizes the economic and nationalist impetus of late nineteenth century British imperialism in the South African expeditions, but this was wedded to the
gentlemanly virtues of duty and honour, made in the crucible of public
schools, ostensibly available to all Englishmen but only economically
viable for a wealthy few who could look for an investment income
abroad. Cain and Hopkins' *British Imperialism: Innovation and Expansion
1688–1914*, argues for an understanding of British society as the *a priori*
necessity for comprehending activity at the far reaches of empire, and
the kinds of public personalities mediating between the two, such as
Rhodes.[28] However, while Cain and Hopkins's work argues compellingly
for seeing British expansion as a reflection of developments in British
society in general, and of a consensus of gentry capitalism in particular,
expansion also revealed differences and conflicts in British society.

Clearly, not all those involved in the scramble for Africa were looking
for lucrative overseas incomes; most had nothing to invest, so the scramble included gold diggers, looters, outsiders – many of them Britain's
rejects – but all eventually encompassed by the necessarily broad conviction that they collectively represented national character. Collectively,
these individuals were what Arendt refers to as the 'mob', a term which
gained a fearful imaginative hold in England during the Boer War.
Only when the scramble for gold had already started did the Uitlanders
and gold hunters turn to the British government for political protection,
so that gold hunger became politicized into the desire for either a
Uitlander republic, which the British government did not want, or a
British Federation of South Africa. An important agent in this process of
politicizing that was already under way was the appeal to national
character, strongly related to Alfred Milner's notion of English 'race
patriotism'.[29]

Proponents of the idea of England as a nation-state with an imperial mission idealized and depended upon the idea of 'national character' throughout the Boer War. Representations of 'national character'
expose changing relations between military and civil society; in such

representations class interests and conflicts become visible. Purveyors of national character as an imperial asset could argue, as did H.F. Wyatt, a regular contributor to *The Nineteenth Century*, for the salutary effects of war as 'the supreme test of national value' and a necessary precondition of social evolution. He states: 'wars in our time are the expression of vast natural forces, having their roots far down in national character'.[30]

Appeals to national character, as exemplified in Wyatt's assertion, appeal to the essentially republican idea of citizens as soldiers, and the Boer War signifies an important moment for a realignment between borders of empire and the concerns of civil society. Images of the soldier in a range of literary and popular forms display nationalist fervours which aspire to unification, but also display political dissent, in which the shifting boundaries of empire and the ostensible fixity and stability of civilian life are both forced together and questioned. The nation-state, nationalism and a sense of imperial destiny were in conflict to the extent that life and politics at the borders of empire could no longer be safely represented as somehow different and safely separate from civil society. The soldier was also a civilian; the army was a civil reality; deeds of empire were civil facts and not tangentially ordered reflections of the nation's own ethical self-justifications, while the simultaneous new alignment of the military and the civil exposed the contradictions of the body politic.

The analogy between the state and the man-as-soldier was useful for those who wished to persuade that not only does national character exist, but that it is, as one commentator in *The Contemporary Review* put it, 'the most precious asset in our national balance-sheet'.[31] Such comments assume a consensus, a subsumed appeal to a politically unified nation. Soldier images, strongly related to ideas about national character in the range of literary and popular forms I discuss, display the imaginary configurations of unification in nationalist fervours and longings, but they also express political dissent by revealing the ways in which the borders of empire and civilian life are forced together, and the ways in which class formation and class interests diverge in war as well as in peace.

The analysis of sources in this book draws particularly upon the work of Edward Said, but I also wish to make three necessary and strong distinctions between my own and a Saidian approach, and return to this in the conclusion.

Said's central argument in *Orientalism*, published in 1978, and refined in *Culture and Imperialism* (1993), has a functional premise: that culture and cultural forms concerned with the Orient and promulgated by the

West are expressions of power and legitimations of authority. The Orient was 'almost a European invention', Europe's 'cultural contestant' and recurring image of the Other.[32] Said identifies three main areas of authority, each of which contributes to a creation of images and meanings that legitimizes power relations between ruler and ruled; in the case of the Boer War literature, adopting a Saidian approach would mean that images are produced which, intentionally or not, literally create an 'Africa' for British rule. Said first identifies an academic approach (the authority on another culture); a more general ontological approach, involving the work of imaginative writers, economists, administrators, who take as their starting point a given distinction between East and West, based on Western superiority; thirdly, a style of domination, based on Foucault's notion of a discourse which, in the case of sources in this book, would be seen as a means of institutionalizing and authorizing British imperial rule. Discourse, as defined by Said, could 'primitivise' Africa as it 'Orientalised' the Orient.

The use of the term 'discourse' is paramount in Said's book:

> My contention is that without examining Orientalism as a discourse one cannot possibly understand the enormously systematic discipline by which European culture was able to manage – and even produce – the Orient politically, militarily, ideologically, scientifically, and imaginatively.[33]

The determinist use of 'discourse' bypasses the problem of intentionalism by arguing that domination is inherent in any trafficking between the authority of the West and the Otherness of the Orient. In this context, 'discourse' is a term which does not allow for consideration of specific literary or cultural form or differences between forms, except in their deterministic force as part of the web of discourse, itself a predeterminant of how something should be read or understood. Discourse is a prescriptively collective rather than a specifying noun and the idea of discourse theory to explain all forms and ideas is a brittle orthodoxy that asserts without detailed explanation.

In the sources I discuss, I do not assume that different forms add up to a monolithic discourse of domination or nationalism; often, forms and representations backfire and politicize when the intention has been to pacify. For example, the hooligan debate in Chapter 4 suggests the complexity of intention in maintaining civil/military boundaries which reveal class conflicts in the idea of homogeneous national character. The 'discourse' of power and domination functions ambivalently; just as the

Other (the object of discursive domination) is not in a fixed position of passivity, so the discourse itself can reveal, in its juxtaposition of the historical, the political and purely imaginative, its own inherent instabilities. Most of the writers and commentators discussed here were, in the momentary mix of history and personality and politics, trying to discover and explain what it was to be English.

Said's own theoretical stance is also problematic in that the theorizing voice is itself part of the problem of power. The discursive voice of Orientalism is a relentless assertion of critical power over the sources it seeks to place within a configuration of Western domination. In both *Orientalism* and *Culture and Imperialism* it is clear that Said's sympathies are with the represented Other, the dominated culture, to the extent that Said's critique of Orientalism has, as Benita Parry points out, 'fed into and augmented colonial discourse analysis'.[34] While this may appeal politically to the Left and to conspiracy theorists, it does not necessarily persuade theoretically, and the discourse of Orientalism should not be uncritically accepted as an all-encompassing concept. Said states, for example, that when Disraeli said in his novel *Tancred* that the East was a career, 'he meant that to be interested in the East was something bright young Westerners would find an all-consuming passion'.[35] This is by no means necessarily the case; given the emphasis upon the word 'career', Disraeli may have been referring to the lucrative possibilities in the administration of colonies without any specific interests in the East *per se*, but Said's insistence upon 'all-consuming passion' subsumes Disraeli's book as part of a larger discourse. Said's central thesis encompasses but does not distinguish.

A Saidian use of discourse is useful in bridging the gap between superstructural and base levels in textual and cultural studies, as he affirms in his critique of current Marxist theory, but it is only by paying attention to the nuances and specific difficulties of sources that fault lines may be perceived in those levels of base and superstructure. As such, in discussing the sources in this book, I am aware of the problems of textual analysis; I both draw from and impose upon the material I am using and accept this as part of the critical disposition. This seems to me to allow for intertextualizing and discursive analysis without appealing to the ostensibly neutral authority of a conceptual term, such as discourse. It is also an appeal for the virtues of practical criticism, whilst not eschewing the bridges theory can build from one set of stories to another.

I am suggesting a need to be aware of ambiguity. In Said's work, function (domination) determines form (discourse), whereas I argue that form can undermine function and that there are discrepancies between form and particular representations, which can undermine the ideological function of the work. It is for this reason – namely, the differentiating relationships between form and representation – that this book has to deal with the relation between the representation of the soldier in a range of literary and popular forms. Comparative analysis identifies both the range of images, their relatedness and points of difference and tension, and how this range is expressed across cultures of the time. During the war the very term 'soldier' becomes contentious, given the adherence to the eclectic idea of national character, in which everyone is implicated in struggles at the borders of empire; as a result it is an imperative term with which to examine the resultant blurring of the borders of the civil and the military.

Key political figures in the war included Rhodes, Jameson and Kruger in South Africa, Sir Alfred Milner (British High Commissioner at the Cape), and Chamberlain and Salisbury at home. There were, of course, several hundred thousand other key players, some of whom are mentioned here. Events which rapidly became part of Boer War mythology include the sieges of Kimberley and Mafeking, the battles of Ladysmith, Poplar Grove, Diamond Hill, and the running guerilla warfare which the Boers pursued both during and beyond the official end of the war. Thomas Pakenham's *The Boer War* is still the most comprehensive and scholarly account of the war, drawing upon hitherto unused sources. *The South African War: The Anglo-Boer War 1899–1902*, edited by P. Warwick, is also a useful historical source, as are B. Farwell's *The Great Boer War*, D. Hall's *The Hall Handbook of the Anglo-Boer War*, I. Knight's *The Boer Wars 1898–1902* and the more populist T. Jackson's *The Boer War*.[36]

I examine specifically two related concerns: first, the concept of national character in its relation with nationalism and patriotism and how this articulates relations between military and civil society and between class interests and class conflicts; secondly, I am concerned to show how images of the soldier in different literary and popular forms variously display nationalist ideals and dissent in which the borders of empire and civilian life are negotiated, affirmed or denied.

These two foci have methodological implications for the selection and treatment of source materials. The argument that nuances of dissent as well as domination are to be discerned in representations of the soldier in ways that discourse theory does not and cannot allow requires attention to the hybrid types of literary forms from popular to high culture. Furthermore, the Boer War itself gave rise to new forms of representation and so, throughout, I am trying to show something of a history in the making, and of a nation both resisting and adjusting to change. Because each chapter is concerned with mostly different kinds of sources, from music hall to novels, and each has its own sphere of scholarship and approaches, the book is less a developing argument and more a circling around recurrent images and concerns from different perspectives, much as a collection of essays might try to achieve.

In Chapter 1, I examine contemporary music hall songs, acts and reviews as primary sources for what they reveal about patriotism and nationalism, and argue that in the geographical location of halls, diversity of acts and audience response, expressions of 'nationness' and national unity also reveal disparity and class distinction. Audience identification with soldier songs and theatrical representations is countered, or at least complicated, by ironic representations and occasional ridicule, suggesting a shifting alliance between military and civil worlds. Soldiers' use of and attitudes towards music hall and popular song reveal as much ambivalence as patriotic fervour, as one might expect. Peter Bailey, J. Ellen Gainor, J.S. Bratton and Dagmar Kift are among those whose work has proved useful in finding a place within which one can usefully think about music hall culture.[37]

Chapter 2 is concerned with contemporary accounts and histories of the war published either during or soon after it ended in 1902. I make some reference to the 'official' histories of the war – the seven volumes of the *Times History of the War in South Africa (1900–1909)*, edited by Leo Amery, and the official eight volume *History of the War in South Africa (1906–1910)*, edited by General Maurice and others – but these are only of value in the recognition of their overt partisanship. I agree with Pakenham's view that Amery's *Times History* is written under the shadow of Milner and a desire for army reform while Maurice's official history was too severely edited for fear of offending both the Boers after the war and friends of the War Office.[38] More useful are popular sources, the explosive result of Anderson's 'print capitalism', which are certainly partisan, but less self-consciously so and without fear of creating offence in high places. These works, part of the enormous canon of Boer War ephemera, had a more popular readership and retain a claim to an immediacy of response to the war, most having been written during it. They are part of a range of Boer War writing, which include boy's adventure stories, journalism and weekly magazines; they seek to circumscribe a new kind of war, with its guerilla tactics on the part of the Boers, its increased technology, its speed of communication for an eager and more literate public, within a desire for chivalric warfare and homogeneous nationhood.

Chapter 3 discusses Rudyard Kipling's work in the context of the Boer War. I begin with a discussion of *The Barrack Room Ballads* and argue that their popularity throughout the 1890s lay in their continuing argument that the military is an integral part of the civil world, and that violence, class difference and conflict are part of what had to be recognized in the bringing together of empire and home. Soldiers' own ballads, borrowing heavily from Kipling's idiomatic use of language and form, are discussed as part of the impact of the *Ballads* on popular culture. Although Kipling clearly supported the war in South Africa, his position does shift from the rhetorical affirmation of the private soldier to a more reflective mode which reveals a more revisionist and cautious attitude towards the empire.[39]

In Chapter 4, I develop the specific discussion of the *Ballads* into a consideration of Kipling's crucial role in the wider context of the hooligan debate during the Boer War. Robert Buchanan's diatribe against the *Ballads* is seen as a determined attempt to recuperate a sense of nation and national character by clearly distinguishing between the proprieties of civilian ethics and the barbarism of extreme militarism.

In Chapter 5, Kipling's treatment is completed by my discussion of his poetry and its effects on the broader context of popular poetry during the war. The Boer War writings of W.E. Henley and Thomas Hardy are taken as different indicators of the problem of defining the nation among a body of popular poetry that includes dissent and belligerent affirmation of England as a militaristic nation. The proliferation of popular poetry is itself a phenomenon worthy of attention.

Chapter 6 discusses novels published around the time of the Boer War but directly concerned with the earlier Indian Mutiny. These novels display a form of nostalgia which avoids having to represent the specific problems posed by the Boer War – such as a white, highly organized adversary, the increased replacement of hand-to-hand combat with strategic and technological warfare – in which there were less obvious opportunities to valorize real or imagined individual heroics. The Mutiny fictions also offer a useful comparison with novels specifically concerned with the Boer War and South Africa, discussed in Chapter 7. In this connection, my claim is that the representation of national character is less certain and the image of the soldier undergoes a transformation, away from the institutionalized heroism of the army and towards a representation of the anti-hero of the twentieth century. As such, the lone hero mediates between civil and military worlds and highlights the contradictions in both; this focus on individuality in popular fictions makes a useful counterweight to a growing and useful reconsideration of history through biographical and autobiographical narratives, the stories of individuals, and which investigate subjectivity as opposed to just class. Christopher Kent's article, 'Victorian Social History: Post Thompson, post Foucault, post Modern', is useful in this respect, as is Patrick Joyce's *Democratic Subjects: The Self and the Social in Nineteenth Century England*.[40]

In the use of soldier images to represent the nation, there is no easy Left/Right distinction. The variety of cultural responses cut across party lines and cast doubt on easily identifiable political oppositions. The sheer variety of texts and source materials is itself part of this argument – what appears to be politically evident in, for example, popular poetry concerned with the Boer War, is countered by themes and representations in novels of the period. The methodological issue of diverse materials is a historical question since the Boer War is itself implicated in the phenomenon of changing literary form. For example, some texts are accounts hastily composed during the war which cannot be placed as journalism, as they were published in book form and do not always profess to communicate or interpret events as they happened, even if they sometimes borrow sentences and reported incidents from newspapers. They are not histories in the sense of being reflective, interpretive accounts based on documented incidents and events. They are part of a range of Boer War ephemera in which the increased speed in printing and circulation could match the extraordinary consumer demand for Boer War materials.

A popular image of the Boer War is that it is the last Victorian war, with proper hand-to-hand battles, and that it is not until some fourteen years later that the slaughter in France heralded a new industry of death in which millions could die without ever making eye contact. My claim is that it is in the Boer War that we see the beginnings of modernity. It is not the last war of the nineteenth but the first of the twentieth, and this straddling of epochs is part of its unique history. It was a new kind of war and new forms of representation arose as part of it.

1
The Music Hall

Critics and commentators at the time of the Boer War express as wide a range of views on the role of music hall as do contemporary music hall scholars. The reminiscences of J.B. Booth assert that 'the music-hall bards reflected the national feeling'[1] and MacQueen-Pope wrote that music hall was the 'fount of patriotism'.[2] Kipling believed that music halls disseminated 'the very stuff of social history'[3] while two powerful figures on the emerging Left, H.M. Hyndman and J.A. Hobson, saw them as part of a belligerent and chauvinistic imperialism.[4] Later research largely focused on the question of whether music halls were deliberately used as agents of propaganda, to both quell possible class antagonism at home and promote a form of race nationalism, as in the arguments of Lawrence Senelick,[5] or if music halls did represent popular sentiments and were therefore a form of class expression, from patriotism to working-class jingoism. This latter view is not new and reiterates the arguments of much earlier commentators, such as Booth, Max Beerbohm and Harold Scott.[6]

Recent work both compounds and elucidates the complexities inherent in examining music-hall culture. The methodological problems of how to approach music-hall entertainment lay in three distinct but related areas: the social experience of music hall which was part of a wider context of theatre; secondly, the problem of form in which songs need to be considered as musical performance within which words do not necessarily take precedence; thirdly, that the primary and economically motivated impetus of music-hall song was to entertain, and that the production of pleasure inevitably complicates without denying any political motivation or reception.

Since the 1970s the study of music hall has largely been pursued by social historians and grounded in sociological theory, as in the work of

Martha Vicinus and the earlier work of Gareth Stedman Jones (though the latter has tended more recently to look at music hall in discursive terms). However, Peter Bailey is right to argue that the 'idea of a single trajectory of development' in music-hall studies 'pays little attention to contradictions and exceptions'.[7] This has more recently diversified into, for example, Patrick Joyce's examination of the language of the halls in *Vision of the People. Industrial England and Questions of Class 1848–1915*, as part of a broader investigation into the symbolic narratives people tell about themselves. Joyce investigates subjectivity, the stories people tell about themselves to themselves, as being as crucial determinants of 'meaning' as are social 'facts'. It is in language, in its multiple forms, that identity as much as class is made.[8] Language and class are, of course, related and it is in this relatedness that much postmodernist thought struggles to remake meaning. Douglas Kift's *The Victorian Music Hall* surveys current approaches and usefully details the halls as arenas of changing social relations in England, in which audience composition provides insights into nineteenth-century society. He contextualizes and analyzes specific music-hall content caught in a mix of 'spontaneous and oppositional people's culture "from below" and commercialized mass culture "from above." '[9] The twin concerns of music hall as a product of specific social structures and a 'history from below' approach are part of a debate that will continue, and in which, as Kift recognizes, there are still often neglected areas: the specific content of acts and the audience's relationship with that content, and with the halls as places of entertainment with their own rituals and symbolic behaviour. It is in those areas that I am trying to work here, examining the detail on a large and often confusing canvas. Peter Bailey's recent work has developed from a consideration of music hall as part of a history of leisure and popular culture to a more extensive examination of specific music-hall practices. He develops fresh perspectives on performance and meaning in *Popular Culture and Performance in the Victorian City*,[10] while rigid sociological categories that tend to define music hall only in terms of social class now coexist with more discursive analyses, such as Joyce's. Christopher Kent discusses the diversity of developments in discursive and contextual studies of popular culture.[11]

The question of what constitutes patriotism and nationalism in music-hall song is a complex one. Civilian reception of military songs and responses to theatrical representations of soldiers suggest, I argue, an uneasy alliance of civil and military worlds. This relationship between the civil and the military in the context of music hall cannot be defined in terms of patriotic and/or nationalist sentiments alone.

To what extent music hall can be considered to have any political meaning necessitates considering how the halls functioned as popular entertainment and theatre, and examining available evidence regarding the
reception of songs and acts. The Boer War marks a significant moment
for the political impact of music hall in that it drew upon and coexisted
with an interest in military spectacle and the technological impact of
film; representations of the soldier then assume a new hybrid dimension
at once intensely theatrical and quasi-documentary.

The large body of music-hall memoirs is a useful source for locating
songs and acts which had considerable currency at the time of the
Boer War. Contemporary critical accounts of music hall, by such as
Clement Scott, of the *Daily Telegraph*, who also wrote regularly for the
Contemporary Review, are useful in gauging how critics who regularly
attended music halls perceived the relationship between performance
and politics. There are contemporary accounts of audience response,
such as W.R. Titterton's *From Theatre to Music Hall*,[12] which are impressionistic while having the value of first-hand experience. Such works
are part of the broad music-hall canon of contemporary performance, response and criticism, and reveal something of attitudes towards
performance and audience response, as well as themselves being a part
of music-hall culture.

Songs and acts have been chosen for specific reasons: those which
foreground the figure of the soldier when the reality and effects of the
war were prevalent and which are most frequently mentioned in music-
hall memoirs as being popular during the Boer War; songs which were
anthologized for public sale and circulation at the time, in publications
such as *The Music Hall Songster*; songs and acts reviewed in theatre publications, such as *The Era*, which is itself a valuable source of information
on songs and performers. Some of the songs and acts discussed have not
been mentioned in any of the existing literature on music hall, but were
published and circulated at the time and are mentioned in sources such
as *The Era*.

One of the central critical questions regarding the relation of music
hall to a patriotic and nationalist ideology concerns itself with whether
entertainments which express patriotic or nationalist sentiments are
motivated by supply or demand. Hobson's argument in *Imperialism:
A Study*, first published in 1902, is that the public house and the music
hall transmitted a crude jingoism, apotheosized in the Mafeking celebrations. Music hall was a 'potent educator', the only ' "popular" art of
the day' which fed and disseminated the 'fervour of jingoism'.[13] This
view has been modified but fundamentally reinforced by later research;

Laurence Senelick argues that music hall was a 'valuable tool' for mould-ing the 'political temper' of the people.[14] Hugh Cunningham argues that in a range of leisure activities, patriotism became the 'key compo-nent of the ideological apparatus of the imperialist state'.[15] As a con-trolled leisure market, music hall inhibited a lively, indigenous and possibly radical working-class culture from developing and sought to pacify potentially antagonistic class interests. Senelick concludes that in the music halls the working class heard imperial sentiments contrary to its own class interests, and cites as supporting evidence connections between the Conservative Party and music halls, such as Tory propri-etors and arrangements with the Tory drink trade.

More contemporary voices offer a rich source of accounts, nostalgias, memorabilia and analyses which are themselves a part of the music-hall credo, from the celebratory testament of W.R. Titterton to Hobson's damning critique of music hall as the expression of a nascent new imperialism.

Penny Summerfield's research indicates that rather than a wide and politically motivated attempt to feed music-hall audiences with a diet of patriotism and imperialist songs and acts, the halls experienced a mix-ture of official controls and a self-censorship which was economically rather than politically motivated.[16] Official controls took the form of fire and licensing regulations, as part of an attempt to create uniformity and respectability. Even though music halls were formally outside the Lord Chamberlain's censoring jurisdiction, it was in the commercial interests of proprietors to avoid antagonizing the authorities and the accompanying risk of any introduction of new legislative powers which may be directed at them should the halls draw too much pejorative pub-licity. The proprietors simply wished to keep their licenses, and to avoid causing offence and the possibility of licensing censure they tended to phase out anti-Establishment or overtly risqué songs in favour of senti-mentality, 'improving' patriotism and appeals to national unity. This distinction between the politics of business and the business of politics is important when assessing songs and acts because it rebuts any asser-tion that the halls simply reflected an existing sense of homogeneous nationhood and allows economic rationalization to explain the nation-alist stridency of some music-hall songs and acts.

In *Marie Lloyd and Music Hall* (1972) Daniel Farson outlines the working-class genesis of the halls, from taverns and penny gaffs to the emergence of music hall as a more 'respectable' entertainment institu-tion, particularly from the 1870s onwards.[17] By the 1890s it was possi-ble to distinguish music halls both in terms of social stratification and geography. In *Harpers New Monthly Magazine* (1891) F. Anstey identified a pattern:

> London music hall might be roughly grouped into four classes – first the aristocratic variety theatre of the West End, chiefly found in the immediate neighbourhood of Leicester Square; then the smaller and less aristocratic West End halls; next, the large bourgeois music halls of the less fashionable parts and in the suburbs; last, the minor music halls of the poor and squalid districts. The audiences, as might be expected, correspond to the social scale of the particular place of entertainment.[18]

New halls were predominantly middle-class and contemporaneous with the production of song as commodity, written mainly by lower middle-class song writers whose sentiments and perceptions of audience requirements were not necessarily those of the working class. Writing of the audience attending new halls, such as the Alhambra and Pavilion, Booth states:

> The black-coated, white-shirted, silk-hatted crowds of 'young bloods' who filled the promenades of the great Leicester Square houses ... differed vastly from those found in the Strand or in Piccadilly Circus; but in each there was an intimacy born of coteries which frequently meet.[19]

Booth does not relate his observation of social and cultural differentiation to his statements about the patriotism of the halls, but Penny Summerfield's discussion of 'patriotic extravaganzas' suggests that the most zealous expressions of patriotism and empire emanated from West End halls. In discussing a patriotic sketch called 'Britannia' at the Oxford in 1885, she states:

> A sketch like the 'Britannia' was an elaborate and expensive type of performance. It would not be shown once only, but repeatedly, and might well be taken on tour of those halls who could afford it.[20]

These halls were not patronized by a working-class audience, nor were they part of a music-hall culture, outlined by Farson, which could be said to represent working-class sentiments. It would be likely that, during the Boer War, public demonstrations of jingoism on the streets of London might be found in areas in which music-hall entertainment similarly affected jingoism; Richard Price argues that it was the lower middle classes which were most visibly jingoistic:

> The truly jingo crowd was that which disturbed peace meetings… this crowd was not a working class phenomenon. It was a typical patriotic reaction of middle class youth… with a status anxiety problem.[21]

Within the 'embourgeoisment' of the music hall, as identified by Anstey, it therefore seems possible to identify both an increase in audience differentiation and to argue that jingoistic acts and songs were largely the product of West End, middle class and 'aristocratic' halls. In Anstey's analysis of audience stratification, he states that it is in the bourgeois halls that the audience, 'not remarkable for intelligence', is pleased with 'dull songs, hoary jokes, stale sentiment, and clap trap patriotism'.[22] Suburban halls, a pale imitation of West End halls, constitute a popular culture distinct from that of the East End, where the concrete detail of everyday life in music-hall songs was more prevalent than an abstract patriotism.[23]

To understand the effects of the Boer War on music-hall representations of the soldier and the military, it is necessary to understand how music halls drew upon an already existing appetite for military plays and sketches in theatres. Some research does draw attention to the fact that music hall can only be properly considered as part of a wide spectrum of popular entertainment during the nineteenth century, and in relation to theatre forms of the period. Circus, broadsheet ballads, melodrama and the sketch, were all elements which music hall borrowed and shaped as part of its own hybrid form of entertainment. However, this alchemy of popular forms as a context for understanding music hall is not an innovative research discovery, for it was perfectly obvious to the contemporary critics and observers of music hall. Music-hall performers were also often used in military dramas, either as characters or as singers. In *The Soldiers of the Queen* two music-hall performers, Tom Pinch and Fred Lawrence, made 'considerable capital' (*Era*, 9/9/99, p. 11) out of their own comic scenes, then using them as independent music-hall acts. It is in this mutual borrowing between theatre and music hall that the latter can be best approached.

W.R. Titterton's *From Theatre to Music Hall*, published in 1912, is a well argued case for the relatedness of theatre and music hall, both in form and tradition. Earlier, in 1893, in *The Contemporary Review* E.R. Pennell argued for an understanding of music hall as the perpetuity of minstrel and theatre traditions reaching back to the Middle Ages and in which '[t]he miracle play was transformed into the variety show against which its existence, at first, had been a protest'.[24] Its function, he wrote, is to celebrate the 'heroes of civilization' but, ironically, in the 1890s, a number of those heroes he cites are soldiers with complaints against civil society or references to soldiers who are the ruination of young women, suggesting that the audience's desire to 'delight in patriotism' is couched in terms in which civil and military worlds are distinct, and the gap between them is a source of complaint, amusement and pathos. Charles Godfrey, in a white wig, 'sings the woes of the old soldier, once England's brave defender'.[25] Charles Coburn gave dramatic force to Kipling's belligerently resentful 'Tommy' and Ada Lundberg both laments and complains that 'Fur me Tommy Hatkins was a fly young man, And 'e's bin the ruingiation of 'is Mari Hann!'[26]

The theatricality of the music hall has implications for any discussion of the politics of music-hall performances. Titterton's descriptive account of going to the music hall suggests that it is the ritualized engagement of the audience, rather than the content of songs, which is being celebrated. Meaning is inherent in the act of singing rather than in the ostensible attitudinizing of song words. Titterton makes several explicit references to the Boer War and each centres on the memorability of performance rather than any explicit social meanings articulated by the words; while discussing Albert Chevalier's costermonger stage persona, he writes:

> How long ago is it when I saw him [Chevalier] last, and we each went world-touring and our orbits refused to intersect? Why, it is two reigns ago, when the Boer War and the London crowd were raging and he had just invented 'Mafficking Night' [*sic*]. Do you remember the quaint, delirious joys of that immortal ditty? Do you remember the rat-a-tat dancing march with loose legs, head stiff on the torso, and arms dangling?[27]

'Mafeking Night' appears to be as much a product of cockney song as historical event; indeed, the event as Titterton describes it is not the relief of Mafeking, but the song in performance, and it is the 'ditty' which is 'immortalized'.

The Boer War signifies an important moment in the relatedness of theatre and music hall, for it was now that the popular taste for the stage conventions of military plays, melodramas and spectaculars could be used to represent current events at the same time as news of the war was being relayed more efficiently and speedily than in earlier wars by the press and publications.

The fusion of melodrama, spectacle and the sketch allowed for both technical innovations in staging and the traditional archetypal struggle of good against evil prevalent in melodrama to complement one another. This was particularly true of military plays and spectacles. *The Era, Era Almanack, The Theatre* and *The Play–Pictorial List,* review and publicize several hundred plays for the few years leading up to and intensifying numerically during the Boer War which have a strong military theme. Titles are revealing in themselves: *England's Flag; Life and Honour; A Soldier's Devotion; The Red Squadron; The Queen's Shilling; Tommy Atkins; A Soldier and a Man; The Soldiers of the Queen; Cheer Boys Cheer.*

Tommy Atkins was one of the most popular and widely reviewed plays, gaining an enthusiastic audience in the East End, where the theme music ensured rapturous applause. It began its run in 1895 and received more column inches of reviews in the *Era* than most other plays, playing at various theatres, including the Adelphi and the Duke of York. Called by the *Era* the 'Military Drama of the Day' it had a long and various run, up to and including the Boer War years, parts of the play being presented as music-hall pieces. There are key moments in the play which, according to reviews, most excited audiences. The hero is a curate named Harold Wilson, but he is metamorphosed into the archetypal Tommy Atkins when he throws aside his church raiments:

> when they bring their hero on the stage in the sable trappings of the church; when they show him flinging off his ecclesiastical obligations and preparing to take the Queen's shilling; when they make him strike his superior officer...[28]

These are moments of distinction, the soldier being marked out by dramatic gestures as a figure dissociating himself from the authority of both the church and the military hierarchy, in ways similar to aspects of 'Tommy' in Kipling's ballads. Tommy Atkins is heroized precisely because he is not specifically identified with a military tradition or an abstract patria. Peter Bailey usefully applies the term 'knowingness' to a certain type of performance dynamic in music halls. A performer can pull the crowd 'inside a closed yet allusive frame of reference' and implicate them in a 'select conspiracy of meaning that animates them as a specific audience'.[29] Knowingness, both drawn upon and created in the performance, facilitates a domain of shared knowledge and secrets about life, custom and behaviour. This lends itself to comic pragmatism – the ironic use of official idioms and language, to nudge-and-wink humour, as well as to more overtly serious forms of shared knowledge.[30] Knowingness activates an audience from being passive consumers to co-producers, confirming the testimony of a regular: 'We went there not as spectators, but as performers'.[31] In *Tommy Atkins* the protagonist is a character who moves and is identified by the audience against specific institutions, including officers, rather than embodying them. He is more aligned with an heroic outlaw status, acting out his own code rather than a prescribed one. Towards the end of the play, when Tommy is saved from certain death whilst fighting in Egypt, at the moment of his rescue the music for 'Rule Britannia' is eclipsed by the melody of 'Tommy Atkins', amid 'general rejoicings' by the audience.[32] The 'knowing' pact between audience and Tommy is often at the expense of abstract institutionalized patriotism and nationalism rather than being subsumed to it.

However, it was in the combined development of the spectacle and morality plays that the gap between the military and civil worlds could most dramatically be embodied, particularly in those plays which depicted India and South Africa. The melodrama offered easy opportunities for racial stereotyping while the spectacle allowed the borders of empire to be depicted as remote exotica, Oriental or primitive centres of strangeness peopled by equally strange and lascivious inhabitants. Later I discuss novels about the Indian Mutiny, or Sepoy Revolt, as a form of nostalgia exactly because it became more difficult to represent the Boer War as a further glorious chapter in the history of Britain's colonial wars. Stage representations of India, and in particular the Mutiny, took on reassuringly diffuse meanings: they could satisfy a need for imperial heroics in a context that made the military world geographically and historically remote, yet victorious.

Plays about India, usually focusing on the Indian Mutiny, tended to depict Indians as both lascivious rascals and figures of fun. *The Saucy Nabob*, *The Nabob's Pickle* and *The Begum's Diamonds* suggest this predilection for pantomime ridicule, and shared with plays such as *The Indian Mutiny* and *The Star of India* an elaborate and ornate use of exotic backdrop, scenery and effects which ensured both India's difference and its status as imperial fantasy. The British soldier in these extravaganzas was dramatically uncomplicated and demanded little engagement from the audience other than unproblematic approval – he belonged historically to another time and represented what Bernard Shaw, writing in the *Era*, called 'ideal, artificial systems of morality' which we would be best rid of.[33]

Mutiny plays utilized simple characterizations and spectacle to represent the historical; Boer War dramas similarly used simple characterizations and tried to capitalize on the contemporaneity of the war. The war was a present fact; news of it was relayed daily and the theatre and music hall could draw upon public interest to guarantee attendance. Audiences were already familiar with sensational military dramas set in South Africa, not dissimilar to Mutiny plays, in that they employed spectacular backdrops suggestive of exotic and alien landscapes, even though the British soldier actors were fighting 'fuzzy-wuzzies' rather than Indians. Zulu warriors were popular in plays such as *Cetewayo at Last* and *The Zulu Chief*, but the Jameson Raid and the Boer War gave rise to over a dozen plays specifically concerned with the war, such as *Briton and Boer*, *The Soldiers of the Queen* and *The Raid on the Transvaal*. Reviews suggest that such plays used pantomime conventions to elicit audience response; the Boer President Paul Kruger would be represented as the villain, treacherous and antagonistic towards the audience, quickly followed by the entrance of dashing 'heroes', such as Dr. Jameson. The *Era*'s review of *The Soldiers of the Queen* stated that 'the references that

Figure 1.1   'Boer president Paul Kruger would be represented as the villain.'
Source: From *Punch*, 13 June 1900.

continually crop up concerning British pluck and Boer treachery generate a sort of electricity in the air, and the Hoxton Britons are swayed
accordingly'.[34]

These plays appear to have taken their racial cue from the huge success of *Cheer Boys Cheer*, by Sir Augustus Harris, Cecil Raleigh and Henry
Hamilton, which began its run in various theatres in 1895 and continued to be performed, either in whole or in part, during the Boer War.
Concerned with the Matabele War of 1893, the villain of the play is an
'Afrikaner' Jew called Meckstein, who is in South Africa to exploit its
wealth but refuses to fight for the British. Boers are portrayed as cowards
and black 'natives' are there as sexual threats to a party of English aristocratic women. The soldier hero is an aristocrat who makes a valiant
and successful last stand against the marauding Matabele natives – a
reference to Captain Wilson's battle with the Matabele which became
part of the folklore of the war.[35]

However, although the play reasserts an aristocratic patriotism, suggesting that aristocratic leadership will resolve all in South Africa, it does
not combine all its elements into a resolution that represents the British
in South Africa as a nationally unified presence. At the beginning of the
play it is made clear that it is a rejection of civil values that leads to
enlistment. The play is also a satire on capitalism, with South Africa as
the foremost playground for city spivs, dubious share deals and ensuing
military adventurism. Life at the border of empire is an adventure, but
a chaotic one, and is simply preferable to the duplicities of life at home.
The sense of nation is of a Britain fragmented, whilst the patriotic elements are clustered around an aristocratic coterie far removed from the
difficulties of society and therefore able to enact a simpler code of heroism. The valiant aristocratic officer figure also coexisted with stage representations of the bumbling officer, and this ambivalent theatrical
presence clearly appealed to audiences, who could enjoy both the nostalgia of chivalric heroism and the satirizing of upper-class officers.

As I discuss in Chapter 2, the British public were used to seeing the
military as pageant on the streets of London and other major cities.
A growing trend for and interest in real military spectacles and public
displays of the Volunteer force drilling necessarily meant that music hall
and theatre had to offer something other than pageant.[36] However,
a sense of 'the real' was engendered more by the advent of film, which
appeared to show real battles during the Boer War, rather than ordered
displays of military prowess in civilian society.

Film makers, such as R.W. Paul, were given special commissions
to make a series of films on army life in 1900 by the Adjutant General,

Sir Evelyn Wood, which suggests that the army quickly realized the opportunities afforded by film to represent the war to a mass audience in a medium which proclaimed realism but which could be edited, emphasized or simply fabricated. Many of the Boer War films, such as *The Scouts in Pursuit of the Boers* and *The Signing of the Peace of Vereeniging*, were made using extras.[37]

The Boer War was the first opportunity for film to offer a mass audience the 'actuality' of war as part of a music-hall programme. The films were an extension of theatrical conventions, using military music and spectacle, and concentrating on British heroism and Boer treachery. Clips from the films suggest that the British soldier is a figure ever advancing, either embarking for the war, or chasing Boers, hauling guns into action, accepting Boer surrenders and moving through difficult terrain. Retreats and reversals are absent and British casualties almost non-existent. Audiences were always left to assume that what they were viewing was the real thing. The truth is these events were as likely to have been filmed on Hampstead Heath with bearded Londoners as Boers, as on a South African veld.[38] Sometimes the use of film, even when it was pure documentation, was introduced by a carefully stage-managed use of spectacle and song as precursors to the film. The *Daily Mail* (16 October 1899) describes a music-hall pageant in which a troupe of soldiers sang 'Up the Old Flag', 'Rule Britannia' and 'God Save the Queen', followed by a biographic film of General Buller's departure for South Africa – all to a standing ovation. The mood is set, with the film of Buller carrying the emotional weight of the songs and performances. Pageant, the novelty of film and the excitement of seeing Buller himself could provide a vicarious sense of being part of the embarkation for the war.

Rather than diminish the status of music-hall songs, sketches and acts, film initially enhanced, until it later usurped them, in that it offered the heightened excitement of a new medium which placed assumed realism alongside overt theatricality. This was an extension of the already eclectic and varied music-hall canon.

Music-hall songs and the theatrical context of their performance create their own problems for the cultural historian. Some commentators, particularly earlier writers, such as J.B. Booth, tend to emphasize a delight in song as an indication of patriotism. What he means by patriotism is not clear, other than vague reference to 'National feeling'. What is clear is that the eclecticism of songs in music hall during the Boer War is charged with a variety of sentiments: a blood-and-soil patriotism and a nationalistic pride in race, but also with what Christopher Pulling calls 'a revealing cynicism' and at times indiscriminate 'admiration for perspiration rather than inspiration'.[39]

However, this is to focus on language rather than performance and the ritual of song and its music which can qualify or override the meaning of song words. Martha Vicinus observes that prejudicial definitions of what constitutes 'literature' hinder critical responses to popular song.[40] The use of cliché, simplistic language, repetition and ostensibly obvious sentiments in song apparently offer no substantial ground for critical manoeuvre. However, the interpretative problem here is one of form; songs are essentially musical forms in which the words do not necessarily take precedence. In performance, they also generate different meanings according to context, the relationship between performer and audience, and the complex nature of performance itself, including nuance, irony and gesture. A primary purpose of any song is to produce pleasure. Vicinus fails to consider the entertainment, musical and performance aspects of song, which are imperative to any comprehensive understanding of the form as it was used in music hall. These aspects of music-hall song, plus the need to distinguish between different kinds of hall, as Kift's work has shown, all complicate the 'patriotism' of the halls.

In *Song and Democratic Culture in Britain* Ian Watson applies Benjamin Disraeli's 'two nations' theory to cultural values and mores, arguing that often, there was reciprocal ignorance between classes which has implications for the reception of song by different classes.[41] Hugh Cunningham argues for a similar distinction to be made in which class experience and expectations lead to different conceptualizing of terms; just as 'respectability' meant different things to the working and middle classes in the mid-nineteenth century, so did the term 'patriotism' have different meanings and associations for different social groups in an age of imperialism.[42]

The imperial polity of ritual, the abstract patria of customs, laws and institutions, and the often localized patriotism of palpable realities, local customs and class allegiance, were qualitatively different expressions of 'nationness' and part of the dense texture of British life. In music-hall songs, this means that Harry Champion's celebration of 'boiled beef and carrots' or Gus Elen's eulogizing of the dustman in song were, to a certain working-class audience for whom the references were 'knowing' mirrors of everyday life, a celebration of a specific class within the nation and an attachment, sentimental or otherwise, to a discrete sense of identity within that nation.

In terms of military songs, Laurence Senelick corroborates a distinction between the 'chanson militaire' and 'chanson guerrière'. The former could include sentimental songs and might be considered as part of a broad repertoire often popular in the armed forces; the latter is the 'song embattled' and was particular to 'aristocratic' and middle-class halls in the West End and 'it tended to be fustian in language, vengeful, and bloodthirsty in tone, spirited in rhythm and monumentally stupid over all'.[43] The jingoistically patriotic songs to which he refers do, therefore, seem to belong to a particular class of society, geographically located outside working-class areas.

A good example of such songs is the Great Macdermott's 'We Don't Want to Fight' from which the term 'jingoism' was coined. The song enjoyed popularity beyond its inception in 1877, and particularly during the Boer War. Ostensibly a response to the Russo-Turkish War, its personification of nationhood and a neo-Darwinian sense of racial superiority is also an abstract confirmation of Conservative imperialism:

The Dogs of War are loose and the rugged Russian Bear...
Full bent on blood and robbery has crawled out of his lair...
As peacemaker old England her very utmost tried,
The Russians said they wanted peace, but then those Russians lied,
Of carnage and trickery they'll have sufficient feast
Ere they dare to think of coming near our Road into the East.

CHORUS

We don't want to fight, but by Jingo if we do
We've got the ships, we've got the men, and got the money too.
We've fought the Bear before, and while we're Britons true,
The Russians shall not have Constantinople.[44]

The aggressive affirmation of collective identity in which 'we' are all soldiers contrasts with the more individualized parodies of Macdermott's professional rival, Herbert Campbell. The two performers performed in the same West End halls, often on the same bill, and Senelick states that Campbell would throw 'cold water on the very sentiments his audience had been bellowing and applauding moments before'.[45] Adopting his comic persona of a 'snivelling recruit', Campbell would decry any notion of heroism:

I don't want to fight, I'll be slaughtered if I do!
I'll change my togs and sell my kit and pop my rifle too!
I don't like the war, I ain't no Briton true,
And I'd let the Russians have Constantinople.[46]

Rather than Campbell being, as Senelick believes, an anomaly in the prevalent patriotic mood, it seems more likely that the 'snivelling' persona of Campbell would act as a parody of the unwilling recruit, thereby presenting the persona to the audience for their derisive laughter. This would then provide tangential support for the strident imperial tone of Macdermott's act. Such dramatically blatant contrasts 'work' the audience and exploit its knowingness. There is a pleasure in responses being manipulated, in knowing and allowing this to occur in the 'nature of a transaction or co-production'.[47] Even if this was not the case, the contrasting attitudes may simply register both the inherent dramatic value of presenting opposites and the pleasure of ambivalence. The eclecticism of music-hall entertainment makes it difficult to assume there was a singular political temper enjoyed by an audience.

If the Great Macdermott's 'By Jingo' was performed with gusto and authority, other songs satirized military authority. The music-hall army officer was derided for his blustering incompetence, epitomizing authority without intelligence. George Bastow's 'The Galloping Major', written by Bastow and Fred W. Leigh, and sung to a galloping rhythm, is a portrayal of a vain and sexually voracious fool, always after a bit of 'Bumpity! bumpity! bumpity! bump!' and concerned with his own imagined dashing figure:

> When I was in the army
> I was a cavalry man, you know,
> And whenever I went on parade
> A magnificent picture I made.[48]

'Captain Ginjah', also sung by Bastow, is a similar character, a ladies man who is also an incompetent:

> A soldier once was I by jingo such admir'd,
> The army lost a treasure on the day that I retir'd.
> They begg'd of me to leave they asked it as a boon;
> They said my fiery whiskers made the guns go off too soon.[49]

Both songs were popular during the war, along with others portraying a similar type, such as J.W. Rickaby's 'Major General Worthington'. 'Ginjah' and the 'Major' have something in common with the effete dandyism of the 'toff', as portrayed in songs such as Rickaby's 'Silk Hat Tony' and Vesta Tilley's 'Algy'. It is a type which allows satire to undermine an upper class which assumes and has bestowed upon it undeserved status and authority.

Representations of incompetent leadership coexisted with reverence for real officers, such as Lord Roberts and Kitchener, and suggests an ambivalence in which the stage type allowed for satire which may have been unpopular were it to be aimed at real public figures. As such, the figure of the officer in popular culture contains contradictions which that same popular culture made palatable, what Colin Macinnes calls 'a barrack-room portrait of the monocled officer who is undoubtedly courageous, and undoubtedly a nit-wit'; a portrait which is 'satirical without being malicious'.[50]

It is worth considering how musical accompaniment complicates and shapes what may be seen as social meaning in song. 'The Seventh Royal Fusiliers' was a popular song performed by Charles Godfrey in the 1890s.[51] The construction is typical of many music-hall songs, consisting of verse and refrain, which evolved from the ballad form. The rhythmic structure consists of four beats to a bar, or alternating long and short beats, which help to create an heroic, quasi-military march accompaniment. There are also repetitions of chord structures, such as the D A7 D Bm sequence in the fifth bar repeated in the ninth bar, constituting a 'sub text' which pulls away from linear progression and hints more at circularity and a return to the same point. The melody suggests a ballad tradition, the lyric sentimental of single notes progressing harmoniously and although the heroic march accompaniment hints at the melody line, it also subjugates it to its own rhythmic patterns. The words form a narrative which relates a battle against the Russians, deriving from the story form of ballads, and which creates a successive series of pictures which pull the listener through the song: 'Through deadly Russian shot and Cossack spears we carved our way to glory'. In this sense, the linear sequence of the words exists in tension with the musical structure that is moving around itself. In Barthes's terms, there is a tension between the completed sign and the free signifier; the words tell of soldier Fred's heroism within a tradition of lamenting balladry, and this is a countermovement to the strident insistence of 'tempo di marcia' which, because it sets the initial tone of the song in the first four instrumental bars, determines the dominant mood of the song as march heroic.

Any reading of song words should, in other words, be considered in relation to internal tensions within the song as a musical performance piece; also, these tensions may account as much for the song's popular reception as the words. Structurally, 'The Soldiers of the Queen', written in 1881 and sung by Hayden Coffin, contains similar tensions to 'The Seventh Royal Fusiliers':

CHORUS

It's the soldiers of the queen my lads,
Who've been my lads,
Who've seen my lads,
In the fight for England's glory, lads
Of its world-wide glory let us sing
And when we say we've always won,
And when they ask us how it's done,
We'll proudly point to ev'ry one
Of England's soldiers of the queen![52]

The song was later used as a recruiting song during the Boer War and in the Boer War scenes in Noel Coward's *Cavalcade*,[53] suggesting how popular songs can become part of a wider cultural formation and that what starts as a piece of popular entertainment may be used for diverse purposes, from mainstream theatre to being given an overtly political function.

As Hugh Cunningham argues, political sentiment in song is dependent upon context:

when political songs were sung outside the conventions of theatre, in the streets ... then the context in which they are sung may be the key to their political meaning. A jingo crowd singing the jingo song may be assumed to share its sentiment.[54]

It would appear that the members of a 'jingo crowd' during the Boer War were not necessarily working class, given that both Conservative party propaganda and socialist anti-imperialist demonstrations failed to capture significant working-class support during the 1900 'khaki election'. Cunningham, following Price's arguments, stresses apathy as a key factor:

in the East End Conservatives had to appeal to more than patriotism to be successful. 'There was ... very little correlation between imperial idea and electoral success', writes Richard Price. Neither imperialism, nor for that matter socialism, were important issues in British elections between 1885 and 1910 according to Henry Pelling.[55]

The more aggressive sorts of patriotism promulgated in West End halls appear to have had little impact politically in the East End and apathy may be the key explanation for this. Gareth Stedman Jones argues that, regarding the popular culture of music hall, the emphasis was on a localized celebration which had no intention of sharing middle-class sentiment, patriotic or otherwise; in writing of working-class music hall, he states:

> Its attitude was a little bit of what you fancy does you good. Music hall was perhaps the most unequivocal response of the London work-ing class to middle-class evangelism … Music hall appealed to the London working class because it was both escapist and yet rooted in the realities of working class life.[56]

The content of many popular music-hall songs suggests that, for a working-class audience, the function of music hall was to reflect a keen interest in localized day-to-day realities and pleasures. Songs which are found in standard collections of music hall songs, such as Peter Davison's *Songs of the British Music Hall* (1971), invariably include titles such as 'Arf a Pint of Ale' and 'Boiled Beef and Carrots' and suggest that the halls were there to celebrate small pleasures, or, as Titterton asserted at the time, to transmute these into 'extravagant happenings'. As Kift has pointed out, patriotic songs can be both 'anti-heroic' (following the Stedman Jones view) and 'heroic' (the Bratton view):

> They were anti-heroic because they refused to glorify war, and heroic because they sang of the heroic deeds not of the generals but of the little man. Here, as in other groups of songs, the audience was able to recognise, endorse and celebrate itself.[57]

He goes on to say that the equivocal nature of patriotic songs disappears into blatant warmongering by the time of the Boer War. This is not the case, as some of the songs here will show. Absolutist statements about music-hall culture tend to collapse because the culture itself was diverse and often contradictory.

Among those songs which create a specifically patriotic image of the soldier is 'Here Upon Guard Am I'. Although no indication of the original performer is given, it is clearly the song performed by Charles Godfrey as part of his repertoire of patriotic songs.[58] The song recounts the heroism of a soldier who stoically remains at his post and is eventually killed:

> Who dares to say that British pluck
> Is somewhat on the wane.
> That British valour never will
> Be seen or known again.
> The Crimean page will yet be read,
> And honest cheeks will glow,
> When learning how we nobly fought,
> And thrashed the stubborn foe.
>
> CHORUS
>
> Here upon guard am I,
> Willing to do or die,
> Fighting for Queen and country too,
> Fighting for home so dear,
> ....
> What matter tho' we lose an arm,
> Through rifle shot or sword.
> 'Tis for our country's good, and she
> Will help us when we're old.[59]

The song then moves into more of a narrative mode, enemy soldiers creeping up on the guard until a bullet finds its mark: 'ah yes – at last,/One's found its way in here'. As the soldier dies, he invokes Heaven to protect his wife and children and rejoices that the battle has been won: 'List, list to the loud ringing cheer'.

The song telescopes narrative to an arrested posture so that the voice of the song is more an object of attention, like a storyteller offering a condensed point of view, rather than a protagonist or character whom we can contemplate detachedly. We are given no specific context other than the soldier's consciousness. W.H. Auden stated that the most apposite words for songs are 'those which require the least reflection to comprehend ... ; verbs of physical action ... or physical concomitants of emotion'.[60] Words gesture at action and the action of performance so that a reader/listener is invited to engage with the attitude and pose of the singer for the duration of the song. The attitude offers a mythology of sentiments, such as the assurance of reciprocal devotion between the state and the individual soldier, a state which will 'help us when we're old' – a promise perennially exploited for propagandist reasons.

Proverbial phrases combine individual and national interests, with the 'stubborn foe' relegated to depersonalized Otherness. The use of simple antitheses and pairings in the song may be seen as a trigger for associative values, which would include: Queen and country; friend and foe, life and death; duty and nation. These pairings and antitheses collectively create a larger suggestion of patriotic values. Death elevates the soldier into an embodiment of heroic self-sacrifice.

Godfrey's acts were immensely popular, the songs often relying on the use of catch phrases which then gained common currency beyond the music hall. For example, the last line of the following song, which lionizes Britain as an imperial force:

> Folks say, 'What will Britain do?
> Will she rest with her banners furled?
> No! No! No! When we go to meet the foe,
> It's the English-speaking race against the world.'[61]

However, one of Godfrey's most successful acts was a sketch and song entitled 'On Guard', which indicts the social neglect of old warriors. Dressed as an old tramp soldier, Godfrey is refused admission to a poorhouse and exclaims: 'No! I am not wanted here! But at Balaclava – I was wanted there!' H. Chance Newton states that in London and the provinces, this 'raised vast audiences to an almost incredible pitch of enthusiasm… I have seen him move the patrons of the "halls" to volcanic excitement and to thunders of applause!' This emotionally charged piece of social criticism incurred the wrath of the War Office, which tried to have the act banned, as it threatened to be 'prejudicial to recruiting'.[62] However, this sort of paradox embodied in the stage career of Godfrey should be understood in terms of the kind of 'knowing' audience involvement discussed earlier. For the duration of the song or act the audience is invited to share the pose, or attitude, held in the performance. That songs and acts articulate different political or cultural perspectives does not necessarily imply a contradiction but a continuum of engagement, a collective suspension of disbelief. Audience involvement is an arresting of personal consciousness by the song, which gives shape to an attitude or mood. Logical consistency is not required, because the ritualizing of engagement is primarily a theatrical process, a collusion between audience and performer.

Other songs are more openly critical of patriotic sentiments, such as 'I ain't a Briton True' and a song in which Wilkie Bard declaimed 'I don't care how soon the bugle calls/so long as – I don't hear it'.[63] Alfred Lester's 'Conscientious Objector's Lament', which was also sung later during the First World War, is even more specific:

> Call out the Boys of the Old Brigade,
> Who made old England free,
> Call out my mother, my sister, and my brother
> But for God's sake don't send me![64]

As I indicated in my earlier discussion of Herbert Campbell, there is an element of parody in such songs which may antithetically affirm patriotic sentiments, but a song like the above also belongs to a broad aspect of music hall and saturnalian humour which ostentatiously celebrates a debunking of noble, patriotic sentiments. Deflating the pomposity of inflated rhetoric and certain stereotypes, such as the officer, the policeman and the magistrate, aligns certain songs with the interests of those usually on the receiving end of authority.[65] Some songs take the form of simple protests at social injustice. In *The Music Hall Songster* (1893), 'A Soldier's Letter' tells of a young soldier 'fighting at the head of his band' while, at home, his mother is being evicted 'by the laws of her land'.[66] Another song, 'He was one of the Light Brigade', tells the story of an old cavalryman who is refused admission to a workhouse, then crushed by a van and, ironically, is finally taken to the workhouse infirmary to die.[67] Songs like these provide a dramatic context within which to protest at blatant injustices in a way which is absolute, gratifying for an audience, and impossible in the real world inhabited by the singer and audience. The song defines the terms of protest and offers the simplest and most appropriate gestures for fulfilling them.

It cannot be claimed that such songs have a subversive role in the music-hall canon, more that they are part of an eclectic dramatic repertoire which takes acute pleasure in variety and contrary states of feeling. However, such songs do suggest what others make more explicit: that military and civil society did not coalesce into a homogeneous idea of nationhood and patriotism, with concomitant associations of a shared culture of values and ethics. Kipling's *Barrack Room Ballads*, discussed in Chapter 3, gave a distinct voice to the common soldier's criticisms of a civil society which both needed yet derided him; some of the Ballads were performed in music halls and other songs too confirmed this sense of a split culture. In 'The Soldier', sung by James Fawn, the singing voice decries the presence of soldiers in London, which is seen as a moral threat to civil society:

> Who is it marches through the streets
> As if he owned the town?

It is the British soldier bold,
A man of wide renown;

...

Who is the giddy Lothario? the soldier!
Stiff as a poker from head to toe, the soldier

...

Who is it cuts the civilian out? the soldier!

...

Who is it mashes the country nurse? the soldier!
Who is it borrows the lady's purse? the soldier!
Getting it toddles towards the bar
Orders a drink and a big cigar,
Hands it back quietly, and says ta! ta! the soldier![68]

The soldier is variously cast as swaggering toff, spurious ornament, sexual adventurer, decadent, drunk, coward, thief and occasional hero. Rhyme and consonantal repetition are constant reminders of the musical purposes of the song. The singer's rhetorical opening is an invitation to the listener to become singer and to share in the cumulative indictment of the soldier. The sheer length of the song would induce tedium were it not a deliberate appeal to indulge in each fresh opportunity for approbation in a way which is musically similar to the repetitive, incantatory pleasure of songs like 'Six Green Bottles' and 'The Twelve Days of Christmas'. The use of colloquialisms and slang, such as 'mash', 'choice', 'tasty'; of familiar situations in the song, such as the Lord Mayor's show; and equally familiar character types, like the 'street arab', all help to create a representation of a known social world for the audience, within which it can enjoy the denigrating of the soldier.

Writing in 1890, Percy Fitzgerald quotes from an act by a performer called 'Fast Fanny Fonblanque' whose work continued to be performed during the Boer War:

> Keep your eye on the military,
> With their faces smooth and hairy,
> Each a-settin' with his fairy
> In the park, in the park.

She then turns and directly addresses any soldiers in the audience:

Ah, I see ye in the park, with Mary and the perambulator, and the baby! That was last Sunday, hey, Corporal? Didn't think I was there, eh, private? P'r'aps the baby told me, never mind, I shan't blab, and so.[69]

The song is then continued. The performer's direct address to soldiers in the audience may embarrass but is also sexually flattering of them. However, Fitzgerald states that the performer then undermines the flattery with a 'rather offensive mimicry of the professional walk...Everyone turns to look at the poor men, and roar. They too laugh, but rather ruefully'.[70] The soldiers are ambiguously embraced as a dubious part of the community, and of the audience, but are also undermined by exposing the absurdity of military forms. The performer accuses on behalf of the audience, in a pantomime gesture which ostracizes the soldiers as distinct types.

The sexual image of the soldier is a persistent element in music-hall song. Winks, clandestine encounters in parks, the appeal of a uniform or military moustache, are invariably part of the sexual code. There is also an occasional element of sexual blackmail, especially during the 1914–18 war. This was most rife in recruitment posters. For example, a poster, now in the Imperial War Museum, portrays two women and a child staring from a window at a group of marching soldiers and carries the slogan: 'WOMEN OF BRITAIN SAY – GO!' The influence of the well known 'Lord Kitchener Wants You' poster, in which the direct visual confrontation of Kitchener's face, as the personification of single-minded power, both accuses and demands a response. It is visual blackmail. Woman as temptress and accuser was clearly believed to have a pervasive influence upon would-be recruits. This was also the case much earlier, both before and during the Boer War. Music-hall songs appeared which suggested that failure to enlist denoted a loss of sexual identity, whilst to enlist was sexually enhancing. Marie Lloyd's single patriotic song epitomizes this:

> Once I though yer meant to grow a Derby curl,
> But they cut it orf and shoved it on your chest.
>
> I do feel proud of you, I do honour bright,
> I'm going to give you an extra cuddle to-night,
> I didn't think much of you, till you joined the army, John,
> But I do like you, cocky, now you've got yer khaki on.[71]

The association of non-enlistment with effeminacy, the promise of sexual favours and the appeal of a uniform are all implicit in the words, yet Marie Lloyd's biographer, Naomi Jacobs, insists that the popular appeal lay in the persona of the performer. Jacobs states that Marie Lloyd was supremely uninterested in strident patriotism, but used the song to create the character of a 'coster woman ... a fine, buxom East End wench ... '.[72] It is possible that what the audience responded to was a fantasy of Marie Lloyd becoming temporarily available to them and the pleasure of this lay in the more suggestive words, rather than in the sentiment of patriotism. Clearly, the song as performance was heightened by the fact that during it, Marie Lloyd danced on stage with a man in uniform. Jacob's insistence upon character creation does not take into account the fact that the audience would also be very aware that this was Marie Lloyd, the music-hall star performing.

Once the music-hall performer became a 'star' in his or her own right, the storyteller disappears and is replaced by the professional, or specialist. The conventions of singing as a shared experience which I discussed earlier may still operate, but a famous performer, a 'personality', can disrupt this process so that the song is actually distanced from the audience. Equally, however, the performer who can seduce an audience into acquiescence and submission to the myth of the performer's persona, can also exploit the potentially unifying power of song for political purposes. Such is the case with Vesta Tilley. Her forte was to create soldier types as a virtuoso spectacle of manners rather than as military heroes. She clearly saw her role as music-hall and variety artist in relation to historical events,[73] believed in the war effort during the 1914–18 war and already had a predilection to 'becoming' a soldier long before her major successes. Booth records an early song, probably performed in the early 1890s and during the Boer War, in which she was:

> Only a brave little drummer boy,
> > Only a smart little lad;
> Only a rough little, tough little chap,
> > As e'er in the service we had
> Only a boy with the heart of a man,
> > Only a mother's joy.
> Marching along with a heart stout and strong
> > Like a brave little drummer boy.[74]

The appeal of this song, performed by a slim, young girl, mingling sentimentality with lion-hearted youth and fresh-faced optimism was to later become enhanced by stylized gestures which critics and audiences alike were mesmerized by. Her two most acclaimed military songs were 'Jolly Good Luck To The Girl Who Loves A Soldier' (1907) and

'The Army of Today's All Right' (1914), though her repertoire had always included other military songs, such as 'The Bold Militiaman' and 'Six Days Leave'. It is her earlier work, performed during the Boer War, which set the tone for her 'war work'.

Titterton's book provides a descriptive opportunity for examining the power of her act. The fascination of Vesta Tilley is primarily with a sexual ambiguity which teases and allures, and is expressed through gesture and song. Her face is 'cherubic round and young' and she charms with her 'freshness, her lightness, her spontaneity, her unspoiled rollicking boyishness',[75] yet this suggestion of innocence barely masks a sexuality which is attractive in its confusion; 'but for a subtle hint of womanly waist and curving hips you might fancy it indeed a round-faced boy. Even so you are doubtful'.[76] The movements of this sexual tomboy are an intrinsic part of the song; 'the gestures move to rhythm', so that the rhythmic characteristics of music, in which, Titterton states, the band plays a crucial introductory role before Tilley enters, are converted into body gestures and she becomes an object of voyeurism – 'and the body wriggles into itself with a foot up'.[77] This alchemy of musical enjoyment and physical presence is managerial, as Titterton is aware; 'How despotically she rules over her audience – dallies with the rhythm, draws it out'; and also highly conscious, for she creates the quintessence of types in which 'all types of fledgeling manhood (I speak in a Pickwickian and artistic sense) are her lawful prey'. The power of these types is that they 'explain ... laugh at ... justify ... They have all the deep truth of uncynical humour'.[78] Her songs are known and exploit the knowingness they engender; once the band plays a chorus the audience are engaged by its familiarity and when she enters the type she is portraying continues to mesmerize visually, 'only there is another person present – the woman artist who unfolds the tale'.[79] The performance of 'Jolly Good Luck to the Girl Who Loves a Soldier' suggests the recruiting power she exploited so successfully, as Titterton writes:

> We join in – this is the song we love. Out steps a Tommy from the wings in Brodrick cap and crimson cloth, striding jauntily with the chest out and a flapping cane ... this is irresistible; these quick-step movements seize us; this merry, saucy face with its sideways jerk sets our blood dancing. With what delicious jerky precision the feet tap heel and toe! How the whole body keeps time within itself as if it were a battalion! This Tommy is so virile, so vain, so self-possessed, so jolly – you long to be up and after him, marching to his drum-tap measure ... Here is the very type of Tommy – joyous, impudent, and imperturbable.[80]

She then proceeds to sing. This is the zenith of late music-hall conventions. Tilley projects a world that is obviously and appealingly faked, offering a view of soldiering as a privileged game for 'joyous, impudent, and imperturbable' Tommies. The tensions between this enjoyment of a mythical type, musical excitement and the charismatic physical presence of the performer are secured for the audience by the knowledge that she is ultimately in control of the performance. She emphasizes, through swagger and movement, a camaraderie which hints at the erotic, at the woman whose body is deliberately imitating gestures of male virility. The audience is supremely conscious that it is the woman Vesta Tilley performing for them and offering back a cameo of male bravado; the storyteller of a ballad tradition is usurped by the specialist who personalizes the song through the creation of a type and the audience allows her this role and confirms it with appreciation. This creates a tension between her actual physical presence and her remoteness as a star and was later to be exploited during the First World War, in this song, by the appearance on stage of a recruiting Sergeant, Horatio, who would appeal for young men in the audience to step on stage and enlist.[81] Audience members may have been co-producers but some were obviously mesmerized into the trenches – whether by the charisma of Tilley, patriotism, drink, or perhaps all three.

During the Boer War, it appears that the ways in which soldiers themselves used songs were far removed from any strident form of patriotism. Music hall and popular song were an integral part of the social structures of military life, including an accompaniment to marching. Contemporary accounts of the Boer War identify soldiers in South Africa as former patrons of the music hall at home. Variety entertainment – mostly songs in which solders participated – was the staple entertainment for off-duty hours[82] in which 'the canteen, from its two-fold nature of music hall and bar ... holds out the most convivial mode of spending a few pleasant and profitable hours'.[83] Not only is the milieu of music hall carried abroad, but the conventions of song are used in ways similar to those discussed earlier in this chapter. The ritual of a song world is imposed on the reality of war. James Milne suggests that the tones of song, as much as the words, are used to express the experience of war. He writes of soldiers singing 'Goodbye Daddy':

'They didn't let it go', we are told of the chorus, 'as they would if they had been in a London music-hall. They sung it in a quiet, soulful way, which showed that many of them felt deeply what they were singing'. Surely, for the concert is at Ladysmith, where men in their isolation have time to think.[84]

What is described here is a ritualistic way of rendering intelligible, and possibly of assuaging, the experience of the siege of Ladysmith. Song articulates a fantasy of longing and regret that can be relevantly imposed on a real situation; it can also express and highlight the disorientating effects of bombardment in an apparently absurdist manner:

> When 'Long Tom' [the nickname for a gun] was dropping ninety-six pound shells round about us, some one started singing 'Why did I leave my little back room in Bloomsbury?' and the whole lot took it up. It did sound funny![85]

The song converts the scene described into absurdist drama, both distancing the experience of heavy shelling and ironically apprehending it as something too shocking, or new, to be articulated and shared by ordinary speech. This may also help to explain why 'Goodbye Dolly, I Must Leave You' and 'The Miner's Dream of Home' were adopted as anthems for the Boer War.[86]

In 'Goodbye Dolly, I Must Leave You', the words speak of leaving and returning, regret and resignation, looks of care, broken hearts, marching and dying. The march accompaniment is still present, but musical accompaniment would obviously be absent for the soldiers who sang, so that the dominant mode of the song is a lamenting ballad in which the emphasis is not on the glorious opportunities of battle, but nostalgia – a homesickness which prevails over the heroic possibilities of being a soldier. The 'inner life' of the song involves a conflict between love of home and a vague sense that 'I am needed at the front to fight', but which, musically, is dominated by the maudlin and regretful. Kipling wrote of Boer War songs that 'Tommy moaned all through his sing-songs'[87] and in 'The Miner's Dream of Home' the disconsolate voice is more obviously prevalent. The song was not new at the time, suggesting that it offered something more than novelty value. It has no mention of warfare or military life, but is a despondent dream-wish for the home of childhood. The dream form implies the impossibility of such a return after 'ten weary years' and that any potential return to a state of innocence, when 'The log was burning brightly – T'was a night that should banish all sin' can only be fulfilled in dreams, or song. From a central situation of isolation burdened by worldly experience, the gap between present misery and an idealized past is heightened by the sentimental but somnolent melody.

These two songs neither exalt the Empire nor aggrandize the image and role of the soldier. They may be seen as either a powerful nostalgic relief from the war or disillusionment with it. The imperialist and nationalist hysteria of many popular songs may actually have been part of the death throes of a declining empire, and a hysteria with which a significant number of Tommies did not identify.[88]

In representations of the soldier during the war we can glimpse variety, the impact of new technologies and the increased significance of the 'star'. In the range of songs, acts, films, sketches and plays which constituted the music-hall repertoire during the Boer War it is not possible to identify representations of the soldier which coalesce into a generally accepted endorsement of the war. Neither can the variety of performances be easily reconciled to a clear sense of nationhood. The soldier figure is both accommodated and distanced, supported and derided, an expression of unity and of class antagonism.

2
The Image of the Common Soldier in Contemporary Accounts of the Boer War

> The sunshine has appeared to rest upon scattered clusters of redcoats, while the background has been enveloped in a sort of chaotic and fuliginous dimness. The redcoats, according to their number, have been palpable and definite, though a great many other things have been inconveniently vague.
>
> Henry James, 'The British Soldier', in *Lippincott's Magazine*, XXII, August 1878, pp. 214–21

Henry James's article, 'The British Soldier', published in the American *Lippincott's Magazine*, attempts to identify the relationship between soldier and civilian, between the palpable fact of the army and the unresolved complexity of civil and moral issues in British society. James argues that, detached from the battlefield and on display in the streets, soldiers provide 'a delightful entertainment' for members of the public, who become spectators and need only identify with the army on a level of abstract national pride. The soldier is an 'ornamental and potentially useful personage'; within the formal enactment of parades, displays and uniforms, he can be part of a reassuring and ritualistic spectacle, but also, James suggests, a covert reminder of unresolved issues. The specific contemporary example James uses is the conflict between Russia and Turkey, in which there was a felt political imperative to 'take sides' and, James argues, an Englishman's self esteem demanded that he 'assume some foreign personality' and be 'either Russian or a Turk'. However, if the army becomes a too obvious presence on the home streets then the entertainment metaphor begins to break down and the values associated with the army come into question, as James observes: 'Certainly, the army may be too apparent, too importunate, too terrible a burden to the conscience of the philosophic observer'.[1] This tension between civil and military worlds is a keynote in contemporary discussions of the war. The attempt to align civil and military worlds to create what Anderson calls a 'new form of imagined community'[2] also underlined inherent contradictions in British society a few years later during the Boer War.

The soldier is obviously the key actor in James's metaphorical description of the army as an entertainment, a metaphor which is dependent upon clear boundaries between the army and civilians, the soldier embodying certain values in the civilian mind. The problem inherent in the theatrical and entertainment metaphor is that whilst ostensibly encouraging in the audience an identification with the 'performance', it also rests upon distinctions between performer and observer, between the action of events and the passivity of watching. The soldier and the civilian may be in the same theatre, but they are having qualitatively different experiences.

Recognition that the army was in fact an intrinsic part of Victorian society, created by the parent society and embodying certain indigenous cultural values, was slow to dawn and did not become a significant concern until the late nineteenth century.[3] That soldiers who policed the colonies were slowly recognized as part of the 'national character', arose partly from the proliferation of images of the soldier in the press, periodicals, and music hall.[4] However, these images had to be placed within a context of events, and this created problems when unexpected reversals and defeats occurred.

During Black Week (December 1899) the British Army suffered resounding defeats and total losses of nearly 3,000 men. During the same week '[p]ublishers complained that no one read any books except war books. The key to the public's mood was disappointment that victory was so long postponed'.[5] The 'war books' were a form of wish fulfilment. A hunger for stirring accounts of the war was also a hunger for heroic soldiers and glorious victories. The desire to read about an essentially imaginary version of the war suggests a tension in the public mind between what it wanted the army to be, and to do, and an awareness that it was patently failing to succeed. The Boer War seemed to be crystallizing a contradiction in the 'national character' between an assertion of its sovereignty on the world stage, and, as the war was showing, an alarming number of reversals and setbacks for the army at the border of its own empire. The desire for print to tell another, preferable story of heroism and victory created a further tension between British civilian and military worlds, the latter failing to fulfil the expectations of the former.

It is in this gap between expectation and fulfilment that many contemporary accounts of the war were written and read, many of them attempting to bridge the gap with rhetorical flourish and an insistence upon the supremacy of the British soldiers in South Africa, whatever the evidence to the contrary. The volume of consumer materials produced during the war is vast,[6] and includes an enormous amount of writing, from juvenile literature to historical accounts. I give some account of the range and volume of writing and a more detailed analysis of certain works, chosen because they represent what is manifest in many other accounts: a use of literary, figurative and rhetorical devices to create images of the soldier which mark him out as a fictitious character placed in a real history.

There were four main areas of publication during the war which overlapped and supported one another: the Press, juvenile literature, educational texts and documentary accounts.[7] Novels about the war embody new elements in military fiction and, for this reason, are discussed separately in Chapter 7, as the most sustained imaginative attempt to create a Boer War fiction and soldier hero within the parameters of a new kind of war.

The British Press played a crucial role not only in reporting the war but in influencing public opinion before it started. By the 1890s mass literacy and cheaply produced newspapers meant that the Press would play a much larger role in establishing and directing attitudes towards major events and current affairs. Both Alfred Milner, British High Commissioner at the Cape, and George Wyndham, Parliamentary Under-Secretary at the War Office, recognized and took full advantage of the need to control and direct the Press. Wyndham was ex-Chairman of the main jingo lobby in England, the South African Association, and brought his influence to bear upon both the Association and the Press, so that he could write to Milner: 'The Press are ready and under complete control. I can switch on agitation at your direction'.[8] He also gained the support of French and German shareholders of the gold-mining companies. Colonial lobbying could be a full-time occupation for those imperialists who 'made alliances with the owners of the new, cheap, mass-circulation press which had the power to sway lower-middle- and working-class opinion'.[9]

Milner was also working hard to force Chamberlain into war. He had the support of such as Alfrid Beit, who had been involved in the Jameson Raid and was, like other Uitlanders, one of the London 'gold bugs', an influential financier of the Rand mining houses. Milner also had formidable support from many big national newspapers, such as *The Daily News, The Times* and *The Morning Post*. A former journalist himself, having worked for *The Pall Mall Gazette*, Milner could count on support from his old cronies. Only Stead was recalcitrant, with his *Review of Reviews*, but he was seen as idiosyncratic by many of his peers.[10]

There is no doubt that the Press effectively excited public opinion just prior to the war. When Kruger finally issued an ultimatum, it was the cue for a number of leading newspapers to insist on war.[11] However, there were oppositional voices and although Milner never disclosed to the Press his close association with gold financiers, some socialist-inclined newspapers, such as *Reynolds News*, informed readers that this was a 'Stock Exchange War', a staged event designed to fuel war fever, and in which this whipped-up patriotism actually worked against the real interests of the nation.[12] Robert Blatchford, editor of the *Clarion*, occupied a singular position in that he was a Socialist and an imperialist in favour of the war. He believed in empire yet knew the healthy maintenance of it depended on national solidarity, observing that while the sun never set on the British empire, there were city slums over which it had never risen. The implications of differing and oppositional views on the war for Press representations of the soldier were that he was stage-managed to occupy a prescribed role in tabloid politics, moving from uneducated outsider to patriotic hero.

The Press was, of course, part of a wider formation of print which sought to persuade readers into adopting a particular view of the war. The school textbook had, since the 1870s, been acknowledged as a potent political force. The Royal Colonial Institute was an effective lobby for promoting imperial studies in schools. By offering prize money for essays on British imperialism and writing letters to educational boards the Institute helped to facilitate a Whig view of history, with the virtues of commerce and business being extolled.[13] Military fictions by writers such as E.S. White were promoted as 'geographical fiction' which taught the civilizing effects of contact with imperialist soldiers. Joseph H. Cowham's *A New School Method*, published in 1900, advocated a new method of approaching history which started from the present, with England as a world-historical driving force, then working back to show, in a highly selective manner, how this position had been achieved.[14] Emphasis was placed on the expansion of the empire and the importance of militarism in achieving this, so that the heroes of history were military leaders, such as General Gordon and Nelson. The work of Regius professor at Cambridge, J.R. Seeley's *The Expansion of*

England, published in 1883, was particularly influential in promoting the rise of the nation-state, with the British Empire as the embodiment of an expanding state in a world political order. Within this view, patriotism was idealized into religious fervour. Seeley's approach filtered down into schools and was coupled with vivid stories of military heroes.[15] Seeley's work took up the imperial baton from an earlier speculative history, Sir Charles Dilke's *Greater Britain* (1869), and pursued the theme that the Anglo-Saxon race had both a special character and a special mission, though few imperialists cared to delve far into the racial stew that constituted the Anglo-Saxon race.[16]

The Boer War also prompted a strong reaction from writers and publishers of juvenile literature. Comics and more seriously intentioned papers, such as *Boys Own Paper*, offered information on real figures in the war, such as Redvers Buller and Lord Roberts, ran storylines on battles and placed their own invented characters in the war. In *Cartoonists at War*, Frank Huggett argues that the war brought about 'a marked change in the attitude to the common soldier in the illustrated comics';[17] the common soldier now rivalled the Officer in terms of popular images and representations and certain publications, such as *Boys Own Paper*, encouraged boys to prepare to fight not for the nation but as the nation:

> In the world of B.O.P., because boys are identified not so much with but rather as the nation, they are in effect entreated to fight for themselves. That is, they are the England they should be fighting for.[18]

This theme, that each individual citizen is a soldier, or potential soldier, is pervasive in many accounts of the war. To represent the self as nation and vice versa is useful in that its appeal to common purpose avoids having to confront questions of specific and antagonistic class and political interests.

Juvenile literature also had a strong relationship with the Patriotic Association. Howard Spicer, who founded the Boys' Empire League, was also the publisher for *Boys of Our Empire* during the Boer War. The League soon gained over 10 000 members, under the Presidency of Conan Doyle, and provided lectures, sermons and cultural visits, all on an imperial theme.[19]

Consumerism was growing, with supply and demand chasing each other throughout the war. The sheer volume of these publications itself indicates the desire for accounts and stories of the war and the desire to provide them, whether to entertain, inform, or for financial or political gain. It is within this climate of a surfeit of print that the works I focus on were produced. They purport to be documentary accounts of the war, with particular emphasis on the soldiers fighting it, and constitute a discrete sub-genre of Boer War literature which has received little attention.

These texts may be considered as part of a public discourse through which the Boer War was not simply reported, but created, for a British reading public. However, this 'discourse' is not a unified body of writing; whilst imagining the idealized nation through representations of the soldier, it also dramatizes social and political tensions and antagonisms. Transcendent appeals to the sovereignty of nation, with the British soldier as both representative and epitome of that nation, sometimes have difficulties with reconciling this transcendence, events of the war, and conflicting interests of the nation and the soldier.

Tommy Atkins at Home, by Callum Beg,[20] is a meticulous account of the soldier's life in civil society, and how this life prepares him for and inculcates in him the kinds of values considered necessary in battle. *The Romance of the Boer War*, by O'Moore and MacCarthy,[21] draws heavily upon press reports, anecdote, and contemporary opinion with which to create a narrative of the war. *The Epistles of Atkins*, by James Milne,[22] synthesizes soldier's letters and authorial interjection in an attempt to represent British soldiers' experience of the war. It is instructive to compare these with weekly publications, such as *The Sketch*, *The Spear*, juvenile literature and other historical accounts.

Tommy Atkins at Home and *The Epistles of Atkins* both use the popular term 'Tommy Atkins' in their titles, a convention they share with many other works.[23] As a generic term it became established in common usage during the 1890s, particularly after the publication of Kipling's *Barrack Room Ballads* in 1892. W.E. Henley co-edited a dictionary of colloquialisms and slang in which he says that 'Thomas Atkins' was used as a sample name on military forms, but was popularized by Kipling.[24] The term embodies a popular myth of the common soldier; although his protean energies sometimes hint at subversion, these are simply the rough edges of a character whose moral being and physical strength are finally the property of the crown when there is a crisis. As I discuss below, the components of the myth, Tommy's heroism and patriotic fervour, his sentimentality and simple Christian faith, were the products of an idealized vision created by rhetorical devices.

The name 'Tommy Atkins' itself crystallizes certain associations: English working class, an easy familiarity, perhaps streetwise, down-to-earth, but by linking these associations to the profession of a dutiful soldier, the name 'Tommy Atkins' is harnessed to a notion of 'national character'. 'Tommy Atkins' is a metaphor for a culture of working-class patriotism, encouraging a response of admiration and identification. In his essay on 'Photography and Electoral Appeal' in *Mythologies* Roland Barthes discusses the use of photography to encourage certain responses in the observer: 'a kind of complicity ... what we are asked to read is the familiar, the known ... but clarified, exalted, superbly elevated into a type ... he is delegating his "race" '.[25] The use of generic names, such as 'Tommy Atkins', may function in similar ways.

In *The Great War and Modern Memory*, Paul Fussell has documented the extent to which the First World War may be viewed, both seriously and ironically, as a 'literary' event.[26] Earlier writings about the Boer War also contributed significantly to popularizing representations of warfare as inherently 'literary' events. Milne begins his book by stating that '[h]ere the common soldier gives his actual version of the business' so that what follows purports to comprise accurate first-hand documentation. However, the actual and the embroidered are conflated throughout the book, to the extent that quotations from letters are so framed by the metaphorical density of Milne's own writing that one can only be read through the other. The opening paragraph sets the tone:

> There is ever light on the hills, a light which even the angry flare of Mauser and Lee-Metford cannot hide. We see its glow in the letters of the common soldier, written when the S. African war was new, big in battle, and he was impressionable.
>
> *(EA,* p. 7)

In ensuing chapters metaphors accumulate prolifically, borrowed from diverse times and traditions, but emphasizing the heroic; Tommy Atkins is a 'young warrior', *(EA,* p. 135) a 'knight' *(EA,* p. 174) a 'young oak', *(EA,* p. 203) 'Samson', *(EA,* p. 204) and according to one unidentified source, a deity:

> To see those great bearded warriors charging up a mountain taking death as nothing, was a privilege worth ten years of ordinary life. In the moment of battle there is something godlike in these men; their faces change to iron, and they seem Fate itself.
>
> *(EA,* p. 50)

Odd because it was the Boers who were famous for their beards, but the imagery establishes the soldier as a transcendent being for whom war provides the means of apotheosis by which men are either transposed into gods or amorphous destiny.

MacCarthy also creates essentially literary images of battle and the soldier's heroism in which Dantean fires of battle are a scenic stage for the 'grim courage and ... stubborn endurance' of the British Private:

> Bullets might drop like hail around him; the zone of fire might surround him like a cyclone; death and destruction might stare him in the face at every turn; but they appalled not him who had gone from home to conquer or to die. The 'thin khaki line', like the 'thin red line' of other days, never sagged with doubt nor quaked with fear.
>
> (*RBW*, p. 75)

The metaphorical extension of 'thin red line' to 'thin khaki line' suggests a tradition of British soldiering, so that what is at stake here is not a specific battle but a heritage. The style borrows from romance and adventure fiction, in which soldiers live 'by the "kill, cook, and eat" adventures, of which every boy dreams. What more can romantic youth desire?' (*EA*, p. 32) and Milne states that 'even the bullets of a lively fight write wondrous tales, tragedies and romances' (*EA*, p. 12). In *Romance of the Boer War* and *The Epistles of Atkins* persistent references to, and quotations from, fiction and poetry, such as Hardy's 'Drummer Hodge' and Henley's 'England, My England', couch the image of the soldier within a literary context; the liberal usage of literary quotations also suggests that Tommy's own psychology is saturated with English literature, and is itself a crucible of literary tradition. Milne tells us that in the heat of battle a trooper has 'plunging cannon fire for accompaniment, and on his lips Tennyson's line, "All in the valley of death rode the six hundred" ' (*EA*, p. 13).

Coupled with this is the soldier's own verbal dexterity: 'Atkins is a master of the graphic sentence, the picturesque phrase; he explodes into literary shrapnel' (*EA*, p. 3). He has a desire to 're-christen all things colonial with names of his own' (*EA*, p. 20). A mountain is nicknamed 'Tintacks and Onions' (*EA*, p. 21) and Boer bullets are called 'Kruger's pills'; Milne extols the soldier whose language suggests he is becoming a 'sage in khaki' (*EA*, p. 8). Here Tommy Atkins is an urban consciousness whose language and values have been created by London topography and urban, ironic humour. Two soldiers, for example, delight in discussing their horse, who used to draw London buses and provides nostalgic comfort:

> My chum called out, 'Mansion House', whereupon my horse stopped dead, and would not move till there arose the cry, 'Higher up, please'.

Then he went on slowly, all of which showed us that he was one of the old London 'bussers'.

(*EA*, p. 19)

Cockney inventiveness, framed by authorial interpretation, portrays an endearing soldier figure whose fondness for familiar names and meanings indicate a sentimental patriotism. Milne sees the soldier's easy humour as the 'pretty spume' on the surface, hiding 'gulfs of despond' beneath; a welter of working-class irony and jokes stoically hide despair and anxiety, which it would be unmanly and unsoldierly to give voice to. The sentimental use of colloquialisms also confirms him as an Englishman whose affinity with his own culture pervades all his experiences in war. He may be mildly subversive, but is pre-eminently safe and a bit of a character. Any pranks he plays are a sign of healthy high spirits in the ranks. Anecdotes include the fooling of officers, and the inadvertent arrest of important persons through an over-zealous adherence to duty and military form.

However, the soldier is also satirized and patronized in ways which convert his idiosyncrasies into caricature. A poorly wrought Dickensian tone is employed to show the soldier as a confirmed subordinate when a regular private criticizes a volunteer for his social pretensions:

'Yus', sez I; 'you're a volunteer an' I'm a reg'ler',
I sez, 'an' you ain't goin' to lord it over me, 'I
sez, 'with yer "me man"'. 'Don't forget it', sez I. 'I
didn't get no freedom of the City', I sez; 'the only
thing the Lord Mayor ever gin' me', says I, 'was
fourteen days for fur'ous drivin'.

(*EA*, p. 132)

The use of cockney phonetics is inconsistent; 'you' and 'yer', 'sez' and 'says' are all credited to the same speaker. Milne's concern is apparently not with fidelity to dialect in order to portray a cockney, nor to indicate individual psychology, but to portray a social type. He implies this earlier in the book: 'His (Tommy Atkins) use of the negative – "the bullets didn't half make my heart patter!" – to secure an emphatic affirmative, telling us of the English peasant in the ranks' (*EA*, pp. 18–19). Milne's book, like others, is directed at a readership for whom the image of Tommy Atkins is that of a different and subordinate creature. By viewing him humorously, he is allotted what Keating calls the 'special status of character'.[27] Bad cockney dialogue is used selectively as an anecdotal embellishment; the soldier is either actor or narrator, but his lack of high culture is often apparent. 'Cockney' circumscribes the working-class soldier in ways which, despite a fervid insistence upon the class unification of patriotism, are a testament to social divisions.

Milne is, in fact, more openly critical of 'drawing-room' generals, but the textual proximity of, for example, Tennyson and the 'literary shrapnel' of Atkins from the urban working class, suggests how we may read the book as a cultural grid, along which the literary and the popular are represented as a unity. The unifying of different language registers implies the unifying of classes which are engaged in the same struggle and are concerned to further the interests of the same culture. In this sense, the English language, whether a line from Tennyson or working-class wit and 'popular songs' from the music hall (*EA*, p. 27), is itself a metaphor for national character in which diversity is also taken to be a sign of unity. Tommy may be a 'peasant' but he is an English peasant. Other radical voices, however, such as *Reynolds News*, criticized the paucity of education and culture in the ranks of the army, and tended to indict the boarding school and the army for deliberately creating 'unenlightened' soldiers:

the typical, orthodox British Tommy is, thanks to his army training, about the finest specimen of unenlightened white humanity extant. Brains are not a desideratum in the army. Both by their mode of stoking libraries and their system of school education, the authorities take no pains to conceal their desire for a not too intelligent army ... Almost any apology for a man is considered fit for a soldier nowadays.[28]

Criticism of the soldier is also criticism of a wider desire to maintain the army as cheaply as possible. This impoverishment of the army, *Reynolds News* maintains, simply shows the cultural philistinism and political agenda of the parent society.

This is a view which *The Epistles of Atkins* is at pains to refute. As the image of the soldier is repeatedly constructed with florid prose, admiration is cumulatively evoked not simply for Tommy Atkins, but for the variegated richness of the culture which created him. After citing the Cromwellian soldier's catechism, Milne states:

So the Ironsides, of an age which still hums to us, were exhorted in the 'Soldier's Catechisme' of the Parliament Army. Now, it is the other way about. Our 'Soldiers' give us a 'Catechisme', well suited to encourage and instruct 'all that have taken up Armes' in the battle of life. Not theirs 'to reason why', but to play the men in all affairs. Here, surely, is the supreme teaching of this legion of dispatches from Atkins, made by the board school, his own correspondent.

(*EA*, p. 8)

Having been enfranchised by history and literacy, the common soldier is now represented as tutor for common values. The value placed upon literature and its use in creating the image of the soldier, serves as a reminder of the tradition which he now both represents and defends. Milne is, albeit crudely, trying to create a sense of Englishness, of what it might be to be this man in this uniform in this war at this time.

The representation of a shared culture and concomitant patriotism is taken to indicate an affinity between soldier and civilian, a narrowing of the gap between what Henry James called the 'palpable' fact of the army and the 'inconveniently vague' concerns of civil and political life. James used the metaphor of entertainment, with the army as a form of institutionalized theatre for civil society. This metaphor depended upon clear boundaries between military and civil society, or performers and audience. In the texts presently under discussion a language of theatre is also used, but to denote more dynamic images of performance in battle, and with which a reader is meant to identify vicariously. The soldier is represented as heroic actor fully engaged in the theatre of war. MacCarthy states that his chief concern is to give an account of 'the humours and chivalry of the fray' a euphuistic and medieval notion of war as a ceremonial rite in which the 'comedy and the tragedy of life are intimately connected' (*RBW*, p. 1). One example of this theatrical dimension is particularly relevant as the description includes the participation of a 'live' audience which watches British soldiers perform the rites of battle:

> The last charge at Wepener is thus described in Cassell's 'History of the Boer War': The Royal Scots saw the Boers rushing, and their warrior hearts beat quick with joy. Shortly, like a man in a dream, their Captain gave the word, 'Fix Bayonets!' It was done in a trice, 'Ready!' The men loaded their rifles. 'A volley, my lads, and then the steel! All together –' The whistle blows, a flame flies along the parapet. Then over the stone wall there sprang the Royal Scots. Once they shouted, once only. Then the slaying began ... fifty thousand throats swelled the chorus. Ever since the siege began, the black warriors had been gathered in their thousands on these heights, watching with fascinated interest the struggle of the white man. Like the spectators at a medieval tournament, they had applauded the gallant deeds of the

combatants, and as they saw the British soldier holding out day after day, night after night, against the assault of enormous odds, they came to have a profound trust and confidence in the 'big heart' of the Queen's Soldiers. When, therefore, they saw the Royal Scots launch themselves like levin-bolt at five times their number, they held their breath for a time, wondering what the end might be. But when they saw the bloody bayonets of the 1st Foot scatter and utterly destroy the hated Dutchman, they opened their throats and yelled their applause across the river.

(RBW, pp. 21–2)

I have quoted at length to indicate how sustained dramatic reconstruction is part of the 'method' of the book. What is clear is that the metaphor of theatre is prevalent and is represented as an authentic mode of describing the experience of a real event. The description of the Captain, 'like a man in a dream', suggests a suspension of disbelief, perhaps a possession, for the actor as he enters the drama.

We are reading a scripted event rather than an historical account. The battleground is seen as a dramatic triumph in which the performance signifies a change in consciousness which ends only when the battle finishes, as one of the quotations in Milne's book suggests: 'You know nothing till you hear the "rally" sounded, and you pull up to find that you are merely a common soldier' (*EA*, p. 13). This is a telling comment which explains much about the 'theatre of war' metaphor. The soldier is a key actor in the drama of battle and has to return to what is 'merely' his everyday status. He cannot logically bridge the gap between the two, can only 'know nothing' in the transference from one state to another. It is in this gap of 'unknowing' that Henry James's observations on the gap between civilian and military worlds become significant. The two worlds are fundamentally irreconcilable and can only exist in the state of either mutual tension or 'unknowingness'. The Imperial Warrior and the British Tommy, with his own concerns, background and interests, are very different creatures. War elevates the common man, it is implied.

It is not unusual for a language of theatre to be borrowed to describe and thereby enhance the dramatic status of war. However, as in the above example from *Romance of the Boer War*, the theatrical metaphor is also harnessed to cultural myths. The individualization of the British Captain is sketched in against an audience of 'black warriors' which draws on the myth of the primitive black man 'fascinated' by the white man and becoming dramatically engaged with his, in this case, British supremacy. The black warriors are given a double role; they are spectators but are also being instructed, through the medium of dramatic engagement, in the superior courage and implied moral worth of the Queen's soldiers. Victory is taken as infrangible proof that the British have and deserve mastery in South Africa. Phrases such as 'the hated Dutchman' indicate a form of nationalism which has a *prima facie* partisan and competitive base, rather than one which is an expression of universal values, often associated with the civilizing mission of British imperialism. In this sense of differentiation between British and others, we can see how a sense of imperial mission is contradicted, as Arendt points out, by an adherence to an exclusive form of nationalism.[29]

Literary devices and a related language of theatre project the Tommy Atkins image into a world of romantic myth, achieved partly through the extended metaphor of war as an embodiment of childhood adventure fantasies, what Milne refers to as 'kill, cook and eat' adventures (*EA*, p. 5). The belief in war as boyhood adventure is taken from juvenile literature and the scouting mythology propounded by Baden-Powell, himself the hero of Mafeking. Baden-Powell articulated what is implicit in Milne's book and in works of juvenile fiction: to be a true scout (i.e. a soldier in waiting), one must conceive of politics only in terms of inevitable imperial destiny, thereby not conceiving of oneself as a political subject, but as an element of Empire:

> You will many of you be inclined to belong to Conservative or Liberal or radical or other parties, whichever your father or friends belong to. I should not, if I were you...be a man, make up your mind and decide for yourself which you think is the best for the country and the future of the Empire.[30]

The ideal scout, like the ideal soldier, believes in king, country and the law. Baden-Powell idealized the boys at Mafeking, who formed their own juvenile cadet corps during the siege, thereby suggesting that the Boer War was an excellent training ground for a new generation of soldiers.[31]

Baden-Powell encouraged his young readers to read Conan Doyle's Sherlock Holmes stories and Kipling's *Kim*. Drug addiction apart, Sherlock Holmes embodied, for Baden-Powell, the virtues of self-reliance and deduction put to service for the law, whilst Kim epitomized pluck and, according to Baden-Powell, his ultimate allegiance to the British Empire. Partial readings, and even more partial interpretations of fiction, become part of Baden-Powell's didactic strategy in arguing that reading fiction should, for a scout, be reading for the Empire. Henty had a similar purpose in mind when he claimed that his writing was designed to create a form of patriotism in his readers which would make them wish to enlist. In 1902 he claimed that 'very many boys have joined the cadets and afterwards gone into the army through reading my stories'.[32]

Romantic projection and memory conspire in this process of glamorizing of war in which 'the colour, the movement, the elan of the charge are still the heroic poetry of war, and so will remain' (*EA*, p. 11); in the use of nostalgia, such as the song of the pipers on the veld crying itself out 'to the winds of Africa, and … carried overseas to the Highland glens' (*EA*, p. 18); and in the assertion that a soldier's death finds its true reality in romance: 'In reality, it may be a romance, for death is full of romance; in death there is love, as well as in life' (*EA*, p. 18). The aggrandizing of the soldier through the use of romantic imagery creates a response to the war, and to the soldier fighting it, which is divested of political concerns and is converted into an appreciation of the 'humours and chivalry of the fray' (*RBW*, p. 1).

Pictorial imagery usually depicted moments of triumph, such as the British entry into Ladysmith and the relief of Mafeking. The *Spear*, for example, which was registered as a newspaper and declared itself to be a 'critical probe of passing events, literary and artistic', carried many sketches of triumphalist moments for the British. A sketch of the British entry into Ladysmith shows a jubilant but orderly relief column of soldiers, each soldier perfectly uniformed and with the same handsome, classical features and moustache. Another sketch shows British soldiers rescuing a distraught woman and child supposedly left behind by Boers retreating before Lord Roberts. There is no contextual explanation but a caption: 'The Retreat before Roberts: Mr Thomas Atkins caring for some little things the absent-minded Boer had left behind him'.[33]

Sketches of battles invariably depicted British soldiers advancing or attacking, while the Boer soldiers are always represented in retreat, being slaughtered or imprisoned. The pictorial images of the British as active and dynamic and the Boers as essentially passive creates an overall pictorial representation of the war which eclipses ambiguity, reversals and defeats. For the reader, complete victory can only be a few editions away.

Soldiers were big news. They were also stars. The *Sketch* ran a series of 'snapshots of celebrities at "The Front"' in which major figures of the war, particularly Baden-Powell and Buller, were either engaged in leading men, or sitting at a desk engrossed by military matters.[34] Sometimes photographs of officers were simply head and shoulders, not in any specific role other than that of celebrity, the property of the nation, in soft focus which was later to be adopted as the standard mode of photo-graphic representation of film stars.

It is now clear that whenever possible, the military authorities con-trolled Press activities in South Africa. Lord Roberts ensured that war correspondents in sympathy with the war were well cared for at the front, while recalcitrant voices were swiftly silenced if it was in his power to do so. Roberts closed down the anti-British *Express* and started *The Friend*, a bilingual newspaper edited by Kipling, specifically to boost the morale of both troops and the British public.[35] Similarly, Baden-Powell ensured that newspaper reports which criticized the British, and in particular his own behaviour in Mafeking, were not published.[36] It is therefore not surprising to find a uniformity of tone in much of the pic-torial and textual accounts by war correspondents, which was part of a wider industry of colonial lobbying, imperialists working in concert with owners of the new, cheap, mass-circulation press, in order to affect public opinion among working- and lower-middle class opinion.[37]

The use of theatrical and literary languages create related images of the soldier as actor, aesthetic object, and as a figure from romance and adventure fiction. He is idealized as an icon of patriotism. Individual utterances are also framed by generalized concepts and selected quota-tions from soldiers which echo each other in what then appears to be a single, sustained voice representing all soldiers. For example, Milne uses quotations in which individual soldiers, usually at particularly dramatic moments, identify themselves with a larger cause, usually through the use of popular catch phrases:

> 'Goodbye', a dying soldier mutters; 'let 'em have some bullets and don't forget that "They can't beat the boys of the bull-dog breed!"' Endless are the lights when the veldt is lit.
>
> (*EA*, p. 14)

MacCarthy interviewed a Private Maxwell, who tells him:

> we silently swore in our hearts that Christmas that we would fight and die for the honour of the flag and hand it down unstained, flut-tering in its glory and its joy, to our descendants.
>
> (*RBW*, p. 71)

The reader is confronted by the ubiquitous voice of a Tommy Atkins, in which the first person pronoun is eclipsed by plurals and personal codes are expressed and authorially framed as national imperatives. As such, the soldier's voice is written in the language of the state.

Figure 2.1 'We would fight and die for the honour of the flag.'

Source: Drawing by S. Begg in *South Africa and the Transvaal War* (author's own print).

In order that the image of the soldier does not blur in remote abstractions, and to consolidate the concatenation of wars abroad and values of home, the reader is constantly assured that domestic life is a fount of inspiration and that Tommy Atkins adheres to family life as the bedrock of all he is fighting for, as Milne writes:

> We have the passage, 'For the sake of you, and our little darling, I will look after myself as well as I can, but I will do my duty for Queen and country'. What better catechism of conduct could there be, than one in which family ties and national duty meet? They are the twin elements of patriotism, a man's home being the portal to his country.
>
> (*EA*, p. 5)

What the soldier could be expressing as a potential conflict of loyalties Milne proposes as commensurate values; the window of the home frames a larger moral outlook, an extension of the protection of personal to national self-interest. Milne's interpretation of correspondence between husband and wife assumes a sense of emotional and spiritual sanctity; a letter from his wife is, for the soldier:

> tenderly sacred; to us it is eloquently silent. But we may hear, full and clear, as bells ring, the calling of heart to heart, soul to soul, across the seas … a sunshine world after all.
>
> (*EA*, pp. 2–3)

This kind of authorial extemporizing overwhelms the content of soldier's letters and comments which Milne, like other writers, uses to try and create a sense of authenticity and the ostensible immediacy of felt experience in the Boer War.

References to mothers are also used to reveal the tender counterpoint to the soldier's heroism. In *True Stories of South Africa*, which is presented as being mainly autobiographical, a soldier (anonymous) describes an incident in which a fellow soldier sets off on a dangerous mission, and offers him a keepsake:

> 'If it so happens that I do not come back, I want you to send this for me: it is to the old mother at home'. And his voice broke. I looked away to give him a chance.[38]

Milne states that ' "Mother" is … "the dear word" which comes to the lips of the wounded' (*EA*, p. 13).

The central female image which unites battlefield and home in the soldier's mind is that of the Queen, which is used to serve as an archetypal mother-figure to all soldiers. MacCarthy states that while visiting wounded soldiers, Queen Victoria heard the story of Private King, wounded thirteen times at Colenso, but who continued to fight; 'the Queen was lost in the Woman, and one or two silent tears found their way down her cheeks' (*RBW*, p. 3). A footnote is included to remind the reader of the connection between the military and the monarchy; the deceased Queen has been laid to 'honoured rest, beside the remains of her "beloved Albert", with soldiers' music and the rites of war' (*RBW*, p. 3). Milne insists that Atkins is a 'knight of tenderness for his womankind' (*EA*, p. 174) and the significance of the Queen's ubiquitous image is that she can embrace as sons all who defend her sovereignty. She can retain her majesty while being overtly maternal, as Milne suggests in describing the soldiers responses to her gift of confectionery:

> To the soldier who is well, that chocolate is an inspiration; but to the soldier wounded or ill, it is sacred. It is the Mother-Queen visiting his bedside, as it were, with a greeting which falls on the ear as home and love and country – all that is dear and true and good.
>
> (*EA*, p. 20)

The rhetorical impulse is always to sentimentalize. Milne's book creates a context of moral triumph for the soldier and scenarios are sketched in as a manifestation of his protean virtues. He is part of a fighting fraternity in which the intensity of war experience creates new relationships bonded by mutual respect and common purpose. The consolidation of close male friendships is an expression of shared values intensified by the physical sensation of war which, Milne states, shows 'the threads that knit fighting men in a common brotherhood, even while they wrestle for mastery, in the scarlet surge of war' (*EA*, p. 21). This camaraderie extends to the enemy, for '[f]ormal enemies, being thrown together on the knees of the gods, may then begin a friendship' (*EA*, p. 21). This friendship, he argues, emanates from an intrinsic morality which is the unique property of the battlefield. The soldier's milieu transcends civil morality and civil relations, but the foundations of his own morality are seen to have been created at home and retain a strong domestic appeal. In addition to his devotion to the home and family, he is also scrupulously kind to children, faces death with the 'composure of a fine mind' (*EA*, p. 14), and when wounded, can maintain inner calm by being attuned to 'the higher things' (*EA*, p. 13) – religion, literature and patriotism. We are told that his physical courage is modulated and civilized by his 'moral courage' (*EA*, p. 12) which issues from English society. The lining of his heart, duty and good citizenship, is the genesis of his conduct:

> Hear him, all generous, on his opponents in the field. Hear him talk of the medals he will lay at the feet of father and mother, making them proud folk. Hear him about his country and the larger duties. You understand then the sort of lights by which he steers.
>
> (*EA*, p. 14)

Filial devotion and national pride inform both his identity and his behaviour. Not only is he morally honorific for his country, but morally prescriptive for civil society, a veritable 'sage in khaki' (*EA*, p. 2).

A frequent commentator on military issues, Colonel Henry Knollys used *Blackwoods* magazine as a platform upon which to voice his own theories on the moral value of the army. In an article entitled 'English Officers and Soldiers – as They Will Be' (*Blackwoods* February 1896) he argues that military control of personal matters, such as drinking, and more overweening controls, such as 'precautions against improvident marriages' create soldiers of a higher moral calibre.[39] By judicious tact, firm insistence and reformatory zeal, he states that he himself transformed miscreant 'young rowdy recruits' into men who behaved 'with the demeanour of gentlemen and the docility of Japs'.[40] Although the soldiers later revert to recalcitrant 'sulks', Knollys still insists on the ameliorative moral influence of military life:

> The English soldier on enlistment is suddenly lifted into a higher sphere entirely at variance with his former modes of life and habits of thought. He is free from his previous sordid cares of providing for his daily bread, and from the anxieties entailed by sickness, injustice, and the mutability of civilian callings. Organised regularity instead of haphazard disorder; self respect applied both to his dress and his demeanour; the development of his intellectual faculties through travel about this wonderful world.[41]

The recruit is morally elevated by the army, which assumes total responsibility for him. His loss of freedom and self-determination is defined positively, for in civil life his only freedom was to enact a cycle of failure. It would seem that for such a recruit loyalty would be to the army and not to the parent society, and Knollys's argument has as its premise a cultural fracture between the army and society, which he then tries to rationalize.

The key word is organization, Knollys's 'organised regularity' as opposed to the 'haphazard disorder' of society, associated with moral degeneration and physical illness. Yet what appears to be simplistic social criticism is a step towards a concern for conservatism and social order based on military discipline. Civil society is denigrated in order to indicate the greater opportunities, the wider tolerance of outcasts and capacity for moral improvement, available to the working-class army recruit. The army is thus recommended as having a strong social role to play and acts as a model for good citizenship. The army is the perfect society. It can inculcate qualities which the recruit lacked before enlistment; social usefulness, self-respect and a sense of duty. The diatribes against civil life are, then, an attempt to identify the army more strongly with society, as an invaluable cornerstone which, because of its apparent insularity and self-government, can be a forcing house for changing the soldier's consciousness and feeding him back into society as a regenerated and useful citizen. The army fashions raw civilian material into disciplined, controllable individuals. It is described in ways which align it with a public-school ethos, a comparison which is implicit in Knollys's thinking.

This process of controlled change is achieved, Knollys argues, partly through an appeal to gamesmanship, sport and 'team spirit'. Competitiveness is frequently fostered through a metaphorical use of sport and the language of games, in which the soldier is part of a military team and an athlete in battle. In his classic assault on imperialism in *Imperialism: A Study* (1902) J.A. Hobson suggests how the psychology of controlling vested interests appeals partly to the mission of civilization, but maintains itself 'chiefly by playing upon the primitive instincts of the race'.[42] The essence of this appeal is the competitive spirit; the desire to acquire and control lands leads, he argues, to a nomadic interest which may conveniently be called a 'spirit of adventure' and finds an appropriate form of expression through sport. More adventurous forms of sport involve a 'direct appeal to the lust of slaughter and the crude struggle for life involved in pursuit'.[43] Hobson quotes Baden-Powell's statement that '[f]ootball is a good game, but better than it, better than any other game, is that of man-hunting'.[44]

Milne's book appears to support Hobson's thesis and offers a considerable number of quotations from soldiers in which they perceive war through sporting images. These range from metaphorical appraisals of whole battles, such as 'they knocked us out like playing skittles' (*EA*, p. 3); seeing particular activities, like sniping, as 'sport' to be enjoyed (*EA*, p. 6), or tactical advance as a 'game of draughts' (*EA*, p. 7). War is frequently referred to as a game, suggesting both internal rules and schoolboy high spirits; Milne quotes one ghastly voice:

> a valiant scribe who bubbles over with, 'Oh, wasn't it lovely! Oh my! didn't I make my bayonet red! It was the best fun I ever had ...'
>
> (*EA*, p. 12)

He is often carried away by sporting rhetoric himself:

> scorpions and tarantulas stir his sporting instincts...The scorpion, being bigger, is invariably the victor, but the struggle does not lack excitement. The cockpit is the 'Open Veldt Hotel, Proprietors, Breeze and Co.'; What a bowling alley is to an hostelry in a London suburb.
>
> (*EA*, p. 6)

Inhabiting the same verbal arena, MacCarthy describes an incident in which two belligerent soldiers 'had a regular set-to with their fists' during the battle of Colenso, until the 'better man won' and they rejoin their comrades and fight the Boers. Football is the single most popular source of metaphor, providing an apt mixture of team spirit, excitement and spectatorial incitement to win. As with theatrical language, the metaphorical patterning of sporting images masks the brute realities of war by transposing the perception of it into a safer world of role-play. Sport is the self-contained rule-bound world which, for the duration of the game, or war, has its own internal logic and rules of conduct which can be stripped of ordinary convention, but can intensify partisan loyalties. By viewing the soldier as a figure involved in an enclosed world of sport, a spectator experiences not his ordeals, but an exhilarating game. The soldier is a member of a team which is duty-bound to win. Moral questions are replaced by sporting language, hence the outrage expressed by some commentators on the Boer's lack of fair play in adopting guerilla tactics.[45] Sport in nineteenth-century England was, of course, strongly allied to class, and underpinning the sporting metaphors are ideas about fair play, order and rules which speak as much of civil cohesion, with everyone knowing their place, as of war. As Lawrence James says:

> By the turn of the century the obsession with games had become a mania. It was the belief of J.E.C. Welldon, headmaster of Harrow (1881–95) and later Bishop of Calcutta, that, 'If there is in the British

race, as I think there is, a special aptitude for "taking up the white man's burden"... it may be ascribed, above all other causes, to the spirit of organized games.'[46]

Sport also promotes identification with a very particular, easily recognized group. Regimental names – The Sherwood Foresters, The King's Own, The Black Watch – institutionalize loyalty to a group which has its own unique identity. Beg's book provides a detailed account of how the army regulates behaviour and disseminates a sporting culture. Football, cricket and athletics are encouraged as a means of uniting the ranks through 'trials of strength'. A manly game, Beg states, 'develops the muscles, sharpens the wits, and, above all things, teaches the player self-restraint' (*TAH*, p. 6). This process creates an ideal man and soldier. A competitive spirit is fostered further through combat games and simulated manoeuvres, and particularly through regimental jealousies. These heavily structured loyalties and prejudices can then be exploited on a larger scale in wartime, aided by concepts of race, national character and moral superiority. The forms of army life outlined here are part of a neo-Darwinian thinking of the kind adopted by imperialist writers who wished to promote the idea that war was 'natural', and part of an Anglo-Saxon spirit of adventure which Chamberlain told the Commons 'has made us peculiarly fit to carrying out the working of colonization'.[47] Biology informed both history and national character: H.F. Wyatt wrote in *The Nineteenth Century*:

if nations did indeed cease, the one to take advantage of the other's weakness, the processes of biological law, and therefore the evolution of man, would come to an end.[48]

The belief that the natural evolution of nations is achieved through belligerent competition is enacted in the individual career of the soldier through the ritualized, competitively based forms of army life.

Sport is harnessed to and expressive of social class. The Officer leads, controls, and dictates the ethos of the war game and depends upon the subordinate Tommies to follow his dictates. His authority, drawn from the upper and middle classes and institutionalized by the army, demands recognition and loyalty from the ranks. Baden-Powell, like Cecil Rhodes, a son of the rectory, and whose father was an Oxford professor, came from a family of long naval distinction, and embodies the officer figure in both personal history and public image. Mafeking gave him a worldwide recognition which MacCarthy celebrates '[o]ut of respect to those who wield the willow'. Cricket, as a social metaphor, is apt for crediting an historical event to the achievement of an officer:

'218, NOT OUT.'

'Ah, "Captain" Baden-Powell! you
Have given them "tit for tat";
You've won the game for Mafeking
And "carried out your bat".

'The while they served "straights, byes, and wides"
To storm your 'cute redoubt,
You "held the wicket" till the score
Was "two-eighteen, not out".

'So give three cheers for Baden-Powell,
Who, answering every "ball"
With "No surrender!" proudly kept
The old flag over all'.

(*RBW*, p. 10)

Credit belongs not to the team, but to the captain, whose supremacy and victory is a result of the individualism of leadership. Sporting imagery transposes war into recreation, but also suggests that sport is the natural milieu of officers like Baden-Powell, who find an apposite expression of the sporting instinct through war. Hobson later wrote that this propensity is the exclusive property of a class whose economic freedom allows them to indulge in an inherited 'lust of slaughter' under the guise of 'sport' or a 'spirit of adventure':

> The leisured classes in Great Britain, having most of their energy liberated from the necessity of work, naturally specialise in 'sport' ... As the milder expressions of this passion are alone permissible in the sham or artificial encounters of domestic sports, where wild game disappears and human conflicts more mortal than football are prohibited, there is an even stronger pressure to the frontiers of civilization in order that the thwarted 'spirit of adventure' may have strong, free play.[49]

Beg, however, drew attention to social gaps in order to affirm that the private soldier was encouraged to have both military and social aspirations. His earlier work, *Our Citizen Army*, shows concern for the relations between civil and military worlds, and in *Tommy Atkins at Home* he develops a magniloquent treatise on Tommy's opportunities for upward social mobility. Part IV of the book is called 'Promotion' and contains three chapters which enact the career of the ideal private; Chapter XIX entitled 'Climbing the Ladder'; Chapter XX – 'The Second and Third Rungs' and Chapter XXI 'Excelsior'. Emphasizing the prerequisites of good character and personal merit, Beg details the rise of the ideal private to the rank of NCO, with possibilities beyond that. Essentially, it means joining the middle classes. His creature comforts are improved when he enters the sergeant's mess, the description of which is a vision of a middle-class drawing room: luxurious chairs; carpets; daily and weekly papers; interesting books and a writing table. Topics of conversation, 'unknown or voted uninteresting in the barrack room' facilitate intellectual growth and the 'social aspect, too, cannot fail to please' as he encounters genial hospitality, dances, smoking concerts and access to desirable members of the civilian population. Social distinctions are thus perceived as 'natural' and ameliorative, because they promote a concept of potential personal progress. It was, of course, a limited upward mobility because someone from the ranks could rarely become an officer.

The books under discussion indicate ordinary soldiers' inherent mistrust of the officer class. One soldier describes officers as 'all bursting for glory' (*EA*, p. 4); another rejects his colonel's address to the ranks for making 'a name for yourselves which will never die' by commenting ironically that 'the cost is very, very dear' (*EA*, p. 17).

There are other indications of the soldier's disillusionment with heroic myth. A London cockney fighting in the war comments: 'Roll on; I suppose when we are done we shall get a medal, or a ticket for St. George's workhouse' (*EA*, p. 130). Unmanageable and complaining soldiers were viewed by Knollys as 'rowdies' who usually fall into the arms of military authority, while those who do not conform are simply outsiders who are not legitimate soldiers but 'rowdy drafts' or loafers[50] who should be dispensed with, as they have failed the army. Similarly, any criticisms from the civil world are treated to vitriolic diatribes; Beg admits to cases of 'riot and debauchery' in the army but states that this does not constitute a social threat at home because most soldiers are 'equal, if not superior, in manners to the mass of their civilian brethren' (*TAH*, p. 5). MacCarthy refutes Boer accusations of British outrages towards women and children. He also criticizes a belligerent press and the subversive intentions of certain works of literature, such as Marie Corelli's bestselling novel, *Boy*, which criticizes Kitchener (*RBW*, p. 56). *True Stories of South Africa*, despite beginning as a vindication of the soldier, suggests the elements of adventurism, racism and self-gain which lie beneath a military code of honour. Confessing that he himself went to South Africa to make a fortune, the narrator's anecdotes also indicate a hedonistic delight in killing and self-glory while posing as a soldier in a land of 'niggers'.

These elements of criticism and grudging acknowledgements or rebuttals of atrocities and problems hint at other possible narratives and accounts of the war which would foreground self-gain, blunders and disparities between the ranks. The nation, like the empire, would not then appear as a unity but as a complex set of tensions and contradictions.

By the turn of the century, the Boer War was becoming an increasing source of embarrassment and frustration for the British Government. An imperialist nation, whose military history during the nineteenth century had been embroidered with endless colonial victories against poorly armed races, took approximately three years to defeat a resourceful white force one-ninth the size of the British forces. Middle-class fears concerning British military supremacy had traditionally been placated by stereotypical heroes, usually generals, whose public images consisted of entrepreneurial displays of courage and personal valour, rather than professional efficiency. This was no longer so easily achieved against an organized, well-equipped guerilla force which preferred hit-and-run strategic attacks and withdrawals to death and glory battles. This was a new kind of war, what Pakenham calls 'this last great (or infamous) imperial war',[51] but also one in which 'a nineteenth century army had to fight a twentieth century war'.[52] The Boers were not seen purely as soldiers, but as a nation of individuals, whose civilian and military identities were indistinguishable. This fusion of identities, with citizens as soldiers, was not true of the British, and when the assumption of a quick victory through superior military powers collapsed, it posed a problem – if the trained soldier cannot beat the civilian, what does this say about the special status of the army?

A major concern of this kind of literature was to compose an image of the Boer War as a military and moral victory. The war was actually won finally through greater numbers and resources, and clearly exposed the flaws and massive incompetence of the Victorian army.[53] In this sense, the literature acts as escapism from the more disturbing military blunders and partial victories. Central to this purpose was to compose an image of Tommy Atkins as an icon of Anglo-Saxon manhood, yet real potential Tommies provided a shock at the recruitment centres in 1899.

There had been little recruitment until 'Black Week' (10–15 December) when the British suffered unprecedented casualties. On a wave of patriotism, a rush of recruits, upon examination, provided a shock for the authorities who were forced to acknowledge the physical degeneration which the working classes had experienced during the late nineteenth century. The majority of volunteers were too diseased or unfit for military service. F.E. Huggett states:

> Years of exploitation, bad food, bad housing, and a lack of medical care had produced a generation of undersized and unhealthy young men – squints, deafness, crippled limbs… As these crippled and diseased volunteers limped into public view from their slums, the establishment was just as horrified and shocked as it had been by the military defeats.[54]

A further anxiety was the relationship between physical decay, social problems and moral obliquity. The working-class physical degenerate implied, for some, a hive of hidden dangers insidious in their implications for the rest of society. Physical deprivation could herald increased hooliganism and possibly, if organized, a concerted threat to society. The work of the slum novelists and social commentators during the 1890s had drawn increased attention to the urban poor and the kinds of responsibilities which should be shown towards them. Eugene Sandow, a fitness expert who began *Sandow's Magazine* was quite clear about the interrelatedness of poverty and social problems, and equally clear about the remedy. Sandow claimed that the hooligan, essentially an urban type:

> is merely the victim of misdirected courage … he is starving, his mental equipment is little … his primitive barbarism, without any moral restraint, prompts him to take what he wants … by force.[55]

Military training, he claimed, can turn the hooligan into 'a really ideal soldier, and not infrequently a hero … the best of pioneers and colonisers',[56] an argument I shall return to.

The military world is here dynamically related to problems of social order. A growing recognition of Tommy Atkins's background grew contemporaneously with an awareness of the effects of material deprivation among the working class, informed by the work of Mayhew, Booth and Rowntree. Much of the literature I have discussed is an assuagement of anxieties about the army and an attempt to create an image of the common soldier which transcends criticism. What this image did bring, however, was a sense that all was not well with the army, the war, and, ultimately, the nation itself.

3
Rudyard Kipling's Barrack Room Ballads: The Soldier as Hooligan or Hero

> There was a row in Silver Street – they sent the Polis there,
> The English were too drunk to know, the Irish didn't care.
> > Rudyard Kipling, 'Belts', in *Barrack Room Ballads and Other Verses*, London, Methuen, 1892

> [Kipling] ... cannot even follow the soldier home into our streets without celebrating his drunken assaults and savageries.
> > Robert Buchanan, 'The Voice of the Hooligan', in *Contemporary Review*, vol. LXXVI, December 1899, pp. 774–89

Robert Buchanan chose an auspicious moment to brand Kipling's *Barrack Room Ballads*[1] as the 'Voice of the Hooligan'. The Boer War was occupying considerable public attention and by the time that Buchanan's article was published in the *Contemporary Review* in December 1899,[2] the term 'hooligan' had acquired sufficient notoriety for it to accede to the status of a debating term. Given that the Boer War was very much in the public mind, the army was a focus of attention. The term 'hooligan' could serve as a rhetorical device for widely differing ideologies, either to illustrate what was feared to be a degenerating social structure with no real centre of authority, resulting in national and imperial decline, or to condemn a government which, it was argued, was as pugnacious in domestic policy as it was in imperialist exploitation.[3] By identifying Kipling with both 'cockney ignorance' and a belligerent imperialism, Buchanan voices contemporary anxieties about both the direction of imperialism and the dangers of forms of culture traditionally associated with the British working class, such as music halls, and which constituted, for some people, a threat to national identity.[4] The fact that Walter Besant was moved to offer a considered reply to Buchanan suggests that Kipling and his creation of 'Tommy Atkins' occupied a notorious place in this debate in the 1890s.[5]

My discussion of the *Barrack Room Ballads* makes specific use of Buchanan's article because his criticisms highlight the issue of civil and military borders. By publishing his article near the beginning of the Boer War, when the army was much discussed and civilian identification with it encouraged by the Press, politicians and elements of popular culture, Buchanan attempted to articulate a gap between army and civilian sensibilities which, in turn, denied the possibility of a homogeneous national character of which civil and military worlds were mutually compatible expressions.

The fact that the *Ballads* gave voice to a specific image of the British soldier as both archetype and individual character, created a double sense of Tommy Atkins as both a historical and fictional presence, and it is the quasi-historical dimension of the *Ballads* which appears to have prompted vituperation from such as Buchanan.

Kipling's earlier verse collection, *Departmental Ditties*, and stories, such as 'Pagget, M.P.' offered images of an English ruling class reproducing their own social and sexual mores at work and play in India. The *Ballads*, and *Soldiers Three*, however, offered a 'view from below' in which the experiences of working-class soldiers are represented through the slang and dialect of their own culture, constituting what is now seen as an innovative perspective on empire.[6] Stripped of the context and pressures of environment within which the slum novelists had fictionalized the London working class, the image of Tommy Atkins was thrown into sharp relief. Also, he was transposed from his conventional role of acolyte in a continuing imperial drama into a site of contention, a point for critical exchange on both the relative values of empire and the duties of criticism.

By 1890, Kipling's stories and poems were being published regularly, and in February, the *Barrack Room Ballads* first began to appear in W.E. Henley's *Scots Observer*. Kipling rapidly became a celebrity, whose status issued partly from the controversy surrounding it, as J.M. Barrie observed:

Two society papers made themselves at one time a debating society for discussing Mr. Rudyard Kipling ... As a result, while *The World* and other papers thought Mr. Kipling such a celebrity that they vied with each other in describing the tags of his bootlaces, *Truth* and other papers talked contemptuously of log-rolling.[7]

The appeal of Kipling's work also crossed traditional cultural boundaries, to include reviewers and critics, literary circles, music-hall audiences[8] and soldiers, who set the *Ballads* to old tunes and sang them on foreign expeditions.[9] Appearing at a time when the 'new Imperialism' was in its ascendancy,[10] it is not surprising that the content of the *Ballads*, Kipling's adherence to the imperial theme and his use of popular forms, should prompt responses which translated literary into cultural and political criticism. Moreover, his own antipathy to what he saw as an exclusive and self-regarding English culture suggests the possibility of an intention to provoke strong responses. Kipling's autobiography, *Something of Myself*,[11] is littered with anecdotes which consistently reject English moral insularity and a narrow vision of culture as defined by the purveyors of literature. Literary coteries are an extended 'dog fight' among disgruntled elderly men which has its parallel in colonial honour seeking (*SOM*, p. 84). English morality, blind to the social realities of violence and prostitution, is epitomized in the 'great fogs' of London (*SOM*, p. 87). Political sympathies are spare: 'gentry' socialists are dismissed for their provincial prejudices and safe sedition (*SOM*, p. 91) and, equally suspect, is 'a mixed crowd of wide-minded, wide-mouthed Liberals, who darkened counsel with pious but disintegrating catch-words, and took care to live very well indeed' (*SOM*, p. 92). His only expressed political sympathies with a literary figure were with W.E. Henley.

This disillusionment found partial expression in 'The English Flag', published with *Barrack Room Ballads*, and which juxtaposes the expansive realities of Empire with the enclosed world of the English at home: 'What should they know of England who only England know?' (*BRB*, p. 174). From this public denunciation of insularity grew a desire to 'tell to the English something of the world outside England – not directly but by implication' (*SOM*, p. 90). However, the *Ballads* represented elements from the inside too, including the London working class. Kipling's discovery of the music hall helped to contextualize his observations on the cockney soldier in India. What appears to have attracted Kipling to music halls was that they enhanced his own sense of working-class life previously represented in the yarn spinning fraternity of the 'Soldiers Three' stories. Listening to the 'observed and compelling songs' of the Lion and Mammoth comiques, he states:

> These monologues I could never hope to rival, but the smoke, the roar, the good-fellowship of relaxed humanity at Gatti's 'set' the scheme for a certain sort of song. The Private Soldier in India I thought I knew fairly well. His English brother (in the Guards mostly)

sat and sang at my elbow any night I chose; and, for Greek chorus, I had the comments of my barmaid – deeply and dispassionately versed in all knowledge of evil as she watched it across the zinc she was always swabbing off. (Hence, some years later, verses called 'Mary, pity women', based on what she told me about 'a friend o' mine 'oo was mistook in 'er man'.) The outcome was the first of some verses called Barrack-Room Ballads.

(SOM, p. 81)

These observations offer some clues as to a possible reading of the *Ballads* as part of a music-hall tradition in which the ballad form, as used by Kipling, is essentially song, with a repeated refrain, an emphasis on sound repetitions and a strong first person voice that delineates the ballad as a 'character' performance piece which presents an easily apprehended view of the world. As Keating has observed, Kipling's attendance of the music hall was contemporaneous with the rise of the coster figure as entertainer.[12] Narrative songs, sung by performers like Gus Elen and Albert Chevalier (the 'Kipling of the halls') reflected a concern with the details of everyday life: courtship, work, privation, endurance and street life.

It is now accepted that the *Ballads* are more than populist verse. A recent biography of Kipling discusses their 'undeniable literary qualities' and reminds us that fifty years after their publication T.S. Eliot singled out 'Danny Deever' as 'technically [as well as in context] remarkable' with its perfect 'combination of heavy beat and variation of pace'.[13] In the 1890s the critical problem which the *Ballads* posed was the extent to which they should be considered as part of a popular, or mass, culture, rather than an exclusively literary one. Furthermore, if they were part of a mass culture, what were the implications of this, especially now that Kipling was a rapidly rising star in the literary firmament? Buchanan was in no doubt; the Ballads were, he stated, articulated at 'the lowest level of music hall effusions'[14] and were symptomatic of a cultural and political regression into barbarity, because they celebrated 'cockney' values of violence and vulgarity with a complete absence of authorial condemnation. Buchanan's diatribe against Kipling's affinity with the degenerative influence of music halls immediately followed a resurgence of moral outrage at the halls.[15] For example, following a magistrate's condemnation of music halls as a major cause of hooliganism, a Board School manager tested the hypothesis by visiting a hall in 'one of the roughest districts of London'. He then wrote to *The Times* about the celebration of drunkenness, crime, prostitution and unemployment in the bill of eighteen turns. Such entertainment, he concludes, 'is likely to appeal with terrible force to the ill-educated, ill-clothed, ill-fed, and often ill-paid hobblede-hoys of the threepenny gallery', and which 'can scarcely help but aid the lawless spirit that it represents'.[16] It seems plausible that Buchanan not only shared but was appealing to such contemporary fears by suggesting that the Tommy Atkins of the Ballads was the embodiment of a 'lawless spirit'. Whatever Buchanan's personal motivations, the *Ballads* do need to be viewed in the prevalent context of this mood of outrage.

The fear of a cultural fall had, of course, been more cogently rehearsed in Matthew Arnold's *Culture and Anarchy* (1869), in which he restated a political problem, that of social order, as a cultural problem and called upon guardians of culture, in a famous passage, to recreate a centre of authority by means of public education:

> Plenty of people will try to give the masses, as they call them, an intel-lectual food prepared and adapted in the way they think proper for the actual condition of the masses. The ordinary popular literature is an example of this way of working on the masses ... but culture works differently ... It seeks to do away with classes; to make the best that has been thought and known in the world current everywhere.[17]

The desire for a classless society has a peculiarly contemporary impetus; for Arnold, it was partly a concern to thwart anarchic tendencies which were embodied in the appearance of such as the 'Hyde Park rough', a 'brawling, ... hustling' type who 'has no idea of a state'.[18] It is not difficult to see how the *Barrack Room Ballads* inflamed the resurgent debate about culture and social order. Critics and reviewers had already, by 1889, com-mitted themselves to an approval of Kipling's work, so when the *Ballads* were published as a collection in 1892 these earlier responses had to be rationalized. The key problem was how and where to place Kipling within established points of reference. Eminent figures, such as Henley, had already made claims for the literary merit of Kipling's work, and now had to acknowledge concern for his use of the 'popular'.[19] He used slang and dialect, not as mere gestures towards realism, but as defining struc-tures for his work; music-hall song patterns were an obvious influence; he was both stigmatized and excused for his earlier schooling and jour-nalistic writing for the *Civil and Military Gazette* in India. Also, the cre-ation of a cockney soldier figure, Tommy Atkins, implicitly challenged the veracity of existing cockney stereotypes – Tommy did not have the same manageable and occasionally servile propensities of a Sam Weller.

Critical boundaries were at stake in the extent to which Kipling could be acknowledged as a literary figure rather than as a celebrated populist.

Attempts to assimilate him into the literary fold constituted an effort to rationalize aspects of a 'popular culture' without being seen to compromise a held view of high art. As early as 1889, Andrew Lang, clearly an admirer, was nevertheless worrying that Kipling's work was 'occasionally flippant and too rich in slang'.[20] Suspicious admiration was a keynote, final judgement being reserved until the new writer graduated from journalism to literature, or, more accurately, until he satisfied critics and reviewers before appealing to a wider public. The literary needed to be sifted from the vulgar, the culturally permissable from the offensive.

His case hadn't been helped by publishing *The Light That Failed*, a novel which he hoped would impress the Savile Club Literati as worthy art, but which failed to impress. Responses were at best ambiguous to this novel about earnest artistic integrity, passion, tragic blindness and finally seeking one's own death in battle. Gosse said the book had 'oases of admirable detail in a desert of the undesirable'.[21]

The aesthetes were 'horrified' at works such as the *Ballads* which, for them, represented an unapologetic and unacceptable relationship between art and practical life which, in this case, explored the administrative labour of the empire.[22] Charles Whibley, who worked in an editorial capacity with Henley, qualified enthusiasm with a warning that a prerequisite for Kipling's initiation into the Temple of Art was to discard what Oscar Wilde called the 'most admirable subject' of vulgarity.[23] Kipling needed to refrain from crossing the cultural line which 'divides art from reporting':

> He seems to forget that the written word does not produce the same effect as the spoken. A duologue conducted in the slang of the mess-room only becomes vulgar when it is crystallised into literary form. Words and phrases have one value in life, another in literature, and it is the artist's business to translate, not to transcribe. The reader wearies of such expressions as 'regimental shop o'sorts', and the jarring note lingers on.[24]

'Vulgar' is a key term in responses to Kipling. The ideal reader is posited as a frequent image of referral, whose jarred sensibilities can only be recuperated through a refinement of style in accordance with prescribed literary requirements. As a sign of literary maturity, a novel was also expected from Kipling, in which the subject of army life would, it was argued, necessarily be relinquished in favour of more elevated subject matter. One unsigned review insisted upon a ' "majora cavere" ... [to] concentrate his undoubted gifts upon the treatment of more important themes than even the amusing vagaries of Tommy Atkins and the risky situation of Simla society'.[25]

In 1892 Stevenson wrote to Henry James, stating that Kipling is 'all smart journalism and cleverness';[26] James's correspondence is fraught with bitingly qualified responses – admiration for the 'diabolically great' talent of the 'infant monster Kipling'[27] and revulsion at the 'steam and patriotism' of later work.[28] Kipling's work could not be easily deposited in the categories of Romance or Adventure and his use of the 'vulgar' denied comparisons with writers like Bret Harte and Rider Haggard.

The Tommy Atkins of the *Ballads* is partially reclaimed from the purely vulgar by emphasizing his heroic traits, but he remains in the critical mind as a parody of refinement, a Caliban who offends the good taste of an imagined reader. Charles Eliot Norton wrote in 1897:

> The recklessness, the coarseness, the brutality of Tommy Atkins, the spirit of the beast in man, all appear in the Barrack-Room Ballads, but not less his courage, his fidelity, his sense of duty, his obscure but deep-seated sentiment. The gist of all these Ballads is the display of the traits of human nature which makes this semi-savage 'most remarkable like you'. Yet it will not be only the fastidious and the super-refined reader who will find that some of the ballads might well be spared. There is more than one in this last volume which offends the taste by coarseness insufficiently redeemed by humour or by suggestion of virtue obscured by vulgarity, and diminishes the charm of the book as a whole.[29]

The recurrent issue in such responses is the remoteness of the image of the soldier from critical sensibilities. That remoteness is confirmed either through accusations of vulgarity or by the use of an emollient rhetoric which is the antithesis of the soldier's colloquial speech. Lytton Strachey called *The Soldiers Three* 'this quaint trio' and asserted that 'Mr. Kipling has a genius for reproducing quaint and characteristic Hibernicisms'.[30] Quaintness, like vulgarity, sets the image of the soldier, and by implication, his culture, at a distance, to be reclaimed through the moral imperatives implicit in critical practice, for Strachey goes on to say that in the image of the soldier, Kipling 'shows how in the grossest natures sparks of nobility may lie hid'.[31]

There is a double intention in the critical responses I have outlined: to maintain distance yet create spaces for the image of the soldier, and, by implication, Kipling himself, to be accommodated in terms which were not only aesthetically but also morally and politically acceptable to the critical temper of the time. At the heart of these responses is an unease about what the empire is, who is policing it, and in turn, what is the nation? Buchanan may have reviled the Ballads as a symptom of cultural regression; others tried to negotiate new relations with the alienating image of the soldier by cautiously extending literary reviews to include issues of national and imperial responsibility:

> We in England seem to take it for granted that India is hot, but scarcely one of us makes any attempt to realize what that heat really means, especially to the men on whom our Power there really reacts, our private soldiers, with their few comforts, their dreary, enforced leisure, and their almost irresistible temptations for getting into mischief... although his [Kipling's] aim is artistic in the first place and practical only in the second, he will certainly not be unwilling that the British government as well as the British people should come nearer to realizing what these terrible conditions of life actually imply.[32]

Yet the *Ballads* persistently proclaim separateness and a refusal to be easy philanthropic prey. The 'Barrack Room' of the title signifies an enclosed world of men, defined by its internal structures, mores and duties, and absolutely different to civil society. It is closed to outsiders yet in the title is yoked alliteratively to 'Ballads', which has associations of a common folk culture and the sharing of stories through a ballad form. Accessible form conveys an uncompromising and often cynical point of view.

The immediacy of an extensive use of the first person voice is not ultimately reassuring for a reader, because we are frequently given an alternative to the view of the soldier as an heroic object of contemplation, such as I discussed in Chapter 2. As dramatic persona, Tommy Atkins is shaped entirely by the language and conventions of the *Ballads*, which subvert the idealized possibilities of either glorious death or ecstatic homecoming, thus overturning a popular convention of the time-expired soldier returning home to a grateful nation, 'English women an' a quart of English beer':

> Then 'ere's to the sons o' the Widow,
> Wherever, 'owever they roam.
> 'Ere's all they desire, an' if they require
> A speedy return to their 'ome,
> (Poor beggars! – they'll never see 'ome.)

> (*BRB*, p. 41)

The use of an extra parenthetical line acts as a dramatic aside, a *sotto voce* reminder of a more ambiguous reality behind the hearty good wishes of the previous four lines. We are reminded that the perspective of this particular folk hero, created indirectly from the vicissitudes of imperial politics, tends towards personal irony rather than patriotic cliché, working in the way that music-hall songs often did. By breaking the four-line stanza form the extra line adds a dramatic dimension to the ballad and underlines a subversive quality in the soldier's voice. That possibility of subversion partly defines the voice in the *Ballads*, with Tommy Atkins acting as a synecdoche for a whole class, and this unnerved critics such as Buchanan.

The soldier's view of the British Empire in the *Ballads* is essentially pragmatic. The organic metaphor of empire as a growing, developing body, with soldiers as sons, such as we find in Henley's poetry, was useful for concepts of expansionism, but the *Ballads* remind us that half of creation is actually constructed from the dead: 'An we've salted it down with our bones./(Poor beggars! – it's blue with our bones!')' (*BRB*, p. 40). Survival is, not surprisingly, dependent upon cultivating a necessary indifference to others in certain times of crisis; in 'The Young British Soldier' the voice of experience advises a young recruit on survival techniques, and what to do if the worst happens:

> When first under fire an' you're wishful to duck,
> Don't look nor take 'eed at the man that is struck,
> Be thankful you're livin', and trust to your luck
> And march to your front like a soldier.
> ...
> When you're wounded and left on Afghanistan's plains,
> And the women come out to cut up what remains,
> Jest roll to your rifle and blow out your brains
> An' go to your Gawd like a soldier.
>
> (*BRB*, pp. 47–8)

Yoked to the machinery of war, the soldier finds in that machinery a metaphor for the ideal military consciousness, based on efficiency and obedience, as in 'Screw Guns', where the narrative voice merges with the voice of the guns:

> For we fancies ourselves at two thousand, we guns
> that are built in two bits – 'Tss! 'Tss!
> For you all love the screw guns...
>
> (*BRB*, p. 17)

Mechanical performance is then related to military training:

> If a man doesn't work, why, we drills 'im an'
> teaches 'im 'ow to behave;
> If a beggar can't march, why, we kills 'im an'
> rattles 'im into 'is grave.
>
> (*BRB*, p. 17)

One result of this induced disengagement from 'ordinary' feeling is a displacement from civil society on returning home. The realities of colonial service do not sit comfortably with civilian sensibilities. The irony, of which Tommy is acutely aware, is that what he calls 'English morals' are ultimately dependent upon such as he:

> I went into a theatre as sober as could be,
> They gave a drunk civilian room, but 'adn't none for
> me;
> They sent me to the gallery or round the
> music-'alls,
> But when it comes to fightin', Lord! they'll shove
> me in the stalls;
> For it's Tommy this, an' Tommy that, an' 'Tommy,
> wait outside';
> But it's 'Special train for Atkins' when the
> troopers on the tide.
>
> (*BRB*, pp. 6–7)

Tommy's complaint in this ballad aligns him with folk heroes such as Dick Turpin and Captain MacHeath, not in respect of the imagined glamour of their outlawed status, but in what their positions as 'outsiders' reveal about the hypocrisies at play in civil society. Conventional heroism is a civilian fantasy, created by keeping uncomfortable realities at a safe distance and Tommy's actual presence is a problem. After chronicling the hypocrisies of his own society, which, according to its immediate needs, exploits, condemns, disowns or adores its soldiers, Tommy makes his accusation explicit to the audience he addresses:

> We aren't no thin red 'eroes, nor we aren't no black
> guards too,
> But single men in barricks, most remarkable like
> you;

An' if sometimes our conduck isn't all your fancy
    paints,
Why, single men in barricks don't grow into plaster
    saints.

(*BRB*, p. 8)

Figure 3.1 'For it's Tommy this, an' Tommy that, an' "Tommy Wait outside";
But it's "Special train for Atkins" when the Troopers on the tide.'

Source: Drawing by R. Coton Woodville, appeared in *South Africa and the Transvaal War* by
Louis Creswicke, published Edinburgh, T.C. & E.C. Jack, 1900.

Rather than being an uncivilized and savage enemy of the empire, the Soudanese 'Fuzzy Wuzzy' is represented as an adversary whom Tommy not only respects, but sympathizes with. The enemy is the audience for Tommy's appeal, which contradicts the remote fictions of what Kipling called, in another poem, the 'old Black Art' of the Press:

> We 'eld our bloomin' own, the papers say,
> But man for man the Fuzzy knocked us 'oller.
> ...
> We sloshed you with martinis, an' it wasn't 'ardly
> fair;
> But for all the odds agin' you, Fuzzy-wuz,
> You broke the square.
>
> (*BRB*, p. 11)

Admiration for the 'Fuzzy's' ability to break the fighting formation of the British square, against the odds, suggests how, in ways dramatically peculiar to the exigencies of military life, the soldier's experience both consolidates and dissolves racial and ethnic boundaries. Where a military ethic predominates, 'Fuzzy Wuzzy' is a 'pore benighted 'eathen but a first class fightin' man'; equally, the more sentimentalized native character of 'Gunga Din' may be a piece of 'Lazarushian-leather' who exists to serve the white soldiers and be flogged for it, but the exhaustively quoted 'You're a better man than I am, Gunga Din' (*BRB*, p. 26) introduces a scale of values which accommodates the heroically masculine but not the racist impetus of imperialism. Gunga Din may epitomize the devoted servant and Fuzzy Wuzzy the heroic adversary, but the British Tommy's subjective experience of empire leads him to identify with these 'uncivilized' types rather than with an elevated concept of racial superiority. Kipling was to return to this theme in 'The Mother Lodge' in which a cockney voice reflects on his experiences abroad:

> An' lookin' on it backwards
> It often strikes me thus,
> There ain't such things as infidels,
> Excep', per'aps, it's us.[33]

The affinity with such as Gunga Din extends to a disenchantment with civilian life in general and a nostalgia for the pleasures and freedoms afforded by places Tommy has known:

> I am sick o' wastin' leather on these gritty pavin'–stones,
> An' the blasted Henglish drizzle wakes the fever in my bones;
> Tho' I walks with fifty 'ousemaids outer Chelsea to the Strand,
> An' they talks a lot o' lovin, but wot do they understand?
> ...
> Ship me somewheres east of Suez, where the best is like the
>   worst,
> Where there aren't no Ten Commandments an' a man can raise
>   a thirst.
>
> (*BRB*, pp. 52–3)

Tommy Atkins is neither rooted in a political vision of the empire, nor is he a radical opponent of it, though he can be fiercely critical of basic injustices and hypocrisies. By concentrating on sensual and concrete detail, such as drinking, women, guns, animals, survival, Kipling suggests that Tommy is one of the dispossessed. He is apolitical beyond certain tribal loyalties and personal affections. The representation of his experiences constitutes a form of folk wisdom and his language is the story of certain class experiences formed by the politics of the empire. The cockney voice nudges itself into history through these ballads to proclaim another version of the empire. That these experiences, shaped by a cockney language, could not be readily assimilated into either a vision of the empire or a vision of culture, was part of the cause of critical disquiet.

The *Ballads'* insistence upon and celebration of violence could only unsettle a view of the empire emphasizing the civilizing mission of imperialism. The image of empire as a party given by Queen Victoria, the 'Widow at Windsor', is exposed as fraudulent gentility; the duality of drawing-room refinements and the literal carving up of men, presented in folk-ballad form, blatantly undercuts the ethos of armchair imperialism:

> 'What did you do for knives and forks',
> 'Johnny, Johnny?'
> We carries 'em with us wherever we walks,
> Johnny, my Johnny, aha!
>
> And some was sliced and some was halved,
> And some was crimped and some was carved,
> And some was gutted and some was starved,
> When the widow gave the party.
>
> (*BRB*, p. 58)

Acts of violence are also an affirmation of a measure of independence, as in 'Cells', in which a drunken soldier expresses an unrepentant bravado:

> I left my cap in a public-house, my boots in the public road,
> And Lord knows where, and I don't care, my belt and my tunic
>   goed;
> They'll stop my pay, they'll cut away the stripes I used to wear,
> But I left my mark on the corp'rals face, and I think he'll keep it
>   there.
>
> (*BRB*, p. 21)

This violent defiance of punitive authority is reminiscent of early music-hall songs; in particular, 'The Ballad of Sam Hall', performed by W.G. Ross, which was the first music-hall song to be given full dramatic characterization. Both Sam Hall and the soldier/narrator in Kipling's ballad are speaking from prison cells and are fiercely unrepentant, wryly fatalistic, and derisive of authority, whilst accepting its judgements.

Buchanan's criticisms also mark a watershed in responses to Kipling and helped to form what was to become a pervasive rejection of the writer on political grounds. Music halls had reached a commercial apotheosis by the time Buchanan was writing[34] and his marrying of the *Ballads* to what he took to be the degenerative ethos of music halls expressed a fear that the literary acceptance of forms associated with popular amusement was to bow to the culture, and consequently to the will, of the masses. The image of Tommy Atkins is framed by Buchanan as a 'hooligan', who constitutes a threat to imperial grandeur and to a correspondingly heroic literature. The *Ballads* are thus, he argues, part of 'a great back-wave, as it were, in the direction of absolute barbarism'.[35]

Buchanan's vision of the role of the critic is strongly related to his sense of nationhood and history. Nostalgic for a time when 'the great name of (Thomas) Arnold was still a living force in our English schools' he maintains that, during times of relative stability and progress, the critic abstains from overtly political issues and devotes himself to the dissemination of 'the gospel of humanity' and philanthropy, exemplified in the works of Wordsworth, Shelley, Chaucer, Shakespeare, Dickens, Wilberforce and Mazzini.[36] These 'great leaders' also inform the ethical humanism of the critic's political outlook, which remains implicit until threatened by political and cultural forces, at which point he moves from the desk to the pulpit in order to reaffirm the political and cultural conditions necessary for literature again to be socially ameliorative. When the moment of crisis is over, literary language can be reintegrated into culture as the basis of humanism. Crucial to this position is the concept of a state in which leaders are men of culture who can create conditions conducive to the mediation of humanist principles to the masses via the critic, who acts as seer and interpreter of literature.

The argument is not unfamiliar, nor the questions it begs regarding who defines the conditions of ethical humanism. The notion of history in this position is that it is something of a problem because it signifies the possibilities of unruly and uncontainable change. Ideally, history is static until another moment of what Buchanan terms, in an undefined way, 'progress' is identified and created. The critic is a baron in a literary outpost, only returning to the political nerve centre in a crisis to hoist his colours. Like Henley, Buchanan's lament is for an imagined past soaked in elevated sentiments that fostered national pride:

> Sentiment has at last become thoroughly out of fashion, and human-itarianism is left to the care of eccentric and unauthoritative teachers. Thus, while a few despairing thinkers and dreamers have been trying vainly to substitute a new Ethos for the old religious sanctions, the world at large, repudiating the enthusiasm of humanity altogether, and exchanging it for the worship of physical force and commercial success in any and every form, has turned rapturously towards activ-ities which need no sanction whatever, or which, at any rate, can be easily sanctified by the wanton will of the majority.[37]

Enter Kipling to prove the case. Although the targets for Buchanan's crit-icisms are universal, the recurrent derisory term which, he argues, is the key to current degeneration, is 'cockney', with its obvious associations of working-class culture. It assumes a metaphorical status of decline as ref-erences accumulate: 'cockney patriotism'; 'cockney humour'; 'cockney vulgarity'; and 'cockney ignorance' which worships a 'cockney Gawd'.[38]

For Buchanan, these terms unite beneath the collective flag of Hooliganism, which is responsible for infecting both culture and the quality of public life. All contemporary tensions are located in the arche-typal image of the hooligan which Kipling was instrumental in creating for 'idle and uninstructed' readers.[39] Worse, by presenting the hooligan as soldier, Kipling linked degenerative social forces at home with the British army, thus soiling 'the true imperial feeling', formerly fostered by the best of English literature in the 'dominion of dreams'.[40] The 'imperial spirit' was clearly very much in the public mind at this time, given that it was being tried and tested on the South African veld, so Buchanan's remarks were timely.

Kipling is seen as the ring-master in a conspiracy of hooliganism which celebrates the 'savages of the South London slums' as protectors of the empire. By celebrating the spirit of the music hall, popular literature and the press in his 'free and easy rattles', he manufactures and mirrors the will of the mob. As a 'drunken, swearing, coarse-minded hooligan' whose 'assaults and savageries' are celebrated by Kipling, Tommy Atkins is the popular image of a violence which threatens the state of culture and the fate of the empire.[41]

Buchanan's article is significant for two related reasons. First, it made an ambiguous appeal to literature as a neutral terrain, but then sought to give it a specific political function. Secondly, Buchanan related the *Ballads* to key terms – cockney, vulgarity, hooligan, which had gained considerable currency, especially in the Press, regarding contemporary fears of hooliganism. Buchanan exploited Kipling's popularity, and these social fears, in order to attack the status of popular literature and, he believed, the potentially subversive and undermining nature of it, especially as he saw it as representing a working class he clearly despised. The debate on hooliganism, in its wider context, which I discuss in Chapter 4, itself suggested parallels between the Boer War and a potential class war on the city streets of England. However, just after Buchanan's article had been published, Kipling's own fears, not about the hooligan, but about the empire, were to be rehearsed in South Africa.

The keynote for Kipling's writing during and after the Boer War is doubt. The Boer War poems betray a wavering of belief in the British nation as the centrifugal force for an improving and ordered empire. For Kipling, men were soldiers as much as they were citizens; national life for an island with an empire was only possible with an army at the heart of it and political life was tribal obligation: these were the informing beliefs in the *Barrack Room Ballads*. The *Ballads* were there to enlist respect for the soldier he had observed in India, and that respect was crucial if the soldier was to accept and be granted citizenship in ways that created and sustained a unified nation and beyond that, an empire. Men of deeds rather than party politics were the touchstone by which the strength of nation and empire could be measured. An English patria of rights and liberties could not be consolidated into a sense of nationhood without human vigilance, tribal loyalty, national daring and good leadership. To dissolve these fundamental truths, or laws, as Kipling believed them to be, would be to dissolve the nation itself in political chicaneries and moral compromise – the stuff of party politics which created a liberalism more concerned with means than ends.

A sense that England had lost its way is expressed in modified images of the soldier, and a changed view of the relationships between the soldier, the idea of national character and the empire. Some of the reasons for these changes are as much biographical as political. When Kipling wrote the *Barrack Room Ballads* he had observed British Tommies, with whom he could mix and talk freely, from the relatively independent position of a little known journalistic writer. By the time of the Boer War, he was an internationally known and revered writer and could only meet soldiers as a celebrity, the laureate of the ranks, to be offered by them diluted versions of the *Ballads* he had written some years previously, such as Edgar Wallace's 'Tommy to his Laureate' which welcomes Kipling to South Africa:

> O GOOD-MORNIN', Mister Kiplin'! You are welcome to our
>   shores:
> To the land of millionaires and potted meat:
>   To the country of the 'fonteins' (we 'ave got no 'bads' or 'porses'),
> To the place where di'monds lay about the street
>   At your feet;
> To the 'unting-ground of raiders indiscreet.
>   ...
>
> But you're our partic'lar author, you're our patron an' our
>   friend,
> You're the poet of the cuss-word and the swear,
> You're the poet of the people, where the red-mapped lands
>   extend,
> You're the poet of the jungle an' the lair,
>   An' compare,
> To the ever-speaking voice of everywhere![42]

Wallace's poem exploits the vogue for Kiplingesque cockney verses, but like all soldier imitators of Kipling, particularly those published in *The Friend*, there was little that was not either predictable or sententious. This is hardly surprising, given that *The Friend* was part of a propaganda campaign by the British at Bloemfontein.[43] In March 1900 Lord Roberts thought wrongly that the war would soon be over and so set about convincing the Boers in the Free State that the British were friendly and that members of the army would behave like gentlemen. There was entertainment, fraternizing and many Boer officials were left in their posts. Roberts closed down the anti-British *Express* and used the presses to start *The Friend*, a bilingual newspaper which was the joint idea of Roberts's and Milner's. A team of patriotic writers and correspondents was brought in, including Kipling, to play a part in the life of *The Friend*, which had two specific purposes: to give the British army a morale boosting voice and to reassure the Boers that the new British regime would continue to look after Boer interests, including the subjugation of Black African rights. Given this overtly political purpose, and the strictures imposed upon content, it is unsurprising that the pages of *The Friend* are mostly full of pale imitations of Kipling's work and uncontentious verse.

What the soldier's poems do indicate is that Kipling had engendered his own school of poetry, what Smith calls 'Kiplingson'.[44] Most of the poems associated with *The Friend* say little of the soldier's experiences, unlike some poems published elsewhere, but do say a great deal about being Kipling's poetic heirs and devotees. Julian Ralph, in his study of *The Friend*, speculates that one in ten soldiers aspired to 'be regarded as a disciple of this inspired and inspiring master'.[45]

The most interesting collections of poetry produced by soldiers were not published in *The Friend*. Among these are 'Coldstreamer' Harry Graham's *Ballads of the Boer War*[46] and T.W.H. Crosland's *The Five Notions*,[47] a title which parodies Kipling's *The Five Nations*. Crosland's work, more than other soldier poets, was a forerunner of the kind of poetry usually associated with World War I, as in a mourning poem entitled 'Slain':

> 'Dulce et decorum est pro patria mori'
> You who are still and white
>   And cold like stone;
> For whom the unfailing light
>   Is spent and done;
> For whom no more the breath
>   Of dawn, nor evenfall,
> Nor Spring nor love nor death
>   Matter at all;[48]

Crosland also wrote of what he considered to be Kipling's naivety, thinking of the war as an 'Imperial beano' and Cecil Rhodes as a transcendent figure who 'went about in white'.

However, Kipling's own role as patriotic and imperial editor of *The Friend* is countered by the poetry he wrote about the war, which carries its own contradictions in the relations between an uncritical enthusiasm for certain key figures, such as Rhodes, Jameson, Milner and Chamberlain, an awareness that the war was far from a success, and a changed representation of the soldier, whose imperial duties now have neither the energy nor the ironic bite of the earlier *Ballads*. Chamberlain is eulogized in 'Once Upon a Time There was a Man' as the dreaming Joseph in Genesis (Genesis 37:5), a prince among doubters:

> He, single handed, met and slew
> Magicians, Armies, Ogres, Kings.
> He lonely 'mid his doubting crew –
> 'In all the loneliness of wings'[49]

Jameson was lionized in 'If' and Milner praised in 'The Pro-Consuls' for what Kipling believed to be Milner's unstinting and thankless work in trying to create a political framework for a South African Federation, using the imagery of Roman law and architecture:

> Through the night when hirelings rest,
>   Sleepless they arise, alone,
> The unsleeping arch to test
>   And the o'er-trusted corner-stone,
> 'Gainst the need, they know, that lies
> Hid behind the centuries.
>
> (pp. 107–8)

Rhodes is the 'Dreamer devout, by vision led/Beyond our guess or reach' and the man who breeds 'cities in place of speech' (p. 209).

However, these eulogies to 'great men' exist alongside an awareness that the war was an imperial failure and it is difficult to reconcile a vision of great men who, if we believe the poems, could not but succeed, with some of Kipling's reformist poems, such as 'The Song of the Old Guard', 'The Reformers' and 'The Lesson', which are apologetics for failure. 'The Lesson' appears to preach national self-honesty, but also suggests that the informing imperial vision in South Africa was deeply flawed:

> Let us admit it, fairly, as a business people should,
> We have had no end of a lesson: it will do us no end of good.
> Not on a single issue, or in one direction or twain,
> But conclusively, comprehensively, and several times and again,
> We've all our most holy illusions knocked higher than Gilderoy's
>   kite,

We've had a jolly good lesson, and it serves us jolly well right!
...

It was our fault, and our very great fault, and not the judgement
  of Heaven.
We made an army in our own image, on an island nine by
  seven,
Which faithfully mirrored its makers' ideals,
  equipment and mental attitude –
And so we got our lesson: and we ought to accept it with
  gratitude.

(p. 299)

The nation and the army are reciprocally bound, the latter reflecting the
ideals of the former, and the war is cast as a failure of those ideals of the
parent society. That it 'serves us jolly well right!' acts as a simplistic
reminder that we are a commercial and a sporting nation which can
acknowledge its own faults.

In 'The Old Issue', written during the Boer War, he reaffirms the strictures of 'Magna Charta' and reasserts the British Tommy's heritage as
protector of the law, the Tommy being the third in line from English
nobility and Cromwell's roundheads:

> Ancient Right unnoticed as the breath we draw
> 'Leave to live by no means, underneath the Law.'

(p. 297)

Here, Tommy is spearhead of a morality writ large, carrying the weight of
tradition and history through to imperial destiny, but the poem is a willed
assertion in which the soldier is yoked to an abstraction with no individuating identity or voice and devoid of any specific historic moment.

Kipling uses soldier ballads as a more specific variant on the admission
that the war was a failure. The voices are not explicit in this admission,
and lack the vigorous nostalgia and appetite for experience and outspo-
ken criticism of the *Barrack Room Ballads*. These are poems without
energy or conviction. It is as if the private soldier, perhaps like Kipling
himself, had lost his bearings and his authority during the Boer War. In
'M.I.' Tommy complains both of the reduction of his status from bearing
a regimental name to being a mere M.I. (Mounted Infantry of the Line)
and the big 'push' he is a part of, but which seems to be going nowhere:

> An' I don't know whose dam' column I'm in, nor where we're
> trekkin' nor why.

I've trekked from the Vaal to the Orange once –
From the Vaal to the greasy Pongolo once –
(Or else it was called the Zambesi once) –
For now I am M.I.

That is what we are known as – we are the push you require
For outposts all night under freezin', an' rearguard all day
   under fire,
Anything 'ot or unwholesome? Anything dusty or dry?
Borrow a bunch of Ikonas! Trot out the – M.I.!
...

I wish I could talk to myself as I left 'im a year ago;
I could tell 'im a lot that would save 'im a lot on the things that
   'e ought to know!
When I think o' that ignorant barrack-bird, it almost makes me
   cry.
I used to belong in an Army once
(Gawd! what a rum little Army once),
Red little, dead little Army once!
But now I am M.I.!

(pp. 463–5)

Khaki and abbreviations are replacing colour and regimental names to
be proud of. Tommy's rebellious energies in the *Barrack Room Ballads*
have atrophied into a whine. In 'Columns' the complaint is that this is
a different kind of war, fought on the run, and for which the British
Army was neither prepared nor competent to fight:

Same 'Which is right?' where the cart tracks divide,
Same 'Give it up' from the same clever guide
To the section, the pompom an' six 'undred men!

Same tumble-down on the same 'idden farm,
Same white-eyed Kaffir 'oo gives the alarm
Of the section, the pompom an' six 'undred men!

Same shootin' wild at the end o' the night,
Same flyin'-tackle, and same messy flight,
By the section, the pompom an' six 'undred men!

Same ugly 'iccup an' same 'orrid squeal,
When it's too dark to see an' it's too late to feel
In the section, the pompom an' six hundred men!

(pp. 467–8)

Another poem, 'Wilful Missing', gives voice to deserters of the Boer War, and offers more sympathy than judgement:

> We might 'ave been your lovers long ago,
> 'usbands or children – comforts or despair.
> Our death (an' burial) settles all we owe,
> An' why we done it is our own affair.

> Marry again, and we will not say no,
> Nor come to bastardise the kids you bear.
> Wait on in 'ope – you've all your life below
> Before you'll ever 'ear us on the stair.

> There is no need to give our reasons, though
> Gawd knows we all 'ad reasons which were fair;
> But other people might not judge 'em so –
> And now it doesn't matter what they were.

(pp. 482–3)

Owing nothing more to the nation, having fair but unknown reasons for desertion and the dismissive 'it doesn't matter' all suggest that this was a war without the unifying principles of national pride and purpose. Kipling's Tommy of the Boer War is now an ambiguous figure, neither for nor against much at all. Unlike his author, he is unimpressed with the political virtuosity of a Rhodes or Milner and the ballads suggest more that he is a displaced character, no longer at home in the army, nor longing for home, neither citizen nor soldier. Kipling's doubts are expressed through these ballads and in this sense of the soldier as being displaced from nation and empire, the Boer War marks a moment when Kipling's dream of empire begins to waver.[50] It is unsurprising that after the Boer War he returned for subject matter to the imagined historic community of a past England and not the more difficult present. Kipling had become aware of the contradiction inherent in the nation-state which aspires to empire building, as outlined by Arendt and discussed in my Introduction. Kipling's return to a recovery of a specific Englishness in works such as *Puck of Pooks Hill* may be seen as a retreat from the dream of empire and a recuperation of the nation and its historic roots before it sought to further its borders abroad.

4
Empire of the Hooligan

The *Barrack Room Ballads* presented images of violence that were not confined to wars abroad, but were also seen, by such as Buchanan, as an indigenous aspect of British working-class culture. In Buchanan's response to the *Ballads* he yoked images of the hooligan and the soldier. The term 'hooligan' gained a wide currency as a barometer of racial decline, and, ironically, as a possible source of renewal. It also became part of a public debate on national character during a time of war fever, and when a new popular readership was emerging for an increasing number of newspapers. The 'hooligan problem' became a variously used dramatic motif for accusations of British troops committing atrocities abroad, fears of crowds at home celebrating the relief of Mafeking, and confusions over race and class.

The term 'hooligan' is indicative of contradictions in late Victorian middle-class imagery and a motif for fears concerning the nation and the empire. The debate on hooliganism was a means of both discussing and distancing the 'problem' of the working class. In a second sense it became a Janus-faced term, used to rehearse both pro- and anti-Boer War arguments and assertions. Fears of the urban malaise of 'hooliganism' could also be seen as either a potential problem for the empire, particularly during the Boer War, or a potential solution to problems in the empire.

Urban crime, alienation, rogue behaviour and social instability have been the stuff of sociological research since the discipline began, and the term 'hooligan' retains its currency. The political context of the debate on hooliganism during the Boer War was partly a question of defining ideological boundaries in relation to views of the British empire. Pro-war propaganda machinery was extensive,[1] while anti-war responses, particularly from socialists, were divided and divisive.[2] Pro-Boer sympathies came from different and sometimes conflicting quarters, and comprised

Figure 4.1 'British troops committing atrocities abroad.'

Source: Drawing by R. Coton Woodville from a sketch by Melton Prior in *South Africa and the Transvaal War.*

old campaigners, such as Dr. Clark, who belonged to the 1881 protest movement against conflict with the Boers, left-wing radicals, such as the journalist and publicist William Stead, and representatives of the emerging Labour Party, like Keir Hardie, who saw the war in terms of jingo capitalism.[3] Intellectuals like Bertrand Russell and G.K. Chesterton represented a liberal humanist condemnation of the war.

According to Richard Price, the British working class had little enthusiasm either for or against the war, but this was part of a wider apathy in exercising its enfranchisement on either domestic or foreign issues. More immediate concerns, such as poverty, overcrowding and poor housing, dampened measurably active responses to the war.[4] Consequently, most pro-Boer and anti-war appeals were directed at the middle classes. The SDF claimed working-class support, though this is unsubstantiated, the ILP was publicly against the war, but the Fabian Society, comprising mainly middle-class intellectuals, could not agree on any united view of the war, although individuals, such as Shaw, Hobson, and Wells, were vehemently against it.[5]

The London Press, which was also to a great extent the national Press because of its large provincial circulation, was mostly supportive of the war. War correspondents had long been in existence, but the growth of circulation and an increasingly literate mass audience meant that the Boer War was a testing ground for the Press in reporting, commenting upon, and to some extent, creating the war for a large readership. W.T. Stead had been an instrumental figure in creating the 'new journalism': a tendency to popularize events and issues using sensationalist presentation and bold headlines for a new readership, although, of course, publications like *Reynolds News* had already paved the way for this kind of journalism.

An expanded Press, and the quick relay of reports, meant that newspapers had a ground-breaking role in reporting a war. Unionists had the support of *The Times* and the *Daily Mail*, and support for the government was forthcoming from the *Morning Post*, *St. James's Gazette*, the *Standard* and the *Daily Telegraph*. Anti-war support was sparse, centred on the *Morning Leader*, the *Westminster Gazette*, the *Star*, the *Manchester Guardian* and organs of specific parties, such as the SDF's Marxist-oriented *Justice*. Later on, the *Daily News*, backed by Cadbury, and the *Echo* were recruited for the peace party.[6]

A wide survey of journalistic responses, and how these constituted part of the hooligan debate in relation to the war, is outside the scope of this chapter. Selected representative voices from journalism, and the work of other writers, such as Clarence Rook and G.F. Masterman, do, however, clearly show the diversity of political and social opinion at the time.

The genesis of the hooligan is in folklore.[7] In *Hooligan Nights*, written in the early 1890s, Clarence Rook describes an ostensible prototype, Patrick Hooligan, an Irish petty criminal from the East End, as the embodiment of a recalcitrant individualism that distils into the stuff of legend. Like Henley, Rook insists on the unifying power of a type that, if it evolves into being a folk hero, can establish a cult:

> with the life of Patrick Hooligan, as with the lives of Buddha and Mahomet, legend has been at work, and probably many of the exploits associated with his name spring from the imagination of disciples ... the man must have had a picturesqueness, a fascination, which elevated him into a type. It was doubtless the combination of skill and strength, a certain exuberance of lawlessness ... which marked him out as a leader among men. Anyhow, though his individuality may be obscured by legend, he lived and died, and left a great tradition behind him. He established a cult.[8]

The protagonist of Rook's book, Young Alf, represents, like his guru, Patrick Hooligan, the traits of an independent spirit; he is streetwise, self-contained, serving no laws but his own. Rook discovers a great deal concerning what Young Alf does, but surprisingly little about whom he is, which adds further apocryphal mystique to the great tradition of Patrick Hooligan, in which local history is embellished by 'the imagination of disciples'.

The sociological and etymological origins of the term 'hooligan' are uncertain. Sources range from a music-hall song to the infamy of 'Hooley's Gang', a name given by the police to a particularly notorious gang that prowled Islington in the 1890s.[9] The very range of possibilities indicate the diverse cultural milieu associated with the hooligan: music hall, criminal behaviour, gangs and street life. In *Industry and Empire* Eric Hobsbawm states: 'between 1870 and 1900 the pattern of British working-class life that the writers, dramatists and TV producers had thought of as "traditional" came into being, but it was new then'.[10] The years 1875–95, usually called the Great Depression, were also the years when a long-term fall in prices led to a rise in working-class standards of living. This helped to consolidate popular amusements, such as music halls, football, penny dreadfuls and penny bloods, which could be construed as threats to a 'traditional' British way of life.

Certainly, increased affluence and liberty were blamed for exacerbating cultural decline. Popular comics offered images of social types that were mildly subversive, such as 'Area Sneaker' and 'Chokee Bill' in

Comic Cuts. Chokee Bill wore clothes associated with hooligans, and both he and Area Sneaker were the sworn enemies of authority, personified in 'Fairyfoot the Fat Cop'.[11] New working-class voices, like Tom Mann and John Burns, and the rise of Socialist doctrine, could also be seen as a threat to dearly held values. Kipling's *Barrack Room Ballads* had offered a perspective on the working-class antecedents of the British soldier that questioned orthodox notions of heroism and, consequently, the empire itself. In *Hooligan Nights*, Young Alf's father had volunteered for the army to escape from his domestic situation, a phenomenon which suggested that the empire was being policed by men more anxious to escape either responsibility or a disreputable past than to serve their country. In turn, the desire to evade responsibility could signify the breakdown of the family and loss of parental control.[12] Criminal elements fighting at the borders of empire and crumbling values at home could mean that the nation was somehow unravelling.

In this context, hooliganism provided a useful collective term for rehearsing social, cultural and political anxieties. In *From the Abyss* (1895) C.F.G. Masterman identifies the causes of hooliganism as specifically social: overcrowding, large families and few facilities inevitably creating new forms of existence. However, Masterman is also aware that character types are created as much by popular imagery as they are by lived history, and those terms such as 'hooligan' can be used to serve ideology. In *From the Abyss* he uses the imagery of earlier slum novelists, that of the explorer in 'savage' and unknown territories, to question the veracity of that imagery. As the narrator of the Abyss he draws attention to the gap between an imposed, metaphorical language, and the subjective experience of its inhabitants. The hooligan, he argues, is not a reality but a convenient precis of the East End for the minds of those who live outside it, a ubiquitous image of their own fears:

> there has been a sudden vague disquietude as of incalculable forces, pent up, some day destined to burst out and ravage and destroy. Men gaze at Hoxton or the Boroughs as on some Western Indian mountain ... Are these eruptions of savagery which blanch the face of the householder as he reads of 'another hooligan outrage' but the revelation through ubiquitous halfpenny journalism of an element that has always been existent? Or do they record the fermenting as in a laboratory of some strange novel explosive destined to change the future history of the world?

> The hooligan is bred in the Abyss, yet in the Abyss we never hear of the hooligan. He is a product created for the world beyond. At the

meetings of the charitable societies he looms large: appeals for new churches are freely garnished with his name.[13]

The Abyss of the title suggests its own fiction of the East End, and by speaking from the inside, Masterman's irony is directed at the myth-making propensities of outsiders. He cogently captures the tone of correspondents, leaders and articles in, for example, *The Times*, in which the hooligan provided a convenient image for a multitude of complaints. Apparent indifference to the problem by the authorities was a further source of complaint. After a spate of 'hooligan attacks' *The Times* (1/11/1900) complained on behalf of St Saviour's Board of Works, Southwark, from which the Home Secretary had twice ignored letters demanding action over hooligan outrages, which are, another correspondent writes, a 'hideous excrescence on our civilisation'.[14] Another report detailed the proceedings of two conferences convened specifically to consider what appeared to be a growing problem: 'for some months past it has been almost impossible to glance on any day at those parts of the newspapers which are concerned with crime without perceiving that 'Hooliganism' has become a social peril which calls urgently for thoughtful and remedial, no less than for severe treatment'.[15]

The main conference comprised those who were considered to have professional expertise, including the chairman of the LCC, several Bishops, eminent ladies from the 'Women's University Settlement', an army Major, Charles Booth and representatives from the Lad's Drill Association. Their conclusions on the hooligan problem suggest a patterning of fears of moral decline and an affirmation of the idealized values of citizenship: the existence of an independent and threatening youth culture against a tradition of family and parental control; idleness versus work; the wilful ignorance of the working class unfavourably compared with the public-school values of fair play and gamesmanship. These antitheses were considered to be both the current situation and the agenda for action, and it was suggested that a body of professionals should act as reformatory and philanthropic workers.

Perceived as a pariah in society, the image of the hooligan had implications not only for London, but for the nation. Supporting evidence for the belief that national life was in jeopardy came from diverse sources. Charles Booth had provided a comprehensive map of urban poverty which helped to define the magnitude of social problems in London's working-class areas. Theories of urban degeneration, often informed by a simplistic social Darwinism, stressed evolutionary decline; urbanization, laxity in the law, a decline in parental authority, had, it was argued, crystallized into what the eugenist, Karl Pearson, in *National Life and Character: A Forecast* (1894) called the 'shallow hysterical cockney of today'.[16] The novels of writers like George Gissing and Walter Besant provided a fictional panorama of urban decline contemporaneous with fears of racial decline. The hooligan could be seen to epitomize the new deteriorative type which had emerged in stark contrast to a former imagined racial glory. During the Boer War, the poor physical conditions of many volunteers strengthened fears of Britain's imperial decline, especially as other European nations were challenging her supremacy. Comparisons with the internal putrefaction of the Roman Empire were a recurrent thesis.[17] An army of ill-fed, ill-bred recruits also led to a conflated view of lower class and lower species.[18]

One way of rationalizing the belief that the hooligan was in fact part of a lower species was to cast him literally as an intrusive foreigner. A *Times* leader expressed an implied doubt about the British origins of a type who displayed greater affinity with Mediterranean outlaws:

> Who or what are we to do with the Hooligan? Who or what is responsible for his growth? Every week some incident shows that certain parts of London are more perilous for the peaceable wayfarer than remote districts of Calabria, Sicily, or Greece, once the classic haunts of brigands.[19]

The cue to disassociate the hooligan from British culture was taken up by others. The *Westminster Gazette* described the Khalifa, leader of the Dervishes, as 'a sort of Soudanese Hooligan'.[20] Masterman describes hooligans as circling around 'in obedience to some primitive instinct, as little comprehended as that which drove their forefathers down from the plains of Asia towards the setting sun'.[21] His later work, *Heart of the Empire* (1901), when the hooligan had been firmly established in popular mythology, describes these 'street-bred' people as 'stunted, narrow chested, easily wearied; yet voluble, excitable, with little ballast, stamina or endurance'.[22] Such descriptions accord with consensus views of other races, considered at the time to be biologically and genetically inferior.[23] Licentious, capable of committing atrocities, the hooligan did not augur well for the future of the British empire, given that the army was obviously dependent upon working-class soldiers for its rank and file. He also possessed a dangerous kind of courage which was the antithesis of the British bulldog, which signified solidity and fair play. Rook says of Young Alf:

> His type of face approaches nearer the rat than the bulldog; he is nervous, highly strung, almost neurotic ... is very bad to tackle

in a street row, where there are no rules to observe. No scruples of conscience will make him hesitate to butt you in the stomach with his head, and pitch you backwards by catching you round the calves with his arm... The Hooligan is by no means deficient in courage... Young Alf has nearly all the vices; but he has plenty of pluck.[24]

Beyond fears of the individual hooligan lay a fear of paramilitary unrest, however chaotically organized it might be. A language forged in imperialist thinking could cast the hooligan as a miscreant heathen, but the same language carried its own fears of an enemy within. Buchanan, as I showed in Chapter 3, expressed horror that 'cockney hooligans' could also be protectors of the empire abroad. He saw the hooligan as a personification of the mob, which itself represented the rabid imperialism of a growing popular press and cheap literature, having little to do with genuine patriotism, and Buchanan feared that this new hooligan voice was, ultimately, anarchic.

Others also thought that the hooligan posed a collective threat. As newspapers gave increased space to his exploits, the hooligan appeared to grow in both stature and number, echoing Arnold's earlier fears of anarchy. Epitomizing 'lawlessness rather than crime',[25] hooligans posed a particularly difficult problem, because, *The Times* stated, they 'hunt in packs too large for a single policeman to cope with'.[26] The hunger and unemployment rallies of 1886–88 and riots in the West End in 1887 had briefly suggested the possibilities of insurrection. Ten years later, after middle-class readers had been further exposed to the magnitude of social problems in the East End, similar fears of insurrection were expressed concerning the hooligan. In 1898 two hundred people were involved in a street fight in the Old Kent Road, but ironically, it was the Mafeking and Ladysmith celebrations, ostensibly occasions to express unity, which exacerbated fears of the mob. *The Times* expressed its anxiety but offered reassurance that the new verb 'to maffick' is 'not really congenial to the British character'.[27] The *OED* states that to 'maffick' acquired the general meaning of 'extravagant demonstrations of exultation on occasions of national rejoicing'. 'Extravagant' suggests that, in the context of late nineteenth-century England, it was a paradoxical term, hovering between the celebratory and the threatening. After the war, the *Daily Chronicle* declared: 'We have no wish to advocate the hysteria of which the name is "mafficking".'[28]

The prevailing sense was of a new and daunting form of 'street people'. In *The Town Child*, published in 1907, Reginald Bray looked back on the

Mafeking celebrations as a new form of street violence.[29] Masterman also saw the behaviour of crowds during the war as a new phenomenon:

> At intervals during the late war events have demonstrated the necessity for a readjustment of our outlook to an altered environment. A change perfected in secret while men carried on their business and their pleasure has suddenly revealed itself with the force of a thunderclap.[30]

This new phenomenon is the mob, 'dense black masses' which, when drunk, 'reeled and drunk and swore, walking and leaping and blaspheming God'.[31] The links between fears of the 'mob' and fears of strident forms of militarism were becoming more synchronized. As early as 1892, the publication year for *Barrack Room Ballads*, *Punch* had recorded, throughout the year, a marked rise in militarism and a decline in traditional forms of authority. *Punch's* satire, called 'Studies in the New Poetry', focused on Henley and Kipling's poetry with the premise that '[b]lood, bumptiousness, and an aggressive violence, are the special characteristics of this style of writing'.[32] Henley's hymn to imperialism, 'Song of the Sword', became 'Song of the Poker'[33] while Kipling's *Tommy Atkins* is rewritten as a belligerent street brawler.[34] By the end of the decade, the image of the street ruffian was, in *Punch's* comedy of manners, related to a general milieu of political unrest and insubordination in the army.[35] It seems that what civil society revealed about the army abroad, and vice versa, was never far from public debate.

Descriptive accounts of hooligans borrowed military terms and imagery, thus compounding the hooligan image as part of an organized fighting unit. In *East London*, Walter Besant describes the boys of Cable Street as 'a small regiment'.[36] Rook elaborated the metaphor in *Hooligan Nights*, discussing a 'small army of pickpockets' in Drury Lane, and a 'colony, compact and easily handled, of sturdy young villains' in Lambeth Walk.[37] The characteristics of hooligan groups suggest that Rook's image of a 'small army' is pertinent. Self-created gang names, such as the 'Velvet Cap Gang' and the 'Dick Turpin Gang' presuppose a form of group identity, not unlike the regimental pride in Kipling's ballad 'Belts'.[38] They wore uniform clothes, derived from costermonger fashions, but given idiosyncratic variants to distinguish gangs. Mistrustful of and resistant to authority, particularly the police, they were jealous of territorial rights; as Besant says, 'the boys regard holding the street with pride'.[39] Ensuing fights over geographical boundaries were planned with military precision.[40]

Masterman extends these implied relationships between the gang and the army, the hooligan and the soldier, by using the concept of empire as a means of understanding hooligan gangs: 'Those who have fought together, like the component parts of the Empire, become bound together with a new tie of comradeship'.[41] The social inevitability of hooliganism, Masterman suggests, also engenders a primitive tribalism within which the worst kind of imperialist temperament flourishes. The hooligan is a student of 'methods of international policy' and has learnt the 'lust of battle' which aligns him with the underpinning belligerence of the Boer War:

> But 'fair play' is an instinct not naturally acquired in the London Street combat. The fight that commenced with fist and teeth speedily, like the war in South Africa, breaks through the amiable regulations of humanitarianism.[42]

The military imagery used by Masterman, Rook and others, became part of a wider approach to and interpretation of the hooligan problem. Army life and the empire could provide both an explanation of and possible solutions to it. If a minority in society were behaving like rebel soldiers, it was argued, then why not subject them to military discipline? The army could provide a model for society. Flogging was favoured by some, providing the moral satisfaction of casting the hooligan as a guilty insubordinate in need of public punishment by his superiors; this also had the added advantage of reducing complex social issues to the demands of military expediency. It also brought out the lunatics and the plain daft. One ex-army officer, a self-professed expert on the subject of juvenile punishments, embarked in *The Times* on a lengthy plan for a whipping machine to carry out 'a uniform administration of the whipping in direct ratio with the age and strength of the culprit', and which could also be used on parents who could not control their children. The colonies could also be useful in subjecting offenders to the 'iron discipline' of military personnel and where, at a safe distance from England, they would either survive or perish under 'a regime not to be trifled with'.[43]

More liberally inclined views advocated educative reform. Aggression could be diffused by sports and games, organized according to a model of public schools, which could also instruct hooligans in values endemic to public-school life.[44] The army, as much as the public school, provided an exemplary blueprint for clubs, boys camps and physical training. The link between schools and the army was self-evident to some, as suggested in a report of Lord Wolseley's address to Pitman's Metropolitan School: 'For the last five years he himself had been the principal of Her Majesty's Army, which was the largest school of the Empire. (Cheers)'.[45]

Organized quasi-military activities could both recruit and train for the empire and alleviate a disturbing social problem. It was a short step from this to advocating conscription, as one *Times* correspondent wrote:

> I am afraid the exercise afforded by athletics and sport would be too mild an outlet for the class in question. The real cure I would opine should be in military conscription, a service which, commencing at 18 or 19, would afford a prospect for the strictest discipline for a period sufficient to carry with it the habits that would make a man of him instead of the wild beast we are gradually letting loose in our midst.[46]

Some commentators went further and, in a rhetorical *coup d'état*, argued that the kinds of characteristics displayed by hooligans, such as territorial jealousies, fighting ability and tenacity, were the very ones required for defenders of the empire. In effect, the hooligan could serve the ideology of heroism as well as that of subversion, and thus become part of the mythology of empire. Baden-Powell, with some shrewdness, conceived of the empire as a source of wish fulfilment:

> We say to a boy, 'come and be good'. Well, the best class of boy – that is, the Hooligan – says 'I'm blowed if I'm going to be good'. We say, 'Come along and be a red Indian, and dress like a scout', and he will come along like anything.[47]

According to this view, hooliganism was merely a symptom of repressed energy which needed an 'outlet for...high spirits'[48] and the hooligan is not a social pariah but a soldier in the making.

Masterman rightly observed that the manipulation of an image is always underpinned by partisan and politically motivated interests, and that the Boer War heightened this phenomenon:

> He [the hooligan] is a useful weapon for agreeable controversy. To the advocate of peace he is the creation of militarism and the fever of war: to the advocate of war, the living example of universal conscription. To ourselves he is a son or a brother.[49]

A single image becomes a focus for confrontation, sharpened by political conflict over the Boer War. The weekly SDF journal, *Justice*, is useful here, not because it was widely representative of public opinion, as it purported to be, but because it suggests how an opposition voice exploits a contemporary debate and a specific term as a means of offering an alternative analysis of the war and events surrounding it. *Justice* proposed the hooligan type as a model for understanding the thinking and behaviour of Conservative imperialism.

Each front page of *Justice* carried a large illustration of a blindfolded statue of justice, a dramatic motif for the journal's stance toward what was perceived as the modus operandi of Tory ideology. Writers for the journal, working along Marxist and Morrissian guidelines established by the proprietor Malcolm Hyndman, present themselves as proponents of social analysis rather than the mystifications they accused their opponents of.

The following vignette is representative of a persistent attempt to cast ostensible patriotism as the embodiment of a hooligan mentality. Following an article on 'howling hooligans called jingoes' is a dramatic parody of a court scene. A hooligan has just been convicted of kicking to death a shopkeeper, raping his wife and daughter before murdering them, then burning down the premises, at which point the accused protests that the shopkeeper may have had pro-Boer sympathies:

> Magistrate, with visible emotion and scarcely restraining the tears: 'My poor dear friend! How sadly I have misjudged you! The officer made a terrible blunder in arresting so noble a patriot as you have proved yourself to be. You have my sincere sympathy for the trying circumstances through which you have passed. I am sorry indeed that you should have found yourself in the humiliating position of a prisoner in this court simply for having done what it was your duty to do, and for which you deserve commendation and reward. These traitorous scoundrels who are not in favour of war at any cost and for any excuse deserve death, and you have done well to rid the world of one of the villains and his family; you leave this court without a stain on your character, and I cannot but regret that it is not in my power to reward you for your brave and glorious deed.' At this point the worthy magistrate broke down, quite overcome with emotion. His remarks were loudly cheered by those present, by whom a collection was made on behalf of the hero of the occasion, who was presented with the sum of £20 on leaving the court.[50]

The satirical portrait of the magistrate embodies what *Justice* claimed to be the hypocrisy of an imperialist patriotism which is prepared to institutionalize criminal behaviour for its own political ends.

The journal adopted hooliganism as a ubiquitous term to indicate what it saw as a conspiracy between major social institutions: the police, the army, government, the law and education. The hooligan was represented as a consciously created product of the School Board. In an article entitled 'Under the Heel of the Hooligan', *Justice* discusses the kind of literature circulated by the Board in schools. One publication, *Scholar's Own*, edited by a member of the Board, includes florid details of thousands of Boers 'swept at the point of bayonet, from positions which few but British troops would have the courage to attack...[adding] further lustre to the records of our incomparable "Tommy Atkins"'.[51] The resultant product of this cavalier approach to recent events was, *Justice* claims, 'jingo hooliganism', the rhetoric of which was useful in both subduing critics of the war and for metamorphosing the social problem of hooliganism into a political tool.[52]

Within this model of jingoism as hooliganism, the 'mob' is seen, not as a sign of potential anarchy, but as a 'patriotic rabble', which, condoned by the police and authorities, could threaten and disrupt anti-war meetings. It is the lone socialist, usually Malcolm Hyndman himself, rather than the Arnoldian man of culture, who faces the vitriol of the 'savage mob', as the following report suggests:

> The wave of jingo madness from which this country has been suffering for some months past appears to have given a lease of life to Hooliganism...the Hooligan, instead of punishment, wins praise and commendation...while those in high places smile at their antics. Quite a number of these Hooligans, disguised conservatives, attended at a peace meeting at Northampton last week and enjoyed themselves in their usual yahoo fashion, by smashing the furniture and assaulting the audience and the speakers...At Mile End...too...at the meeting addressed by H.M. Hyndman. Here, however, they reckoned without their host.[53]

As a 'playful performer in these dramas', the hooligan is in collusion with his traditional enemy, the police: 'At Highbury, last Sunday, as the hooligans were not strong enough to break up the meeting the police did it for them, and dispersed the supporters of the meeting so that they could be assaulted by the roughs.'[54]

The former recalcitrance of the hooligan has been reclaimed through the agency of jingoism. His enlistment into the 'Jingo Reign of Terror'[55] legitimates acts of vandalism and, like the Conservative working man, the hooligan becomes an anachronistic image of ruling-class imperatives. The sources of hooliganism apropos of the war lie in Chamberlain's policy of 'brutality and ruffianism', Aristocratic 'blackguards', the 'Gold-Greedy Ghouls'[56] epitomized by Cecil Rhodes, investors, bankers, speculators and political control of the Press.

Figure 4.2 '…and the most excellent pig sticking ensued for about ten minutes.'

Source: From *The Spear*, 11 April 1900 (author's own copy).

The army itself derives from an Etonian hierarchy with the 'ethics of the pirate and the highwayman'.[57] Officers are seen as ringleaders in a hooligan ethic, protected by an institutionalized code of honour and the mythology of the hunt. *Justice* quotes an officer's letter which appeared in *The Times*:

> After the enemy were driven out, one of our squadrons (not mine) pursued and got right in among them in the twilight, and the most excellent pig-sticking ensued for about ten minutes, the bag being about sixty. One of our men, seeing two Boers riding away on one horse, stuck his lance through the two, killing both with one thrust. Had it not been getting dark we should have killed many more.[58]

The letter itself needs little comment, but illustrates *Justice*'s condemnatory use of materials to reorientate the genesis of criminal behaviour.

Justice attempts to free the hooligan image from working-class culture and place it within its own perception of a ruling class. The history of England is condensed into a catalogue of ascending tyranny culminating in hooliganism; from 'ruffianly mercenaries' hired by barons in the thirteenth century, to wars between 'aristocratic rascals', to the advent of hooliganism which is the latest manifestation of a class war:

> The history of this country during the last 800 years shows the transition of a nation from feudalism ... to commercialism, with its machine production, its factory system, its women labour, child labour, sweating, adulteration, armaments, blighted agriculture, Protestantism, Hooleyism and Hooliganism.[59]

Exploiting a contemporary obsession with the war in South Africa, *Justice* offers an image of society at war, not with the Boers in South Africa, but with itself. Through the rhetoric surrounding hooliganism, British soldiers could be either heroes or criminals, and the borders of the empire rippled not with victory but political antagonisms.

5
Popular Poetry of the Boer War

The 1890s saw the publication of more anthologies of popular war poetry than in any previous decade, and the Boer War was the apotheosis of this phenomenon. Several decades of literacy created this hunger for both reading and writing poetry, hence the volume of publications. Soldiers could write of their experiences of war, and clearly wished to do so, as testified by the vast number of contributions to newspapers and journals, plus published collections in the British Library.

The proliferation of poetry in newspapers and periodicals suggests that editors recognized that it was both popular among readers and could serve the political stance of the publication. Here I indicate the major themes in Boer War poetry and concentrate my discussion on the works of Henley and Hardy. Henley is important in that his work embodies much of the pro-imperialist poetry of the period and he was a major public and literary figure to the extent that there was a 'Henley School' of Boer War poetry.[1] Hardy's Boer War poetry constitutes a major critical view of the war which is both historical in its themes and ideas, and immediate in its publishing strategy.

It is outside the scope of this chapter to offer an adequately detailed survey of Boer War poetry, an undertaking already partly fulfilled by M. van Wyk Smith in his book *Drummer Hodge: The Poetry of the Anglo-Boer War (1899–1902)*. Smith states the obvious: it is possible to view war poetry through the ages as a constant oscillation between two opposing views: war as 'either heroic and ennobling or tragic and brutalizing'.[2] However, while much of the Boer War poetry does subscribe to either of these views, they are not mutually exclusive. Hardy's poetry, as I argue, finds a certain heroism in the very fact that the war was brutalizing. That this was a new kind of war in a new kind of political climate also

meant that the heroic/tragic opposition was often perceived as politically and aesthetically inadequate in representing the war.

The political context of the poetry included voices on the Right,
such as Alfred Austin and Henry Newbolt, who championed the soldier
as protector of the nation, and voices on the Left, who argued for a
democratization of militarism which would inhibit the soldier from
being marked out as a figure of special heroic or tragic significance.
The editorial voice of *Justice* maintained that armies were instruments
for repression at home and aggression abroad, and should be abolished
in favour of a citizens army which would further the humanitarian
and republican ideals of the Revolution. In *Justice*, (06/01/1900), an editorial demanded: 'We must aim at democratising militarism by the abolition of the barrack system, and by abolishing the army altogether,
while fitting every citizen for the duties of the soldier'. Similar arguments were also put forward in the *Labour Leader, Commonwealth* and
Reynold's Newspaper. Enhancing the image of the soldier as protector of
the state, as Smith points out, 'firmly drew civilians into the ambit of
conflict'.[3]

Aesthetically, heroic images were best embodied in character and narrative poetry, either real or invented, but some of the Boer War poets
anticipated a major theme in World War I poetry in the recognition that
it was not the distinguished hero but the 'undistinguished dead' which
constituted the major casualties of war, and in which even national
identity is effaced as Briton and Boer are indistinguishable in death.
William Watson's 'The Slain' articulates such a theme:

> Already is your strife become a nought;
> Idle the bullet's flight, the bayonet's thrust,
> The senseless cannon's dull, unmeaning word;
> Idle you feud; and all for which ye fought
> To this arbitrament of loam referred,
> And cold adjudication of the dust.[4]

Watson's self-imposed task was to reject military imperialism and
reassert what he saw as lost liberal values. He criticized Kitchener's
'burnt earth' policy of burning Boer homesteads and farms and rightly
warned that such a policy would only kindle resentment and ultimately
lead to a resurgence of Boer domination. It served Watson's purpose
to image the soldier as an unnamed victim of British imperial policies,
a view shared by others and expressed more directly in periodicals like
the *Pall Mall Magazine* and the *Westminster*.[5] Criticisms of poor military

leadership added fuel to the sense of the common soldier as victim, as in a poem published in *Truth*:

> Small use it is for 'Tommy', brought to bay,
> To fight until he's got another cartridge,
> If those who lead him show of common sense
> No more than moves the average driven partridge.[6]

Those in favour of the war drew upon various themes to support their views. The diversity of themes suggests that the 'patria' of the poetry is complex, often combining a fraternal patria which appealed to brotherhood and comradeship as a precursor of nationhood, with the patria of the state, in which British institutions and law are idealized to signify reciprocal service between the state and the individual. The importance of the homeland, the relatedness of blood and soil, or individual and nation, was also a prevalent theme, as was loyalty to authority, whether represented by the monarchy or by revered military figures, such as Lord Roberts.

These themes in patriotic poetry were often harnessed to images of the soldier, but the same themes also created a problem for writers: what exactly were soldiers fighting for here? The true patria is by definition boundaried and signifies a particular homeland and a particular set of values which the writer had to reconcile to the universalizing aspirations of empire. G.K. Chesterton recognized the problem during the Boer War when he argued for the relatedness of art and passionately felt dogmatism. He maintained that 'human nature is so constituted that it can get no real hold on the universal excepting through its particular and instinctive expressions'. Hence, '[i]f we hate a poem of Kipling's from political passion, we are hating it for the same reason that the poet loved it ... '.[7] In its imaginative preference for solid and known local detail, the kind of patriotism advocated by Chesterton could not possibly be extended to an expanding and therefore formless and alien empire. The empire was not compatible with a transcendence of patriotism of the kind he espoused and to persuade British men in South Africa that they were fighting for their country was only to compound the contradiction inherent in the circumscribing qualities of patriotism and the expansionist doctrine of empire, which was a 'sort of heathen notion of a natural law'.

Chesterton accepted that adherence to nation could create enemies:

> If you do not think your nation a solid entity and a holy soil, then do not call it your nation. But if you do, you must admit that it might be as much hated by others, as it is loved by you.[8]

However, this was different to imperialism, which, Chesterton asserted, actively sought enmity and carried its own 'vile assurance of victory'. Neither could he find an affinity with Pro-Boer Liberal critics of imperialism, finding speakers such as Hobson 'nagging' in their criticisms and loving humanity only as an abstraction.[9]

Estranged from both imperialists and Liberal voices, Chesterton nevertheless identified the contradiction in a patriotism which adhered to empire, and it is this contradiction which is apparent in much of the popular poetry of the war. For example, the 'Transvaal War' by Henry Bate, which runs to sixty-nine verses, persistently confuses nation and empire, especially in its diatribes against 'Little Englanders':

> ... some Britons,
> So-called, steadfastly oppose
> Every effort of the nation
> To resist invading foes.
> 'Peace!' cry they, 'and not resistance;
> Peace! Whate'er may be the price!'
> Even such are in existence,
> 'Little Englanders!' how wise.[10]

Given that the 'invading foes' are in South Africa, the heavy-handed irony depends on a concept of nation which knows no boundaries and which denies nationhood to all except the British.

M. van Wyk Smith's work shows that in Boer War poetry, which was part of the daily fare of most newspapers, one of the persistent themes is that the empire is as much of a calling as the Church, as in Alfred Austin's 'Spartan Mothers' which claimed that '[w]ho dies for England, sleeps with God'.[11] Of course, this view also found its opposite, as in an untitled poem which scathingly criticized an appeal to troops for cathedral building funds in Cape Town, after troops had themselves been left wounded:

> They left him wounded, in the lurch –
> The Priest and Levite, sleek and fat;
> Now they build themselves a Church,
> So send him round the earnest hat.[12]

Those men who occupied the role of 'public' poet, in that they were known figures and published writers, invariably commemorated the war in terms which emphasized England's 'special' place in world history, as an ancient island with a global destiny. Henry Newbolt championed the public school hero as soldier, as in 'The Volunteer':

> He leapt to arms unbidden,
> Unheeded, over-bold;
> His face by earth is hidden,
> His heart in earth is cold.[13]

The evocation of reckless yet admirable daring could easily be recouched in terms of folly, as others, such as H.C. Macdowell, acknowledge:

> We mourned his curious lack of brain;
> We judged him stupid, judged him slow;
> How much of what he knew was vain –
> How much he did not know![14]

However, Newbolt's purpose was not to specify but to simplify, to celebrate common action in a common cause, which exhorted heroes and soldiers who:

> ... fought to build Britain above the tide
> Of wars and windy fate;
> And passed content, leaving to us pride
> Of lives obscurely great.[15]

'obscurely great' is a useful phrase in that it can generalize from what is already an abstraction, as in 'Vitai Lampada':

> The river of death has brimmed his banks,
> And England's far, and Honour a name,
> But a voice of a schoolboy rallies the ranks:
> 'Play up! Play up! and play the game!'[16]

To advocate 'Playing the game' suggests how, for writers such as Newbolt, poetry too was a practical activity, a marshalling of images to further a common cause rather than a linguistic search for *gravitas*. Other lesser known poets, such as Norman Bennett, pursued similar themes, using the names of real soldiers as an exercise in reclaiming an imagined 'Merrie England' which delights in a good scrap. His poem, 'The Little Bugler' is placed alongside a photograph of Bugler Sherlock, a fresh-faced young man who enlisted:

> Hurra for merrie England in the thickest of the fight!
> Hurra for merrie England in the battle for the right!
> And the bugler boy he sounds a blast, the veldt takes up the
> cry,
> While Britain's sons, in brave array, to conquer or to die. [17]

Many pro-Boer War poems follow similar lines: sing-song rhythmic patterns which could be set to march tunes and an adherence to imperial destiny and valour which the soldier has inherited and now embodies.[18]

As Smith has shown, the Boer War marked the 'evolution of the soldier from 'rough campaigner' to articulate "war correspondent".'[19] He argues that mass literacy and the mingling of classes created both a sense of novelty and an altering of social perspective in which the voice of the individual soldier, from any class, gained in significance. Unsurprisingly, the 'poets of the veld' used the popular poetic conventions of the time, usually in the form of simple narrative ballads, with iambic quatrains, often borrowed from Kipling and the music hall.[20] Unlike Boer War novels, there is little awareness of the ambiguous status of the army. Most were written during the war in situations where information was limited, as Lord Roberts' attempts to control the Press indicate.[21] Some of the volunteers had contracts with the Press and were expected to contribute stirring accounts directly from the front, although many 'authentic' accounts were either invented or were actually concocted at home.[22] Many newspapers which did publish soldiers' poems presumably chose to publish those which reflected their own editorial and political preferences.[23]

However, it is worth referring to those poems and collections of poems which, as far as it is possible to ascertain, were privately printed, unpublished, or published by independent publishers with no obvious affiliations with the Press, and were therefore less subject to selection on political grounds.

Sergeant Jim Smith's *Ballads of the Boer War* is a collection which seeks to affirm solidarity, albeit in a slightly forced vernacular, between officers and men, as titles of individual poems such as 'Comrades' suggest. However, the affirmation appears unintentionally to undermine itself, particularly in its defence of the officer class. Smith writes of camaraderie between himself and officers:

> There's many a drink I've taken
> Of a h'orfcer's waterbag,
> An' many a tot, when the winter comes,

> As I've 'ad o' the h'orfcers' ration rum,
> And a-many a screw o'shag.[24]

However, by the time we reach this stanza, we have already read nine stanzas which catalogue public criticisms of the officer, from having 'no bloomin' brains' and being stupidly reckless and throwing away the lives of his men. This catalogue of disaster is there in order that the speaker in the poem may refute it, yet the refutation pales beside the weight of criticisms, leaving the image of the officer more tarnished than defended. There is further irony, presumably unintentional, in stanzas such as the following:

> Stoopid? By Gawd, they may be!
> An' long let 'em so remain,
> If they gives us lads o' the bull-dog breed,
> Lads as is born, not learned to lead,
> No matter 'ow small their brain.

The reverence for brainlessness is both humorous and telling. Other poems, such as Private Smith's 'The Battle of Batersfontein', are more prone to accuse directly and bitterly:

> Such was the day for our regiment
> Dread the revenge we will take.
> Dearly we paid for the blunder –
> A drawing-room General's mistake.
>
> Why weren't we told of the trenches?
> Why weren't we told of the wire?
> Why were we marched up in column
> May Tommy Atkins enquire.[25]

Such poems find their corollary in archive materials in the National Army Museum, some of which include a number of letters and diaries which are critical of officers, particularly when soldiers become aware that it is the higher ranks that get the praise for victory. A member of the Royal Dragoons wrote, after a battle at Spearman's Hill in January 1900, that '[i]n every fight we have had, some large blunder has been made'. Buller, he believed, had an uncanny knack for getting things wrong, and the Dragoon resented any glory he may be given, as in the relief of Ladysmith:

I hope that Buller does not get too much praise for this as the praise [is] all due to the lower officers and especially the men... they have not been backed up by the generals nearly enough.[26]

Another soldier, Gunner H. Hayes, complains of officers putting more energy into punishing recalcitrant soldiers for petty offences than into acquiring food for the regiment.

A pervasive voice in the poems, also corroborated by letters and diaries, endorses Pakenham's view that many soldiers dismissed or were ironic about their circumstances. 'The curious thing is how absolutely indifferent you get as to what is going on' wrote a member of the Royal Dragoons.[27] 'The Ballad of the Bayonet' by P.T. Ross suggests the private soldier's refusal to take seriously his officer's questions regarding the use of his bayonet:

> 'Tis my mighty Excalibur, sir,
> I've used it in joy and grief,
> For digging up many a tater,
> Or opening bully beef.
> ...
> Has it e'er drawn human blood?
> Yes, once, I grieve to say;
> It was not in any battle,
> Or any bloody fray;
> 'Twas just outside Pretoria,
> The deed was never meant,
> I slipped and fell on the point, sir,
> 'Twas quite by accident.[28]

However, the majority of poems which appeared in newspapers and periodicals were simple expressions of support for the war and for the whole enterprise of British imperialism. W.E. Henley was in many ways the self-appointed spokesman for this mountain of verse.[29]

W.E. Henley

For William Ernest Henley, the health of English culture was dependent upon a concept of heroism. His work is an attempt to crystallize a range of political, social and aesthetic issues in the creation of heroic types, such as Rhodes and Kitchener:

To the national conscience, drugged so long and so long bewildered and bemused, such men as Rhodes and Kitchener are heroic Englishmen ... Both are great; and that is much. But both are, after all, but types; and that is more.[30]

Henley also sought to harness the popularity of the image of Tommy Atkins to his own belief in the heroic:

> its [the publication of R. Kipling's *Barrack Room Ballads*] real interest consists in its revelation of the lyric possibilities of Thomas Atkins and – what is vastly better – in its recommendation of Thomas as a man and a brother to a superior, high-sniffing world. In so many words, once, not so many years ago, Thomas was nothing; now, thanks to this book and to the author of this book, Thomas is everything, and there is none so great – none downwards from his venerable Queen-Empress! – but is glad to do him reverence.[31]

As man of letters, editor and poet, Henley was an important voice during the 1890s and spoke for an intellectual community dissatisfied with the *fin de siècle* writers of the time.[32] He found solace in powerful images of historical and literary figures and attempted to marry these to contemporary life, partly in reaction to what he saw as a decadent decade informed by effete aestheticism. He was discontented with the status quo of his own historicism, in which the glorious past accentuated the paucity of the present, and the 'New Imperialism' offered imaginative scope within which to reinvent the past through literature, culture and politics. The task was to translate the values carried by art into action. It was a stance which was biological in origin, Romantic in disposition and Tory in commitment.

During 1873–75 Henley completed the sequence of poems entitled 'In Hospital'.[33] They dramatize his personal fight against tubercular arthritis while a patient at Edinburgh Old Surgical Hospital. Already an amputee, having had his left foot amputated in 1868, he placed himself under the care of Joseph Lister, in the hope of saving his right foot.[34] The age of Simpson, Lister, Routgen and Pasteur transformed medical treatment, and Henley's early personal attachment to Lister's then radical ideas provided a regenerative source of hope for him, much as, in moral and political terms, Roberts, Kitchener and an idealized vision of the Englishman as common soldier, were to do in later years. These early poems indicate the physical basis for action in Henley's thought, and constitute a biological metaphor for the informing belief in a warrior spirit.

The 'In Hospital' poems have the authenticity of direct suffering; a chronological and symbolic structure creates a dramatic context for a fight against disease and death, in which the vicissitudes of human character are reduced to elemental values. Extremes of stoic fatalism and optimism are part of a militant struggle for survival which constitutes the conceptual framework of the poems. Henley is the hero-rebel whose physical handicap becomes the battleground within which to assert the assumed masculine virtues of defiance and protest over conventionally feminine characteristics of acceptance and passivity. The use of a mock-heroic persona – 'Patient' – objectifies, to some extent, the sufferings endured, but also prepares for struggle as a self-dramatizing performance: 'BEHOLD me waiting – waiting for the knife' ('BEFORE', p. 6). Surgery intensifies the sense of personal experience as public spectacle:

> Then the lights grow fast and furious,
> And you hear a noise of waters,
> And you wrestle, blind and dizzy,
> In an agony of effort,
> Till a sudden lull accepts you,
> And you sound an utter darkness ...
> And awaken ... with a struggle ...
> On a hushed, attentive audience.
>
> ('OPERATION', p. 8)

The plight of the patient is heightened precisely because he is being observed; the revelatory display of sensations and his open declaration of suffering create a continuous dialectic of pain and elation, a mock-epic journey through illness to recovery which is unfolded only to the reader, as a privileged member of the audience. The struggle of his illness begets forms of self-knowledge which are constitutive of individual identity and a form of heroism.

The cumulative effect of this concentration on the minutiae of pain and the emotions aroused by it is a portrayal of endurance from which emerges the hero hidden in the invalid, struggling to maintain dignity and fortitude even as he recognizes the irony of his situation:

> ... nothing all-too dear
> Unmans me for my bout of passive strife.
>
> Here comes the basket? Thank you. I am ready.
> But, gentlemen my porters, life is brittle:
> You carry Caesar and – his fortunes – steady!
>
> ('BEFORE', p. 6)

In these poems, Henley created his own heroic myth, with his own persona as soldier of fate, battling against illness and the despair it can engender.

Sickness and health were to become overriding metaphors for Henley in later years; in 1898 he returned to the idea of the body as an embodiment of the effects of imperialism on life in England. Comparing the signing of the London Convention of 1884, which relinquished the S(o)udan, to the later public exoneration of Cecil Rhodes, he states: 'the difference between England in 1884 and England in 1898 is as the difference between a man hocussed and a man with all his wits'.[35] The Theory of Dismemberment, or the relinquishing of colonies, is, to Henley, a literal dismembering of a corporate body and personality. Unity of empire, essential to unity at home, is achievable only through the emergence of a 'great man' who not only embodies the imperial idea, but is the actuality of his followers and workers. An obsession with empire is thus related directly to an obsession with the blood and fibre of a single heroic figure, whose task is to 'make our vast and scattered Empire one in fact as it is one in sentiment, one in practice as it is one in blood and speech and theory and name'.[36]

Activism and heroism are also seen as a matter of style. The dialectics of illness and health, hope and despair, resolution and uncertainty, are informing features of his poetry, which rejoices in antithesis. His later imperialist propaganda, as Buckley states in his comprehensive study of Henley, 'carried virilism to pathological extremes',[37] but the style was hewn much earlier in his critical essays on art and literature. On their publication, George Meredith wrote that the 'In Hospital' poems had a 'manful ring'[38] and it was this quality which Henley sought in the works of others. In his essays there is a persistent thread of imagery concerned with virilism, the heroic and the soldierly. Art signifies action, or the potential for action. In this sense of an heroic and masculine culture, Henley's essays are a blueprint for imperial adventure. In Constable's work, he approved of what he saw as the directness of masculine perception which tamed the feminine world of nature: 'He had looked long at truth with no man's eyes but his own: and having caught her in the act, he had recorded his experience in terms so personal in their masculine directness and sincerity as to make his leading irresistible.'[39] Disraeli's literary works are admired because they signify a protean, worldly, healthy manliness; they 'teem with examples of all manner of vices, from false English to an immoral delight in dukes; they prove their maker a trickster and a charlatan ... Their author gives you no time to weary of him' (*ER*, pp. 20–1). Equally, Henley's diatribe against George Eliot is achieved by creating an idealized male sceptic, 'an apostate, and an undoubted male', who reacts against 'nearly all the governesses in revolt it pleased her to put forward as men', and who reads her books in 'much the same spirit and to much the same purpose that he went to the gymnasium and diverted himself with parallel bars' (*ER*, pp. 130–1).

In Henley's vocabulary, the term 'manliness', as opposed to 'masculine', has moral implications; it circumscribes a nature whose propensity and conscious goal is self-fulfilment, the achievement of which is visibly manifested in a life of passion, action and adventure. For Henley, art forms, particularly literature, offered a compensatory opportunity for vicariously experiencing a tough, idealized form of existence. He found in Byron a self-mythologizing activism, a gospel of labour and admiration for heroes in Carlyle, a classical ideal of heroism in Homer, and a capacity for romance and adventure in Walter Scott.

The idealized personality in Henley's works is an image of imperious masculinity, capable of a healthy belligerence which can inspire others to action. Such prototypes are representative of the kind of society he wished to see evolve – one which transcends what he considered to be 'mere' politics and adheres to principles. In this transcendent sense, principles are personality or character in action.

Henley advocated a model of a society propelled forward by the inspiration of natural leaders, whose characters embodied the principle of activism. The image of such a leader was hewn from his conception of the isolated, but superior, stance of the Romantic artist. Napoleon was, Henley maintains, a tyrant and a despot, but more importantly, a figure who combined an awe-inspiring life of action with cultured and literary sensibilities – he was both a soldier and a man of culture. Beethoven, Delacroix and Dumas epitomized energy, tempestuous emotion and the heroic and tragic struggle of man against the forces of fate, while the quieter cultivation of a lyrical sensibility was discernible in the harmonious works of Constable. Beethoven, in particular, gave 'the modern tendency…its most heroic expression' (*VR*, p. 10); Alexander Dumas was a 'lion' among 'jackals' whose authoritative distinction lay in his transcendence of the common crowd: 'It pleased the great man to consider himself of more importance than any and all of the crowd of collaborators whose ideas he developed' (*ER*, p. 33). The mythical heroes of Homer and Theocritus are antithetical reminders of the paucity of modern life, with 'its poverty of men, its innumerable regrets and ambitions and desires' (*ER*, p. 92). Rabelais, like Burns, offers a ribald sensuality, heroic because it is unashamed in its appeal to men of experience:

> Rabelais is not precisely a book for bachelors and maids – at times, indeed, is not a book for grown men … In him, indeed, the humour

of old France – the broad, rank, unsavoury espirit gaulois – found its heroic expression.

(*ER*, p. 98)

Tolstoy is admired as a martial writer, who created an epic language suitable for the panoramic exploits of heroes, 'rich in the common, simple, elemental qualities of humanity'. The elemental qualities allow life to be seen as a morality play, a conflict of circumscribed, uncomplicated forces, particularly in battle:

> None has felt and reproduced as he has done what may be called the intimacy of battle – the feeling of the individual soldier, the passion and excitement, the terror and the fury.
>
> (*ER*, p. 227)

Walter Scott epitomizes 'an incantation of chivalrous and manly duty', has passion, humanity and 'magnificent moral health'. He is, Henley maintains, responsible for the historical element in Romanticism, in teaching pupils 'to admire and understand the picturesque in character and life, to look for romance in reality, and turn old facts to new and brilliant uses' (*VR*, p. 14).

The principle of manliness is then, for Henley, largely a matter of style. His essays are vehicles for an idealist philosophy and a mirror to his own Romanticism, in which writers and artists are, as historical signs, a compendium of types from which to construct the idealized man. It is to Byron that he looks for the fullest expression of a Romantic hero, and he who provides a totem for the culmination of Romantic forces with which Henley sought to justify imperialism. In the figure of Byron, the self is an adventure, flaunting its own egoistic immorality in order to shock convention. He epitomizes a defiant, recalcitrant individualism, and is; 'one of the greatest elemental forces ever felt in literature – Byron was the lovely and tremendous and transcending genius of revolt' (*VR*, p. 12). The 'extraordinary precocity' of the Romantic movement's heroes is, Henley states, due mainly to Byron:

> the modern element of Romanticism – the absurd and curious combination of vulgarity and terror, cynicism and passion, truculence and indecency, extreme bad-heartedness and preposterous self-sacrifice – is mainly his work.
>
> (*ER*, p. 56)

Reverence for the decadent but free individualism of a dispossessed aristocrat is enhanced by the disfavour of the public, or 'common fool', who
simply reveal their own inane respectability and poor judgement. Byron
is the archetypal man's man: 'He lived hard, and drank hard, and played
hard' (*ER*, p. 57) and it is this very image of reckless immorality which
elevates him into the transcendent type:

> who set what seems to be a horrible example, create an apparently
> shameful precedent, and yet continue to approve themselves an hon-
> our to their country and the race.
>
> (*ER*, p. 56)

Byron's art is seen as the disruptive manifestation of a 'private revolution...liberty and self-sacrifice...dictated by a vigorous and voluptuous
egoism'. The apparently conflicting demands of egoism and self-sacrifice
are reconciled by an elevated view of personal desires which, Henley
maintains, find their fullest expression in acts of passion or heroism
where personal safety is at risk. As the embodiment of this expression,
Byron becomes the 'passionate and dauntless soldier of a forlorn hope'
(*ER*, p. 60).

In harnessing his belief in the heroic individual to imperialism at the
turn of the nineteenth century, Henley argues that imperialist work,
because it requires cooperative effort from a single nation, offers scope
for the creation of a nation of heroes. Individuals both transcend and
create history. A workforce of soldiers can therefore fulfil their individual natures through the medium of national destiny – a view which has
provided the fulcrum for many appeals to patriotic instincts. Thus, the
rewards of imperialist work are a conflation of Romantic possibilities
and principled self-sacrifice: 'the chance of a nameless death, the possibility of distinction, the certainty that the effect is worth achieving, and
will surely be achieved'.[40]

The conviction that self-fulfilment is inexorably linked to imperialism, particularly the wars of imperialism, allows national policies to be
converted into moral self-interest. Not all can achieve the fame of a
Napoleon, Cecil Rhodes or Kitchener, but subsumed to the wealth of
popular images, including that of Tommy Atkins, who is, Henley wrote
at approximately the same time, 'everything now',[41] those who fight
have personalized the destiny of their nation, and are aware of the value
of commitment to it. Social regeneration is engendered only by powerful individuals.

The problem with the naturalistic morality summarized in Henley's
adherence to 'overbearing triumphant individuality' (*VR*, p. 12) is that it

requires such an elevated view of the self for it to be a morality at all. That elevated view had been secured in 'The Song of the Sword', written in 1890, and dedicated to Rudyard Kipling. The poem appears with the 'In Hospital' poems in the 1898 edition of *Poems*. Written in the first person, the poet is identified with the sword, itself seen as a manifestation of the will of God. In the form of a creation myth, the poem exults in the power of the sword. God creates man, yet sees him:

> Prone there and impotent
> Fragile, inviting
> Attack and discomfiture.
>
>   ('SONG OF THE SWORD', pp. 49–50)

He creates the sword as 'proof of his Will', as an expression of the triumph of the will over moral and physical threats. In the context of the poem, God's creation is specifically English, and God himself is the retributive, authoritarian Jehovah of the Old Testament. The poem crudely glorifies violence, the sensual fulfilment of battle, and a transcendent sexual authority it bestows upon men:

> ... the sense
> Of his strength grew to ecstasy;
> Glowed like a coal
> In the throat of the furnace;
>
> Bringer of women
> On fire at his hands
> For the pride of fulfilment,
> Priest (said the Lord)
> Of his marriage with victory.
>
>   (p. 50)

The sword is a soldierly persona, a masculine assertion against the effeminate and weak, a 'fatuous ... fungus brood'; violence is sanctified by the amount of sensual pleasure it excites, legitimated by governmental power:

> Edged to annihilate,
> Hilted with government,
> Follow, O, follow me,
> Till the waste places
> All the grey globe over
> Ooze, as the honeycomb

> Drips, with the sweetness
> distilled of thy strength.
>
> (p. 53)

All who follow the phallic sword in 'sifting the nations' automatically become heroes in this primitive ritual of slaughter:

> Follow, O Follow, then,
> Heroes, my harvesters!
> Where the tall grain is ripe
> Thrust in your sickles!
> ... Thus, O, thus gloriously,
> Shall you fulfil yourselves!
>
> (p. 53)

The crudely narcissistic image of the sword, as a personification of the ego, is partly Old Testament, partly mythic. The personal fight for survival and identity of the 'In Hospital' poems becomes here an obsessive concern for national survival and the surgeon's knife has metamorphosed into an almost laughably symbolic sword, as 'Arch-anarch, chief-builder' (p. 55), an instrument of control and purgation on an international stage. The poem is portentous, so overwhelmed by its crass sexual symbolism, that it almost lapses into self-parody.

Poems such as this adumbrate the self-absorption of the 'New Imperialism' of the 1890s, in which aesthetics are sacrificed to assertion. In a desire to dominate and extend one's own world, the image of the sword as self creates its own myth – a flight from the unexciting reality of common experience, '[t]he absolute drudge' (p. 55) which Henley loathed.[42] In sifting the 'slag from the metal', the image is a reaction against the possibility of social degeneration, by creating a willed identification with objects of power and aggression; like other key images in popular poetry of this period (the Flag, the Lion, the Queen), political antagonisms are apparently resolved in the dominance of the image. In love with literature because of what Henley perceived as its heroic aspects, he nevertheless recognized that it was also, in some respects, a substitute for action and heroism, reducing life to 'a kind of review' (*F'S*, p. 4).[43] He responds to this by conceiving of the self and the social system it inhabits purely metaphysically; in this case, with the sword myth. Bearing in mind the erudition of some of his other work, it is difficult not to conclude that the coarsely conceived and even more coarsely articulated poem is deliberately written so. Crude assertion is precisely the point of it.

It is here also that the Byronic obsession becomes an informing feature of Henley's work. The role of the writer as hero becomes priestly; divine purpose is kindled in the language of the poet and, by implication, all who accept the power of images. The exhibitionist hero who publicly displays his wounds and suffering, as did Henley in some of his works, is presented as the ideal personality, one who epitomizes yet contains conflicting forces, or opposites. Anarchic, creative individualism and a flirtation with death become the only causes worth fighting for, hence the sword as 'arch-anarch, chief-builder'. Romantic restlessness finds potential fulfilment in the conquering, extension and protection of territories abroad. By identifying with his own image of Byron, Henley's attack on the complacent 'national conscience, drugged so long and so long bewildered and bemused'[44] is an attack from above, from a Romantic, authoritative and heroic position.

During the Boer War, Rhodes and Kitchener were seen by Henley as 'heroic Englishmen' precisely because they were types, and, in his own mind, carried the full weight of Romantic individualism which sets an example to the nation and cuts through 'smiling self-complacency'. After years of being 'bloated with peace'[45] such types, he states, have ignited the national conscience and renewed national pride, which necessarily means a replenishment of the armed forces which had been held back in the past by a 'few old women of both sexes'.[46] Equally, Tommy Atkins offers the stalwart image of a rough diamond antithetical to the liberal and monetarist values which had emasculated the imperialist drive. He praises Kipling in particular for individualizing Atkins from the amorphous mass of the army, thus providing a popular motif for a resurgence of national pride.[47] Rhodes, Kitchener, Tommy Atkins, and the values Henley wedded to his image of them, become mediating images which transform reality into an idealized concept of national cohesion.

Theoretically, then, war was a matter of principle rather than politics, and important because it increased the potential for heroism and awakened the nation from spiritual sloth. An idealized death seemed far more attractive to Henley than a sedentary, materialistic life. The image of a creative human personality which he had constructed from his essays on the Romantics and imbibed into his own poetry is instinctively patriotic, loving England from feeling rather than intellect:

> Take us and break us: we are yours,
> England, my own!
> Life is good, and joy runs high

Between English earth and sky:
Death is death; but we shall die
To the Song on your bugles blown,
England –
To the stars on your bugles blown!

('PRO REGE NOSTRO', *F'S*, p. 7)

It is as if Henley had been hoping for war. It would provide a vindication of his own ideas on national character. The enemies were at home; complacency, the reductive 'severe uniformity' and 'dreary pessimism' of socialism, and Gladstone.[48] During the attack on him in the 1890s, following his proposal to give Ireland independence in 1886, a new verb circulated among imperialists and conservatives – 'to Gladstone' (to throw everything away).[49] Henley took the risk of publishing Kipling's attack on Gladstone in the *Scots Observer* (8/3/1890), but for him, the disgust with Gladstone was again largely a matter of style. Just as war was a matter of principle, politics was a synthesis of principle informed by style. While Disraeli's novels had 'abounded in action', Gladstone is an ornate poseur and to his ideal worshipper:

His deity is a man of many words and no sayings. He is the prince of agitators, but it would be impossible for him to mint a definition of 'agitation'.

(*ER*, p. 23)

He epitomizes the deteriorative language of sentimentality:

How comes it that Mr Gladstone in rags and singing ballads would be only fit for a police station? ... the bleat of the sentimentalist might almost be mistaken for the voice of living England.

(*ER*, p. 96)

In planning his editorial policy for *The Scots Observer*, Henley decided to subtitle it 'An Imperial review', thus clarifying its political stance. Despite Disraeli's death in 1881, the Gladstone/Disraeli conflict permeated late Victorian politics and probably appealed to Henley's sense of antithesis, for he took sides with energy and venom. It was a short step from admiration of Disraeli's literary gifts to an identification with Tory idealism, as art absorbed and became expressive of political outlook, hence the use of such mediating terms as 'taste' and 'mental attitude' in

Henley's own commitment:

> Toryism, as I conceive it, is as much a matter of taste as a body of doctrine, and as much a mental attitude as a set of principles.[50]

This Toryism consisted of individual liberty within a social context of ameliorative and imaginative authority – a radical Toryism opposed to anarchy and chaos and identified with imperialism as the ideal adventure of conquest, romance and exertion of moral superiority. The moral criteria which appealed to Henley, and which Kipling was largely responsible for, was a self-imposed responsibility inherent in the idea of 'The White Man's Burden', a desire to maintain, civilize and control other peoples. He was delighted to publish Kipling's early work and to include him in his circle of 'young men' with whom he wished to share artistic and political ideas.[51]

When the Boer War began, Henley's Romantic conception of war crystallized into *For England's Sake* (1900), a collection of poems, including 'Pro Rege Nostro', which remonstrate, rally, and, at times, degenerate into declamatory hysteria. Throughout the poems is an insistence that the war is essentially concerned with idealism. Heavily influenced by Kipling and music-hall verse forms, they constitute an appeal to what he hoped were prevalent popular sentiments. Earlier, Henley had written of his aversion to 'popular culture', so the publication of these verses could indicate a capitulation – a sacrifice of style for sentiment.[52]

The collection is dedicated to Lord Roberts '[a]nd the many valiant souls whose passing for England's sake has thrilled the ends of the world with pain and pride'. The Romantic eulogizing of earlier works is largely displaced by a simplistic call to arms. Even if the cause is a 'Rag of Rags', 'O, we'll go in a glory, dead certain that we're/utterly bound to be right' ('The Man in the Street', p. 5). Apart from the exemplary model of Roberts who, echoing Henley's earlier enthusiasm for Lister, is 'Chief of Men' ('Our Chief of Men', p. 17), the idealized individual here is the 'man in the street'. The common man's heritage of '[o]ne race' which 'dares and grows' ('A New Song to an Old Tune', p. 16) metamorphoses him, through the agency of war, into a soldier hero:

> O, your whelps wanted blooding, they cried to come on
> And – Hark to them chorusing: – Storm along, John!
>
> Storm along, John! Storm along, John!
> Half the world's yours, and the rest may look on,

Figure 5.1 'O, your whelps wanted blooding.'

Source: Drawing by John Charlton in *South Africa and the Transvaal War.*

> Mum, at the rip, from Quebec to Ceylon ...
> Storm along, storm along, storm along, John!
>
> ('MUSIC HALL', p. 14)

There is a contradiction, however, in the doctrine of 'one race'. The idealized common man is the rhetorical culmination of the Romantic archetype, now democratized into the 'man in the street', but he does not have the embellishments of a literary canon to sustain his image into posterity. As such, he lacks the recalcitrant uniqueness on which the Romantic hero is founded. This uneasy alliance between the Romantic hero and the 'man in the street' is a significant aspect of Henley's response to the Boer War.

Henley uses language in an incorporative sense, in which the shared myth of activism is, by definition, inclusive of all Englishmen – 'a mighty breed of men' ('PRO REGE NOSTRO', *F'S*, p. 6) so that by the end of the sequence, strident identification has overwhelmed the tenuousness of vicarious experience. It becomes 'our' war, including Henley and the 'man in the street':

> What if the best of our wages be
> An empty sleeve, a stiff-set knee,
> A crutch for the rest of life – who cares?
> So long as the one flag floats and dares?
>
> ('TO AN OLD TUNE', p. 16)

The One flag, like the Sword, constitutes the myth of a chosen race and the soldier is an abstraction created for empire.

By casting the English as God's chosen ones, a direct relationship is perceived between their 'natural' place in the world as leaders, and their moral, cultural and military superiority. For example, in 'The Choice of the Will', it is impossible for the fame of the English to 'fade and die' because they are the chosen ones:

> We are the Choice of the Will: God, when He gave the word
> That called us into line, set at our hand a sword;
> Set us a sword to wield none else could lift and draw,
> And bade us forth to the sound of the trumpet of the Law.
>
> ('THE CHOICE OF THE WILL', *F'S*, p. 11)

The image of the sword is used, as in the earlier 'Song of the Sword', to create a myth that deifies the English outside of history; in this case, the

Boer War is simply an expression of God's Law. The informing belief of the whole sequence of poems is that if things go badly for the English, it is because reality is not satisfying the conditions of the myth, which is, in turn, itself the means for creating a preferable reality. In 'Remonstrance', written when the British army was suffering heavy losses, the first stanza professes bewilderment at what is seen as a denial of nature:

> HITCH, blunder, check –
> Each is a new disaster,
> And who shall bleat and scrawl
> The feebler and the faster?
> Where is our ancient pride of heart?
> Our faith in blood and star?
> Who but would marvel how we came
> If this were all we are?
>
> ('REMONSTRANCE', *F'S*, p. 2)

The poem proceeds to re-establish the English as the finest race, thus setting up its own internal argument in order to fulfil the conditions of superiority it assumed in the first stanza, with the result that the last stanza is more confident and controlled:

> But in the calm of pride,
> That hardy and high serenity,
> ... And, if they challenge, so, by God,
> Strike, England, and strike home!
>
> ('REMONSTRANCE', *F'S*, p. 3)

The logic Henley employs is one of simple opposites, such as the English versus other races. By analogy, the English are 'a breed' (p. 6); a 'race' (p. 2); and, significantly, 'the lion' (p. 12), while the Boers are derogatorily termed 'silly sheep' (p. 18) and 'rats' (p. 18). Within the terms of the myth of superiority, as Said would have it – a colonial discourse, such terms do not simply describe, but also seek to confirm the English as a distinct, superior species, and here draw upon the associations of a jungle hierarchy.

Clearly, the images of a sword, a lion, a pure race, imply a united nation, yet there remains the problem of why, in *For England's Sake*, Henley chose to identify with a 'popular' form of poetry, with a simple vocabulary, apparently unambiguous sentiments, and verse forms and refrains which are a cross-fertilization of ballads and music-halls songs, as in 'Music Hall', quoted earlier. As Buckley suggests in his study of Henley, despite the imperialist clamour of the 1890s, Henley's *Observer* did not reach a wide audience because his editorial standpoint meant that many, in spite of their adherence to imperialism, were not up to the sophistication of Henley's magazine,[53] yet this was the moment, during the Boer War, when Henley could embrace populist forms and the class for which they were produced.

It was Kipling who facilitated the change in Henley, from Romantic aesthete to avenging populist. His joy at publishing Kipling's *Barrack Room Ballads* and at the subsequent success of the image of Tommy Atkins, offered two distinct possibilities. First, it provided a motif with which to attack the 'high sniffing world' of respectable, safe bourgeois culture which failed to serve as an adequate centre of authority.[54] Secondly, it was a means of reconciling him to popular culture and, by implication, the masses for whom it was produced, without sacrificing aesthetic principles, for the ballads were by a literary figure whom he admired, and Tommy Atkins was a potent image: dynamic, ebullient, a soldier fighting for Queen and country. His rough edges were less lordly than Byron's, but belonged to the England of Byronic energy and immorality. As a soldier, a man of action fighting a real war, the common man was elevated to heroic dimensions and, because he was from the working classes, offered the possibility of social cohesion. It thus became acceptable, even profitable, for Henley to write popular verse and in so doing, be identified with the twin principles of victory and unity. In one of the Boer War poems, he makes this idealized vision of unity explicit:

> Mates of the net, the mine, the fire,
> Lads of desk and wheel and loom,
> Noble and trader, squire and groom,
> Come where the bugles of England play,
> Over the hills and far away!
> ('A NEW SONG TO AN OLD TUNE', *F'S*, p. 15)

The medium of popular poetry was an ostensible means for Henley to align himself with the masses. More importantly, it suggested an ideal means of producing a common culture, based on an imperialist ethic, which would create a bridge between England's 'two nations'.

The problem was that without knowing of the intimate connections between Henley's more personal 'In Hospital' poems, the ideology of character inherent in his essays and his Boer War poetry, the latter could simply appear as yet another contribution to the morass of 'call to arms' popular poetry. The belief in the soldier as a bearer of Henley's own view of literature, culture and history was too rarefied and personalized, and his own Boer War poetry too undistinguished, to carry the myth of soldiering and empire he had wished for.

Thomas Hardy

In his book, *The Poetry of Thomas Hardy*, J. Bailey documents the use of local detail in Hardy's ballads on the Napoleonic Wars, which represent an early attempt to dramatize the responses of a rural culture called upon to serve war efforts.[55] In a sense, the ballads are indicative of Hardy's own intellectual predicament which becomes increasingly prominent in later poems; how to reconcile a love of England with a detestation of belligerent nationalism, particularly during wars which it may appear necessary to fight. In this ballad sequence, confusion of loyalties is embodied in the duality of soldier and civilian, people who are victims of decisions they cannot comprehend, and who cannot always reconcile themselves to the personal sacrifices which war demands.

The ballads had provided certain key themes: the nature of heroism, which may be as manifest in a domestic and private world as on a battlefield; and the ways in which national events create individual tragedies. Hardy's own voice is largely absent. The war experiences are presented through the dialect of country folk talking to each other about themselves. In an article on Hardy's own cultural position, Raymond Williams argues that Hardy's education and status as a writer detached him from the rural world he passionately responded to.[56] He is a man caught by his personal history in the limitations of both the educated and the ignorant, in the tension between 'intelligence and fellow feeling', which Kipling, to a great extent, reconciles in *The Barrack Room Ballads*. Both *Tess of the D'Urbevilles* and *Jude The Obscure* are, of course, dramatizations of the kind of alienation Hardy experienced and both novels represent educated classes as having remarkably little understanding. Williams states that the ballad forms Hardy employed carry the implications of these tensions. They are also part of a 'prolonged literary imitation of traditional forms of speech' which serves as a 'tradition for the reading public'.[57]

While I agree with the analysis, it is essentially static and does not indicate the chronology of events which progressively qualify Hardy's position and, in the Boer War poetry, indicate a changing involvement with the reading public. His was an analytical as well as an expressive use of popular images. His dissatisfaction with easily caricatured social types was prefigured in an essay entitled 'The Dorsetshire Labourer', written in 1883, roughly the same time as the Napoleonic ballads.[58] In the essay he tries to unveil the popular image of Hodge the agricultural labourer. Seventeen years later, during the Boer War, he attempted to do the same for Hodge the soldier who, in some respects, embodies a rural parallel to Kipling's Tommy Atkins. Hardy's professed concern in the earlier essay is to release the individuality of Hodge and his like from the amorphous and limited identity of caricature, imposed by 'persons of progressive aims', urban philanthropists from the 'Olympian heights of society'.[59] The image of Hodge as a docile, degraded and inarticulate yokel is an inaccurate burlesque; the real labouring class, Hardy maintains, is 'infinite in difference'.[60] The desire to loosen the bonds of the stereotype is an important antecedent to an understanding of Hardy's Boer War poetry, but the essay is also useful in highlighting two other tensions which concerned him, and which were exacerbated by the advent of war. Firstly, the decline of established tenant communities had, Hardy maintains, led to the emergence of a new wandering agricultural proletariat who were less stable and unique, increasingly coming to resemble a dull, degenerate, urban poor. For Hardy, this implied an inevitable shift in values towards the urban and metropolitan, the real seats of political power. One result of this was that by 1899, when the Boer War began, he needed to find a more appropriate means of defining relations between the soldier drawn from rural England and the decisions and controls of government. If Hardy wished to speak more directly to the nation about contemporary events, the image of an idealized rural innocent needed reformulating if it was to have aesthetic and political credibility. Secondly, the essay includes an adherence to a conception of nature, of which the village is a human focal point, that provides melioration and refuge. 'A pure atmosphere and a pastoral environment'[61] are, Hardy states, necessary for physical and mental health, and are the agricultural labourer's birthright. The loss of rural communities is to be regretted because they are a 'last refuge on earth', ironically so, 'since it is among them that a perfect insight into the conditions of existence will be longest postponed'.[62] Hardy clearly felt pessimistic about the quality of such conditions in a civilization which had, he felt, invalidated its own relationship with nature. The implications of this statement are explored in his Boer War poems.

When the war began in 1899, Hardy appears to have formulated a strategy for publishing his responses to events.[63] He also sought new ways of dissolving the stereotypical image of the soldier. Harold Orel has argued that the self-righteous militarism which issued from some quarters during the war placed Hardy in an ambiguous position; his love for England and professed internationalism conflicted with his hatred of belligerent nationalism.[64] Kathryn King and William Morgan, in an article which discusses Hardy's public role as poet during the Boer War, suggest that the conflict was between moral and political awareness.[65] They argue that the immediate publication of poems as responses to specific events was part of a rhetorical strategy designed to transfer the war quickly into public consciousness, and more particularly to raise apposite moral questions concerning it. Certainly, the choice of popular rather than literary publications suggests a desire to reach a wide audience, and the immediacy of Hardy's responses capitalized on the significance of events still fresh in the public mind. The method of publication, and the poems themselves, indicate that the war had crystallized his sense of the social responsibilities of a poet. The desire to connect his own responses to society was a purely personal project and he did not affiliate himself with the more strident popular movements, even those in literary circles.

In the Boer War poems different personae are used to explore the central themes of war and patriotism. All but one were written between October and December 1899, and continue some of the concerns of the earlier ballads on the Napoleonic wars, particularly the devastation of private lives by public events. The first four poems are concerned with the departure of troops, poems five to eight with war experiences and poems seven to eleven with both private and public appeals for the termination of the war. As a sequence, they reach towards a narrative resolution and, I shall argue, dramatize a personal sense of failure to rationalize the war. The first three poems are concerned with the departure of troops from Southampton Docks during October 1899. The first, ' "Embarcation" (Southampton Docks: October 1899)' creates a divisive atmosphere pursued in later poems. In sonnet form, the poem moves from past to present tenses, from past wars to the present one. Hardy implies that because the rationalist apparatus of civilization has failed to evolve beyond warfare, military heroism has now become an historical anachronism: 'this late age of thought, and pact, and code/Still fails to mend'.[66] Individual soldiers are subsumed into pack names; 'legions', 'army', 'battalions', and whereas King Henry's army apparently 'leapt into battle', the present volunteers merely 'tramp' deckward. Even their energy is ambiguous; they are 'alive as spring' yet 'yellow as autumn leaves', the pale echoes of past glories. All that the 'vaster battalions' of the modern army can do is to unquestioningly pursue their own tragic inevitability:

> And as each host draws out upon the sea
> Beyond which lies the tragical To-be,
> None dubious of the cause, none murmuring.

(CP, p. 86)

War is a repetition of the 'selfsame bloody mode' and the concept of victory degenerates into a territorial 'press for further strands'. The root of the problem is seen as unquestioning nationalism; only Hardy is apparently 'dubious of the cause', yet he shares an as yet unconscious community of feeling with the soldier's families, who smile '[a]s if they knew not that they weep the while'.

In 'Departure' the unquestioning 'tramp of the bands' in the first poem becomes articulate. What the soldiers cannot themselves ask is articulated in their repetitive marching:

> Keen sense of severance everywhere prevails,
> Which shapes the late long tramp of marching men
> To seeming words that ask and ask again:
> 'How long, O striving Teutons, Slavs, and Gaels
>
> Must your worth reasonings trade on lives like these,
> That are as puppets in a playing hand?'
>
> (*CP*, p. 86)

What was implied in 'Embarcation' is here intensified into a plea for an internationalism in which the dream of 'softer polities' could be realized and patriotism, 'grown Godlike', girdle all nations and seas. The didacticism of the poem lacks the subtleties of precise observation in the earlier poem and substitutes for it a biblical and authoritarian voice. In both poems the soldier is not individualized, and is a representative, a victim of historical patterns and contemporary politics. The following two poems use more dramatic forms of personae. In 'The Colonel's Soliloquy' the history of warfare is personalized in the figure of an ageing colonel whose cheerful stoicism becomes less certain and more reflective throughout the poem. On hearing 'The Girl I Left Behind Me' he considers how the suffering of parting is unmitigated by time:

> ... Her tears make little show
> Yet now she suffers more than at my leaving
> Some twenty years ago!
>
> (*CP*, p. 88)

The colonel's initial 'Hurrah!' dwindles to a note of uncertainty:

> Though when
> The girl you leave behind you is a grandmother,
> Things may not be as then.
>
> (*CP*, p. 88)

The colonel embodies a fading ideal of battle, wearily preparing for another conflict, having become more human than heroic. Personal lament is made more specific in 'The Going of the Battery', written one month later and subtitled 'Wive's Lament'. The wives accompany their soldier husbands to the point of embarcation, past cannons which appear to them as 'living things ... Throats blank of sound, but prophetic to sight'. The poem culminates the departure sequence in a tone which registers an emotional appeal against the war.

The soldier is created as a figure of longing and regret:

> – Yet, voices haunting us, daunting us, taunting us,
> Hint in the night-time when life beats are low
> Other and graver things.

> (*CP*, p. 89)

The persistent rhyme of the first line, which occurs in two other verses, and choric sound repetitions, echo the tread of marching feet and potential thunder of the 'upmouthed' guns. They also provide a somnolent counterpoint to the increasing emotional tension of the poem. Without being over-explicit, Hardy is creating various voices which constitute a criticism of the war. By concentrating on the feelings of those left at home, the departing men only gain identity through their domestic roles in intimate relationships; as soldiers they are unrealized presences, a 'tramp of mounting men' and 'puppets in a playing hand?'. Heroism apparently belongs to those at home who '[h]old ... to braver things' (*CP*, p. 87).

The foreboding of the wives is realized in the next poem, in which the sequence moves from Southampton to London, from a world of 'feeling' to the mechanical worlds of military administration. 'At the War Office, London', subtitled 'Affixing the lists of killed and wounded: December 1899' (*CP*, p. 89), provides a salutary reminder of the consequences of enlistment. It was written very close to 'Black Week' when the British suffered heavy losses and the voice of the poem reflects on the imminence of war a year earlier, when it seemed the 'darkest unthinkable'. Now, as a reality, it is a purely mechanical process of 'hourly posted sheets of scheduled slaughter'. Other poems attempt to regenerate a moral sense which has collapsed into routinized death. 'A Christmas Ghost-Story' is dated Christmas Eve 1899, the significance of which is reiterated in the poem. The 'puzzled phantom' of a 'mouldering soldier' inquires by what right the Christian Law of Peace 'was ruled to be inept, and set aside?'. It is, he argues, neither logical nor truthful to tack 'Anno Domini' to the years while ignoring fundamental Christian principles. His own death becomes an indictment of the reader: 'your countryman/Awry and doubled up are his grey bones' (*CP*, p. 90).

The move towards individualized fate is sustained in the following poem, 'Drummer Hodge', the most anthologized in the collection. The anonymity of the soldier is here given archetypal significance. As a Wessex lad, Hodge may be seen as one of the embarking troops in the first poems; in death he is given the penultimate anonymity: 'They throw in Drummer Hodge, to rest/Uncoffined – just as found'. The same ironic anger which Hardy used to free the agricultural labourer from the limitations of a stereotype in the Dorsetshire Labourer essay here informs a diatribe against a war which discards the unknown dead. Hodge's death and alienation in an unfamiliar landscape is part of a larger incomprehension which points to the futility of that death:

> Young Hodge the drummer never knew –
> Fresh from his Wessex home –
> The meaning of the broad Karoo,
> The Bush, the dusty loam.

> (*CP*, p. 91)

Hodge's identity is nominal to the army, the 'they' of the first line of the poem, and nature itself furthers the anonymous manipulation of the drummer boy in the disturbing image of his heart and brain becoming part of a foreign landscape; his 'homely Northern breast and brain growing to some Southern tree'. The organic relationship between a Wessex boy and the land is perverted by the impersonal forces of war and nature, reducing him to the vegetable status of a 'portion of that unknown plain'. The complicity of warfare and nature is given a metaphysical dimension in the motif of stars, the central image of the poem. As a Wessex countryman, Hodge would have intimate knowledge of the stars. His grotesque burial beneath stars which appear as foreign is thus given ironic force. Each stanza contains a progressively alienated and phantasmal vision of stars. They are 'foreign constellations' in stanza one, 'strange stars' in stanza two and 'strange-eyed constellations' in stanza three, suggesting an omniscient consciousness indifferent to the fate of Hodge. They give Hodge a dual status; as a specifically tragic soldier figure and as man in an indifferent universe. With Hodge as both Everyman and as an individual casualty, Hardy's irony has a double function; it is both universal and strategic. Hardy is trying to contextualize the war within a larger vision, yet retain the importance of a humanist perspective on individual tragedies at a time when a flood of verse was mainly concerned with perpetuating the braggadocio of empire.

From here, the consequences of the earlier departure poems are ful-filled. The sequence gains its reciprocity from a consideration of what is sent out and what returns from the war; living men embark but only news of death returns. 'A Wife in London' records the receipt of a telegram telling of her husband's death (*CP*, pp. 91–2). The next poem is visionary; geographically accurate, the landscape is personified and linked with the narrator's consciousness. Actual place becomes inner condition:

> The thick lids of Night closed upon me
> Alone at the Bill
> Of the Isle by the Race –
> Many-caverned, bald, wrinkled of face –
> To brood and be still.

(CP, p. 92)

The Race is the turbulent sea area off Portland Bill where contrary tides meet in very shallow water. This conflict of natural forces achieves, not stasis, but 'a continual bubbling and rippling', suggesting the turmoil of the narrator who overhears the spirits of the dead, which in turn also constitute his own troubled consciousness. In dialogue form, the souls of dead soldiers speak as they journey northward home to 'feast' on their fame. They encounter a 'senior soul-flame' of the general who once led them in battle. He voices disillusionment with the war and usurps their expectations of being remembered as military heroes. Fathers mourn the deaths of sons in 'a dire crusade', some sweethearts have found new loves and wives remember 'Deeds of home; that live yet/Fresh as new' (*CP*, p. 95). The men are remembered as sons, husbands and sweethearts and not as soldiers. Heroic myths have here only a superficial value to a few women who revel in reflected glory. Those souls who had a valued home life return, while those of 'bitter traditions' plunge down into the ocean to be forgotten. Like the first two poems, the observer is detached from the scene itself, but here he has internalized the emotional impact of the war and it has become his own moral crisis.

King and Morgan state that the poems adumbrate a failure to connect with any sense of moral conscience in the nation during the Boer War,[67] and become increasingly personal and philosophical, ending with a public statement of a private wish in 'The Sick Battle-God'. In a contrast to this view which makes one doubt the feasibility of practical criticism,

James Hazen argues that these poems express an assured optimism: 'Hardy's hopes seldom shine as brightly as they do here'.[68] The critical problem arises because of the movement from precise observation of events to a stance which is both personal and abstract in the sequence, which may be interpreted as either a failure to sustain a perspective on real events, or an intensified grasp of the moral issues involved. It would be a mistake to read the poems purely as a direct commentary on social reality. They embody a variety of voices which attempt to create a collective moral consciousness, as well as a search for a suitable aesthetic means of writing about the war. Suffering is not used as a prelude to heroism among the soldiers, but remains unvindicated and unendorsed. By focusing on the suffering of women in, for example, 'A Wife in London', Hardy avoids conventions of male heroics associated with some war poetry.

The narrator does become increasingly isolated in the sequence. A community of bereaved women and the souls of the dead create an imagined solidarity against the war, but in the final proposal for a more complex moral awareness of war, resolution is achieved on a conceptual level which conflicts with earlier poems. The insistence that the Battle of God is dead and that men have become too civilized to pursue war does not seem a logical conclusion to a sequence which repeatedly suggests the inevitably dehumanizing effects of modern warfare. The Battle God appears in a different guise, but claims more victims and at the heart of the sequence is moral indifference, exemplified in 'At the War Office: London'.

The capacity of natural forces to reflect the fate of soldiers, yet remain indifferent to them, is counterpoised by the indifferent postings of casualty lists at the political heart of war planning in London. Those who make decisions are an invisible 'playing hand' which we can only condemn by observing the effects of military and political decisions in the slaughter of soldiers and grief of families. As 'puppets in a playing hand' the soldiers are capable of only a limited awareness of their predicaments. Even in death, their souls are puzzled and often unquestioning and, as such, provide apposite images for the reader to question the virtues of nationalism on the soldier's behalf. Early in the war, Hardy had been proud to declare of his poems that '[n]ot a single one is Jingo or Imperial'[69] and he congratulated George Gissing on his diatribe against Swinburne's bellicose sonnet, 'The Transvaal', which appeared in *The Times*.[70] By 1901, however, he could write to Florence Henniker: 'I cannot rise to war any more'.[71] The disillusionment expressed to Henniker suggests that, two years after writing the Boer War poems, his hopes for an increase in 'crescent sympathy' which would facilitate the death of the Battle-God had not been validated, morally or otherwise. By trying to appeal to a wide audience with these poems, he had presumably hoped to meet with a mutually supportive response which would subvert what he saw as a belligerent nationalism. The profusion of nationalistic verse and rhetoric which accompanied the war, and the cult of the hero, personified in Generals like Roberts and Kitchener, may have appeared as too large a popular force to counteract.

Literature (28 October 1899) published instructions for writers to serve the war effort. Poets in particular were asked to supply rousing songs of 'pure patriotism, ... songs for the soldiers on the battlefields, songs for serious upstaging masses to sing at great assemblies'.[72] Henley, Austin and Swinburne could respond to such a propagandist plea, but Hardy could not. In his poetry the soldier embodies a nation not acting in its own best interests, a nation pursuing an imperial design at the expense of its own people. The localized patriotisms of the soldiers in the Boer War poems are the expressions of regional and domestic interests, which qualify their national status. More importantly, the imperial temperament is implicitly undermined throughout the sequence of poems and is seen as both archaic and destructive of the nation and the values Hardy believed should both create and support a sense of nationhood.

6
Disoriented Fictions: Indian Mutiny Novels

Orient. Adj. Bright; shining; glittering; gaudy: sparkling.
Dr Johnson's Dictionary

Orient. Vb. fig. to adjust, correct, or bring into defined relations, to known facts and principles. refl. to put oneself in the right position or relation; to ascertain one's bearings, find out 'where one is'.
Oxford English Dictionary

Chapter 1 discussed how stage representations of India and the 1857 Mutiny were part of the music-hall credo at the time of the Boer War, providing opportunities for exotic spectaculars and the depiction of Oriental stereotypes. The Mutiny also gave rise to a distinct sub-genre of fiction which has been documented,[1] but not studied in detail. There are over one hundred Mutiny novels and over a third were written around the time of the Boer War. There was also academic interest in military novels about India at this time.

I examine here those Mutiny novels which were published in the late 1890s and early years of the twentieth century for two reasons. First, to argue that while there were specific problems confronting the Boer War novelist, as I discuss in Chapter 7, the Mutiny novels could both avoid those problems yet still satisfy a desire for military fiction when war was very much in the public mind. Secondly, the Mutiny novels afford a useful and necessary comparison with the Boer War novels, which casts a shadow over them. The Mutiny novels are an attempt to reclaim certainties about nation and nationhood when the Boer War was in fact complicating imperial politics and making many certainties ambiguous.

'The Orient was almost a European invention', claims Edward Said in *Orientalism*.[2] His concern is to show how the West produces images of the Orient which are neither picturesque tapestries in which Europeans can read of their own colonial antecedents, nor genuine attempts to 'know' the Orient, but part of the rhetorical strategy which attempts to control it. The 'Occident' can define itself, and ascertain its own bearings, against this textually produced 'Other'. India in particular has been consistently used as a referent for Western conceptions of mystery, decadence, and unconscious sexual impulses, often in terms which stress its 'inscrutability' and thereby increase its power, as a 'sign', for endless suggestion. For much of the nineteenth century it was seen by the British as a place where they could experience romance, adventure, dreams, abandonment, quick profit and career advancement; it could satisfy both material and more exotic passions.

The Mutiny novels may be referred to a wider conglomeration of texts which collectively maintain a style of domination visible not only in fiction but also in the apparently diverse works of historians, administrators, missionaries and adventurers. The Colonial discourse identified by Edward Said may be applied to any situation determined by power relations between colonizer and colonized, or ruler and ruled, and the war with the Boer people was essentially fought to determine who should have geopolitical preponderance over South Africa and its peoples, just as the Mutiny was fought by the British to maintain its Indian Empire and to prevent the independent militarization of the sepoys. Said identifies three main areas of authority, each of which contributes to a creation of images and meanings which legitimize power relations between ruler and ruled; in the case of South Africa, this would mean that images of it are produced which literally create an 'Africa' for British rule. Said identifies first, the academic approach (the authority on another culture); a more general ontological approach, involving the work of imaginative writers, economists, administrators, who take as their starting point a given distinction between West and East, based on Western superiority; thirdly, a style of domination, based on Foucault's notion of a discourse which, in this case, institutionalizes and authorizes British imperial rule.

However, while Said's work does help to identify an intertextual presence between novels and other kinds of works, there are important distinctions to be made and contradictions to be identified. The publication of Mutiny novels could offer readers a wistful rendering of a time when the borders of empire were threatened but then contained, and of a time when the army was apparently in the hands of politically and militarily competent leaders. The Mutiny had entered the mythology of empire by the 1890s and could be represented as pure adventure and obstacles overcome, the empire secured and the nation proud.

The 1857 Indian Mutiny gave rise to a distinct sub-genre of fiction, including recent works by M.M. Kaye and J.G. Farrell, and over a third of these were written during the period of 'the New Imperialism', when fears for a declining British Empire and an accompanying fear of racial decline frequently spawned novels and poems which are notable for their belligerence.[3] Kipling's works, although he is usually cast as the prophet of this tub-thumping phenomenon, often suggest a more sophisticated grasp of the realities of the Empire than those of many of his contemporaries, such as W.E. Henley, and 'popular' writers such as G.A. Henty. Given the historical context of imperialism, late nineteenth-century novels about India can represent a colonial style of domination in which literary devices and the administration of the Empire appear to conspire.

The uprising afforded an opportunity to reaffirm the moral and political strictures of the Empire, suffused with the excitement of living memory. It had sufficient historical distance for many writers to assume a narrative voice of knowing retrospection. In J.E. Ruddock's *The Great White Hand*,[4] the author argues:

> Of course, in a work of this kind, history must necessarily be used simply as a means to an end; therefore, while it is not claimed for the story that it is a piece of reliable history in the guise of fiction, it may truthfully be said it records certain stirring events and incidents which are known to have taken place ... Those who know India as I knew it in those lurid and exciting days, will probably admit that there is scarcely an incident introduced into my book but what might have happened during the enactment of the great tragedy.

History is there to serve fiction, not inform it. The appeal to personal experience and a shared view of 'lurid and exciting days' assumes that 'what might have happened' is as much an adequate representation of the uprising as could be provided by 'a piece of reliable history'. What we then read, however, is a formulaic racial confrontation between Indians, 'slimy things ... in search of prey', and British heroes whose comments are usually limited to statements such as 'Nothing like impressing these black wretches with a sense of our superiority'. British racial superiority is a predicate of this novel, an historical 'fact' within the incidents related.

Such writers share a common vocabulary, a language itself formulated in British history. The term 'Orient' began to acquire its increasingly pejorative associations during the last quarter of the nineteenth century. In the *Contemporary Review*, for example, R.H. Hutton used it to indicate a paucity of rigorous (i.e. Western) thought: 'St Paul "orientalizes" in ascribing to the personal agency of Christ what he would, had he been used to our more discriminating western analysis, have ascribed only to the fascination exercised by his own thought of Christ'.[5] 'Imperial' and 'Empire' are obvious examples of words which proclaim their own innate superiority, and continue to do so. Such words tend to attract a constellation of related figurative and metaphorical terms. In *The Great White Hand*, apart from the title, we have the British as 'the God of Vengeance' and 'Goliath'. In *On the Face of the Waters* by Flora Annie Steel, they are 'the Master' and 'the Master Race'.[6] The use of the term 'Mutiny' (often included as part of the title) in itself can reduce the complexity of racial and cultural antagonisms between two nations to an impertinent insubordination from the lower ranks or races.

Those novelists who did acknowledge a problem of terminology usually did so in order to maintain an image of the Indian population as a sectarian, chaotic community incapable of organized revolt. In the preface of his *A Hero of the Mutiny*, Escott Lynn states: 'It would be more correct to speak of the outbreak as the "Sepoy Revolt" than as the "Indian Mutiny", for it should be borne in mind that the Mutiny was one principally of the Sepoys of the Bengal Army'. In the course of two pages, however, his own semantic confusion is revealed in diverse references to 'the Mutiny', 'the Great Rebellion', 'the Revolt', 'the Rising', and the apocalyptic 'struggle against Vishnu, against Shiva, against Brahma'.[7] The editors of *52 Stories of the Indian Mutiny* similarly claim that the uprising was 'not a national revolt – no political cohesion indeed was possible among the heterogeneous races of Hindustan'.[8]

Cohesion was the ostensible prerogative of the British rulers, which is why the uprising rocked the Empire. More significantly, it challenged the whole idea of Empire. The reassuring thought that a mere handful of British administrators and soldiers, supported by loyal Indian troops (sepoys), could effectively maintain a centre of authority in a land as large and as amorphous as India was dependent on a host of assumptions. Most of these were social, political and moral refinements of a central belief in racial superiority – the 'Sahib complex', which embodied a conviction of its own unassailable authority (hence the frequent use in these novels of terms like 'Master' and 'Master Race').

The substantial realities of military and economic force controlled by the British were glossed by a belief in this mythologized British 'character', a concept now receiving serious attention by historians.[9] An anonymously written article entitled 'The Indian Mutiny in Fiction', which appeared in *Blackwood's Edinburgh Magazine* in February 1897, argues that one reason for the uprising having taken 'the firmest hold on the popular imagination' was that men of the period 'had something titanic in them, something that recall older and stronger ages than our own'.[10]

An important aspect of the 'Sahib complex' was a self-referring and myopic view of history which subsumed India to the history of the British Empire. Yet a paradox occurs here. In order to vindicate the continuing moral preponderance of the Sahibs and the stability of British rule and Imperial 'cooperative policies' regarding indigenous peoples, the uprising must be dismissed as a localized outbreak, yet the needs of fiction demanded that it be shown as a tempestuous event affording numerous opportunities for displays of superhuman British heroism.

One strategy allows a British character, usually the officer-hero, some prescience of the Mutiny: expectations of an impending apocalyptic event are created, without the necessity of fulfilling them in historical terms. Storms and abrupt changes in weather and landscape are a useful 'literary' means of creating an atmosphere of widespread disturbance without having to confront the historical problem of the magnitude of unrest. 'You surely cannot be blind to signs which rise on every side, that a storm is approaching', warns the hero's fiancée in *The Great White Hand*.[11] A further strategy – the simple claiming of the Mutiny as a 'British' event – allowed the British to consolidate their self-image and their power. In *Flotsam* by H.S. Merriman, the hero on getting his commission offers up a prayer:

'Please God', he said, 'to send us many wars'. And God in the hollow of his hand had the Crimea and the Indian Mutiny for England.[12]

Thus too Lord Roberts, in his *Forty One Years in India*: 'The Mutiny was not an unmitigated evil, for to it we owe the consolidation of our power in India'.[13] Contemporaneous with these novels was the ascendancy of Imperial History as an important academic field of study, largely due to the work of J.R. Seeley, Regius Professor of History at Cambridge, and Sir Charles Dilke. In *The Expansion of England*, first published in the early 1880s, while discussing the British 'construction' of India, Seeley claims that: 'The fundamental fact then is that India had no jealousy of the foreigner because India had no sense whatever of national unity, because there was no India and therefore, properly speaking, no foreigner'.[14] India comes into historical existence only when British imperial feet first step upon it.

Seeley's ideas were not confined to a rarefied academic world; he was a popular historian and a public figure whose 'romantic approach to history' was widely acclaimed.[15] The Mutiny novels – ethnocentric, romantic and parasitic – made liberal use of histories, biographies, letters and diaries, and it is possible to refer them back to a wider conglomeration of texts, including Seeley's work, which create an India only within the context of British imperialism. India is denied autonomy; it serves merely as an expression of Empire. More than the Anglo-Saxon mythologies of Macaulay and Carlyle, or the oracular historiography of Seeley, Mutiny novels sold to a very large audience who presumably imbibed from them ideas of Empire and India which had the intellectual support of many professional historians.[16]

As Indian history is subsumed to British history, so the image of India is seen as a chaotic terrain – Kipling's 'great, grey, formless India', which needs to be governed and written into order. The myth of a strange 'inscrutable East' is a source of romance and allure for the British, yet also a sign of insubstantiality. The opening sentence of *A Hero of the Mutiny* frames the uprising with 'India, the land of mystery and romance; date April 1857...', and the preface to *The Great White Hand* informs us that '[t]hese incidents and events have been coloured and set with a due regard for the brilliant and picturesque Orient, which forms the stage on which the dramatic action is worked out'. The theatrical metaphor is apposite, for India, created as the place of illusions and absurd posturing by would-be Indian rulers, such as the Nana Sahib and the old Moghul king in Delhi, Bahadur Shah, is essentially an incomprehensible topographical dream. Book IV of *On the Face of the Waters* is subtitled 'Such Stuff As Dreams Are Made Of', and attempts to chart the impossibility of Indians involved in the uprising ever being successful in overthrowing British rule. The King's palace in Delhi, a 'veritable Palace-of-Dreams', houses the equally insubstantial desires of its occupants, and adumbrates, for the European mind at least, an image of this enervating, dazzling, but 'unreal' India:

> The outer court of the palace lay steeped in the sunshine of noon. Its hotel rose-red walls and arcades seemed to shimmer in the glare, and the dazzle and glitter gave a strange air of unreality, of instability to all things: to the crowds of loungers taking their siesta in every arcade and every scrap of shadow, to the horses stabled in rows in the glare and the blaze, to the eager groups of new arrivals which, from time to time, came in from the outer world by the cool, dark tunnel of the Lahore gate to stand for a second, as if blinded by the shimmer and glitter, before becoming a part of that silent, drowsy stir of life.
>
> (*OFW*, p. 249)

We move on to cameo portraits of the old 'Dream-King' (who whiles away his time writing fatuous couplets), his self-seeking Queen, a drunken Prince, 'dissolute eunuchs', and a 'blood-drunk soldiery'. In 1908, Edward Farley Oaten, an Oxford Scholar, wrote a prize-winning essay, published as a book, on Anglo-Indian Literature. As well as suggesting how much Mutiny novels had achieved academic respectability and historical credibility, Oaten's essay makes it clear that what the general public had so eagerly seized on was a product of the British Romantic imagination, a created India; for 'in things Indian, qua Indian, English people are, or were, profoundly uninterested'. The reader's interest is directed, not to an understanding of India itself but to an appreciation of a British writer's way of perceiving and defining India:

> the halo of romance with which the mind instinctively encircles the name of India, though largely dissipated by actual acquaintance, seldom wholly fades, and always tends to inspire the visitor with a desire to give concrete expression to his thoughts and imaginings.[17]

Oaten's standpoint is ostensibly 'neutral'; he seems to be unaware of his own epistemological acceptance of this romantic India.

Within the fictionalized geography, Indian place-names come to signify British values and (since the uprising was suppressed) British victory. Like the association of 'the Black Hole' with Calcutta, places like Meerut, Lucknow, Delhi and Cawnpore, create and commemorate a British India, and ratify the Mutiny as a British experience. In *Barracks and Battlefields in India*, the editor, the Rev. Caesar Caine, declares: 'Lucknow! This name, together with those of Delhi and Cawnpore, comes to mind instantly the great Indian Mutiny is mentioned'.[18] Of the monument at Delhi and the Residency at Lucknow, Lord Roberts says: 'These relics of that tremendous struggle are memorials of heroic services performed by her Majesty's soldiers' (*FOY*, p. viii). Collectively, the titles of novels, such as Lucy Taylor's *The Story of Sir Henry Havelock: The Hero of Lucknow*, *The Siege of Lucknow* by Lady Inglis, and *A Hero of Lucknow* by F.S. Brereton, helped to mythologize a British India.

So too did the representation of Indians. When British writers turned their pens eastwards, says Oaten, the 'greatest literature on earth' came face to face with 'the dreaminess and mysticism of the Oriental temperament'. Indians are not given the ambiguous dignity of being 'noble savages', but are defined either as an amorphous mass, as children, or as figures of confusion. The elusiveness of this temperament, like the culture it embodied, apparently needed controlling and organizing.

In *A Hero of Lucknow*, a swashbuckling British officer, Claude Watson, is sharply defined against a backdrop of Indians whose solvent, mass identity serves to underline his own racial distinctiveness: 'it must be remembered that he was dealing with men of the East, men who had learned to look up to the British, whose force of character and moral courage stood out prominently when compared with theirs'.[19] *A Hero of the Mutiny* has Indian soldiers literally becoming blacker (a sign of increasing guilt) as the novel progresses, until they are reduced to 'swarms ... [of] black faces' and 'black snake-like trains' (*AHM*, p. 116).

The Indian as child confirms a self-comforting paternalistic image of the British, the concept of 'manbap' which is so ironically undermined in Paul Scott's *The Raj Quartet*. In order to govern India properly, says a British officer in *On the Face of the Waters*, one should recognize that Indians 'are really children – simple, ignorant, obstinate'. These characteristics are underpinned by the appearance of older officers as father figures, such as General Wilfred Elton in Charlotte Despard's *The Rajah's Heir*, to whom the Indian sepoys are 'his children. Big children and little children'.[20] One advantage of this image is that it suggests the Indian/child needs educating, civilizing and disciplining and can therefore be used to rationalize imperialism as a civilizing force (though the practice of lashing sepoys to the mouth of a cannon and blowing them to smithereens is overreaching benevolent paternalism, even for a mid-Victorian father figure). Such paternalism conforms to the broader image of the British Empire as an extended family, a politically expedient image which implies a 'naturalness' in relations between colonizing and colonized nations.

Related to this paternalistic stance is the Indian as a figure of confusion, an 'inscrutable' being incapable of self-determination. Hinduism in particular is interpreted as a failure to comply with Western notions of 'rational' intelligence, and therefore in need of managerial rule. In *The Devil's Wind*, by Patricia Wentworth, a Hindu, Sereek Dhundoo Panth, joins the uprising because he is persuaded by a mutineer that it is his fate to do so; an action viewed in the terms of the novel as irrational gullibility.[21] Tara, a Hindu widow in *On the Face of the Waters*, cannot dine with other Hindus because she has not committed suttee, the convention of self-immolation on the husband's funeral pyre:

> Such a mental position is well-nigh incomprehensible to Western minds. It was confusing, even to Tara herself; and the mingling of conscious dignity and conscious degradation, gratitude, resentment, attraction, repulsion, made her a puzzle even to herself at times.
>
> (*OFW*, p. 27)

The uprising not only questioned the 'naturalness' of British rule but occasioned dismay by suggesting that there was more to the dubious alchemy known as the Indian 'national character' than confused, idiosyncratic religious beliefs and the naughtiness of recalcitrant children. If the Indian deviated from the identity allotted to him by the British (i.e. the 'true' identity) then clearly he could not be trusted. The uprising necessitated a redefinition of terms. Inscrutable Orientals became heathenish dangers to British rule; Hindu passivity was apparently a cunning veil; the Indian/child had progressed from naughtiness to delinquency.

By August 1857 British newspapers were loading their editorial guns with the rhetoric which was to appear in Mutiny novels. *The Times* stated indignantly:

> When men astonish you with their wickedness... when malignity surpasses itself, when they lose everything and behave like demons, in nine cases out of ten in history it turns out that they have been under the stimulus of what they choose to call religion.[22]

The Mohammedan is 'a ferocious animal, and made so by his creed, which inspires him with a blind, vindictive exclusiveness, that makes him a true demon on occasion', while the Hindu's ostensible passivity and formerly useful servitude were, according to *The Times*, merely a cloak for malicious intentions: 'The more cringing and servile they were before – the more they crouched under the commanding eye which controlled them then – the more boundless is their insolence now'.[23] *On the Face of the Waters* displays an increasingly derogatory authorial attitude towards Indians, a move from consideration of possible British misrule to the bland indictment of all rebellious sepoys as 'Murderers'. Christian demonology, as in *The Great White Hand*, is used to condemn the Hindu's essentially 'evil' propensities, confirming *The Times*'s earlier diatribes:

> The devil, that had so long been kept down by the bonds of civilization, was rising now, and the ferocity of his nature was asserting itself. All the examples that had been set him, all the kindness of Christianity that had been breathed into his ear, were blown to the winds, and he was simply the Hindoo, burning with hatred for the white man, and thirsting for his blood.
>
> (*GWH*, pp. 51–2)

Failure to respond to kindness and prayers confirms his infernal nature and justifies the need for a more authoritarian rule, in keeping with the kind of 'muscular Christianity' fostered in British public schools. After listening to a long treatise on the cause of the uprising, delivered by a British doctor, two young officers in *A Hero of Lucknow* feel suitably enlightened:

> They realised that the actual cause was not the issue of greased cartridges, as they had heard, but that the anger and arrogance of the sepoys was the result of years of weak government and foolish panderings to caste, to which wrongs, fancied or real, were added.
>
> (*HOL*, p. 127)

This version of Christianity, replacing 'godliness' with 'manliness',[24] identified the British with a retributive Old Testament Jehovah – appropriate to Romantic conceptions of the 'mysterious East', as the British could also be seen to epitomize 'Fate'. *On the Face of the Waters* has John Nicholson, a man 'in the grip of Fate', leading the assault on Delhi, which itself becomes an issue of faith:

> in the ears of many, excluding all other sounds, lingered the cadence of a text read by the Chaplain before dawn in the church lesson of the day.
>
> 'Woe to the bloody city – the sword shall cut thee off'.
>
> For – to many – the coming struggle meant neither justice nor revenge, but religion; it was Christ against Anti-Christ.
>
> (*OFW*, p. 21)

The Nana Sahib is portrayed in *The Great White Hand* as a drugged, licentious coward who suffers agonies from imagining the retributions of the 'Supreme God of the Christians'. Moslems at least shared with the British the distinction of having been 'conquerors' of India, but the Hindus represented the antithesis of a virulent Christianity which found such 'effeminate' practices as piety and asceticism mystifying and intolerable, perhaps partly because they constituted a sexual threat to the British self-image of manly fortitude. As a religious being, the Hindu was therefore truly and unknowably the 'Other', but behaviourally he could be cast as cowardly and cunning. In *A Hero of the Mutiny*, Ali Beg is such a figure; he moves too softly and lightly, has eyes 'set very close together', speaks in 'oily tones', and is altogether a 'nasty, slimy scoundrel'.

A further means of sustaining the Indian's Otherness was to emphasize his sexual decadence; this, in turn, served to confirm the moral superiority of the British and the need for racial purity. In particular, the defenceless body of the white memsahib was used as an image to propel narrative towards self-righteous indignation against the imagined desires of the Indian. 'Stupid business marrying a native', comments one officer in Patricia Wentworth's *The Devil's Wind*, and his prophecy is borne out by the narrative. Frank Manners, half-caste nephew of the Nana (a double moral indictment), agrees to save Adela, a British girl, from the sepoys, if she will marry him. As he declines into a fever of drug abuse, so she declines into a moral torpor and eventually dies – the only fitting end for a white woman fallen enough to prefer intermarriage to a noble death. In Lucy Taylor's *Sahib and Sepoy*, the Nana Sahib is cast as villainous seducer: ' "Kill all the Sahibs", he said. "We will have no infidel dogs here, but the memsahibs keep alive; march them up to the Savads Kothee to await my pleasure" '.[25] Fears of rape and intermarriage intensify the East/West dichotomy and help to consolidate the image of the 'decadent' East.

These racial stereotypes and images of India claimed the status of historical 'truth'. An appearance of verisimilitude is provided by the inclusion of odd Hindu or Urdu expressions; not that these constitute an 'Indian point of view' – they usually serve to confirm the British view of Indians. In *On the Face of the Waters* the cry 'Deen! Deen! Futteh Mahomed!' ('For the Faith! For the Faith! Victory to Mahomed!') is used whenever a particular Moslem leader appears, conveniently waving a sword to indicate his fanatical intentions. 'Oriental' terms are also colonized; Lord Roberts is fond of using Indian words such as 'ikbal', a word which he cannot define precisely, but which he believes was used to suggest the intractable authority of the British. In *Gunner Jingo's Jubilee*, by T.B. Strange, Jingo has to supervise the execution of some sepoys. They are to be 'blown from the guns' and their remains will be collected by sweepers from a lower caste; as Strange points out, for a Hindu this would mean 'ages of degraded transmigration for his soul'. At first, Jingo is spattered with blood and so moves further behind the guns:

> The difficulty was solved by a reduced saluting charge instead of the service one, and no more remains flew back. The disagreeable duty completed, the force marched back to breakfast, and the sweepers gathered the remains. Brahman, Rajpoot, and Musselman – 'In one red burial bent'.
>
> None had flinched. It was kismet.[26]

Not surprisingly, 'kismet' favours the British: after shooting a sepoy who, inexplicably, fails to fire his rifle, Jingo reflects ' "It might have held my life", he thought; "but my kismet was not rammed down with that bullet." '

The usual means of representing Indian character through 'his' language is to use hyperbolic or archaic English. The former convention occurs in most novels in which Indians are given dialogue; for example, the last speech of Tara in Flora Annie Steel's *On the Face of the Waters*, where the language counterpoints the creation of Tara's character as mysterious, passionate and volatile:

> Oh! Guardians eight, of this world and the next. Sun, Moon, and Air, Earth, Ether, Water, and my poor soul bear witness that I come. Day, Night, and Twilight say I am Suttee.
>
> (*OFW*, p. 424)

An earlier writer, Colonel Philip Meadows Taylor (1801–76), whose *Confessions of a Thug* is often seen as one of the most significant early novels of India, may have set the precedent for the use of archaic English with exclamations such as: 'My son, thou hast taken upon thee the profession which is of all the most ancient and acceptable to the divinity', and 'Peter Khan, Motee, and myself perambulated the bazaars'.[27]

As the British succeed in subduing the rebellion, invariably they appear to exercise a new control over the Indian landscape and climate. Blistering heat and sudden storms are converted into a new light from the East, smiling upon Victoria's children. Illusions of post-Mutiny harmony are not simply a literary softening of the merciless reprisals perpetrated by the British, but by implication contextualize such reprisals as part of a return to a natural order: British rule, Indian subjugation. G.A. Henty's *On the Irrawaddy* is quite explicit about the need for a firm hand:

> It may be very well to be lenient when one is dealing with a European enemy, but magnanimity does not pay when you have to deal with Orientals, who don't care a rap for treaty engagements, and who always regard concessions as being simply a proof of weakness.[28]

The assimilation of such literary versions of India, coupled with a tough policy towards policing British colonies, may have a connection with later British excesses in subduing potential unrest. Edward Thompson related General Dyer's slaughter of Indians in Jallianwalla in 1919 to a 'reading' of the 1857 uprising: 'At Jallianwalla and during the outcry which our people made afterwards we see the workings of imperfectly formed minds obsessed with the thoughts of Cawnpore and of merciless, unreasoning "devils" butchering our women'. While the emotive creation and punishment of a fictional India during the years following the uprising appealed to a popular audience, realities of foreign policy could draw upon what was called the 'scientific fact' of Indian racial inferiority: 'The ideas forged in the crucible of 1857 were hammered into shape on the anvil of racial and political theory.'[29] As such, the Mutiny novels have insinuated themselves into East/West relations and the making of more modern foreign policy.

Images of empire

In these novels, abstract ideas concerning the authority and superiority of the British are usually yoked to specific concrete images of power, such as a sword, cannon, or to generic metaphors, such as 'the Great White Hand'. These, in turn, are given a special relationship with the hero. In my discussion of W.E. Henley I argued that the dominance of the image becomes its own justification for power; in the Mutiny novels, images of empire are similarly evoked by creating special relationships between object and 'character'. The symbolic value of places and objects reveals the superior qualities of he who perceives their value. In *Flotsam*, for example, the hero Harry Wylam, is born in India, but when he comes to London, as still a young child, his perceptions are shaped by significant signs; a picture of the Duke of Wellington, the great East India House in Leadenhall Street, the Royal Exchange. This selective perception, which unites commerce with heroic tradition, a unity which is itself the lynchpin of empire, crystallizes into a belligerent patriotism personified by a sword. While talking to his guardian's daughter, Miriam, and still under the influence of these impressions, '[h]e told little Miriam bravely that he would one day be a soldier and bear a sword for Queen Victoria, and Miriam thought that she would like to be a court lady' (*F*, p. 28). The sword then becomes a motif of Harry, and by extension, of empire. Years later, his first commission is ritualistically confirmed when he receives his own sword and therefore his 'new' identity, which is then divinely sanctioned when he prays for 'many wars' and God obligingly provides the Crimea and the Indian Mutiny. Both wars are subsumed to the hero's personal sense of identity, itself an image of empire. For Harry, the sword is both the empire and a conferer of identity which underlines his 'manhood'. When he meets Miriam after a two year absence, the sword allows him a sexual bravado which both embarrasses and attracts her:

> Egad! he exclaimed, unbuckling his sword-belt and laying the virgin weapon aside ... Miriam blushed a little.
>
> (*F*, p. 44)

The sword crudely defines both a sexual and, in the later context of the Mutiny, a military and racial superiority. Harry's swashbuckling sexual bravado is a means of preparing the reader for his virtuoso performance in battle.

Flora Annie Steel also uses the sword image in *On the Face of the Waters*, as a personification of John Lawrence, who inspires the British forces prior to the siege of Delhi:

> like all Delhi, under the shadow of the lifted sword which hung above the city. A sword, held – behind a simulacrum of many – by one arm, sent for the purpose; for John Lawrence, being wise, knew that the shadow of that arm meant even more than the sword it held to the wildest half of the province under his control ... And all India waited too. Waited to see the sword fall.
>
> (*OFW*, p. 390)

Sword and character conflate here, as in Henley's poem, 'Song of the Sword', to confirm what is a commonly held premise in many of these novels – that British power in India depends upon structures of character rather than structures of government. Such a 'character' is a morally and physically intractable compelling force which administers harshly but consistently. Flexibility denotes weakness, particularly if it tolerates the unacceptable customs and beliefs endemic to Hinduism and Islam. The mystique of a constructed 'character' becomes not simply an image of power, but a justification of that power, for it is such men, the novels claim, who 'saved' India. The editors of *52 Stories of the Mutiny* (subtitled *The Men Who Saved India*) state that the book has 'a special regard to the personality of the men who endured the struggle and saved the country' (*52S*, p. 5) and the author, Merriman, intrudes upon the narrative of *Flotsam* with: 'Looking back now to the Great Mutiny in the cool repose of historical reflection, we arrive at the same conclusion. It was those who dared who saved India' (*F*, p. 149).

The expression of power, and its concomitant associations with 'manliness' usually depends upon an indifference or hostility to anything outside a familiar frame of cultural reference. In *A Hero of the Mutiny*, an evocative image of empire occurs which illustrates this; Dick and Brian, the two main protagonists, enter a Hindu temple and defile the holy water by bathing in it:

> 'This shade is delightful', cried Brian, wiping his forehead, 'and the water in the tank is too tempting to resist. There are no niggers about, and I'll have a splash in the holy liquid if I die for it.'

In five minutes they were both in the tank enjoying a refreshing swim in the cool, clear, water, in which thousands of gold and silver fish disported, shooting hither and thither in alarm from the two monsters who had so unceremoniously invaded their domain.

(*AHM*, p. 3)

Their antics are meant to indicate insouciant irreverence; two ebullient, schoolboyish, young Englishmen flaunting convention by giving free play to their desires and displaying a spirited independence. Significantly, they have penetrated to the heart of Indian culture, a temple, and used it for their own purposes, dispersing the fish, whose confusion and alarm at the two 'monsters' metaphorically anticipates later battle scenes in which Indians are thrown into confusion and dispersed by a few British officers. As they are aware, the water they have defiled would have to be purified by a high caste Brahmin, but the seriousness of their offence and their complete disrespect is vindicated by the following scene in which they overhear some sepoys, outside the temple, secretly planning the Mutiny, thus indicating the cunning and subterfuge of Indians and invalidating the symbolic 'holiness' of the temple.

The hero

Heroes are created in ways which also shape, either directly or indirectly, a view of the Indian, to the extent that the Indian only exists as servant, friend or enemy, through his relationship to the British, who are seen as epitomizing the sovereign consciousness. The novels, in seeking to redress the blow to British prestige occasioned by the Mutiny, frequently emphasize the innate superiority of the British and often blame the outbreak on a pre-Mutiny paternalism which needs to be replaced by a harsher rule over the Indian.

The typical hero is unacademic and inclines towards sport rather than thought. His exuberance marks him out, at an early age, as a potentially striking military figure. When Harry Wylam, in *Flotsam*, is sent to England, we learn that '[h]e was never the boy to mope in the corner of the playground with a book, but he drank in greedily at second hand the tales of adventure and daring' (*F*, p. 32). Friends suggest to his guardian that such high energy lends itself to the army and 'truly there seemed no other career for one so full of life and spirits' (*F*, p. 49). As I discussed in Chapter 2, the relationship between public schools and imperialism emphasizes the virtues of sport and character, rather than an intellectual and therefore 'unmanly' life. School and army life have obvious parallels, as Lord Roberts suggests, when discussing the camaraderie among officers in India: 'the great majority have been educated at Sandhurst and Woolwich, and all feel that they are members of the same army' (*FOY*, p. 65). The protagonist as schoolboy hero gives him the advantage of ostensible boyish innocence, a quality which the narrative can then endorse and extend by presenting the Mutiny as a game; in *Flotsam*, for example, the narrator describes his hero during a battle:

> He was more like a boy leading some school escapade than a man moving towards danger with his life in his hand … he was already a marked man among those whose business it was to select fitting officers for a dangerous mission.
>
> (*F*, p. 184)

The hero is also a 'moral' figure which, in the novels, is a term partly defined by physical appearance and racial superiority. In *A Hero of the Mutiny* it is these qualities which intimidate the sepoys:

> The position of the lads was one of immediate danger; but such was the calm and steadfast front presented by them, such the effect of their quiet, almost contemptuous bearing, that the moral ascendancy of the ruling race asserted itself, and the sepoys drew back.
>
> (*AHM*, p. 10)

It is this sense of moral presence and transcendence which confers leadership, thus conflating race and class, since to be an officer was the prerogative of the British ruling class. In *Flotsam*, Colonel Sir Thomas Leaguer is cast as the archetypal leader of men: 'his moral presence was uprightness, an unflinching courage, a deep insight, and a most perfect comprehension of discipline' (*F*, p. 98). Given this already unimpeachable 'moral' stature, the officer figure becomes a site around which mythical and classical allusions can be clustered. In *The Great White Hand*, Scully, the soldier who fired the magazine at Delhi, is apotheosized through the act: 'But for the flush upon his face, and the heaving of his massive chest, he might have been taken for a stone statue representing the God of Vengeance about to inflict a terrible retribution' (*GWH*, p. 60).

The retributive role of the British in these novels concurs with the fabulative instinct to achieve swift transitions from history to religious myth. For example, in *On the Face of the Waters*, Hodson, who shot three Indian princes after Delhi had been taken, thereby preventing any future claims for Indian sovereignty in Delhi, is identified with the will of God by, ironically, an Indian crowd, which acts as Greek chorus:

> The crowd was electrified. They saw that with this pale, stern, Sahib there was no trifling. 'God is great', they cried, 'and this is His will'.
>
> (*OFW*, p. 340)

In an indictment of Lord Canning's appeal for clemency towards Indians, Strange indignantly rejects any impulse towards reconciliation after the siege of Delhi:

> As soon as the telegraph had been righted, one of the first messages was 'from that amiable gentleman and scholar, the Governor General of India, "Clemency Canning" ... it was characteristic – inculcating mercy to the conquered, and finishing with a quotation from Shakespeare'. The quality of mercy, etc ... That day, the 32nd took no prisoners.
>
> (*GJJ*, p. 272)

It is the officer class which is given full credit for victory over the Indians. Escott Lynn makes explicit in his introduction to *A Hero of the Mutiny* what he sees as the virtues of class distinction: 'the saviours of India during the revolt belong largely to the ruling class, for while the British soldier fought, conquered, or died with all the majesty of his predecessors, it was the magnificent example of his officers that inspired him with such heroism' (*AHM*, p. vi). We later see the hero-officer, Dick, looking after some British women from his own class: 'They sat upon the ground, and some sometimes gave way to despair. But there were indomitable spirits among them; they were of the ruling class' (*AHM*, p. 138).

Collectively, the officer class acts as an image of authority over both the Indian population and its own troops, drawn mostly from the British working class. The British private is given little space in these novels; he is usually described as brave, has an unquestioning loyalty to his officers and is motivated by a simplistic moral and racial code, but, like the Indians, exists only in a subservient role to the officers. In ways similar to the creation of the hooligan, lower-class Britons and 'savages' jointly affirm a ruling heart of officers. As I have indicated, a typical Indian response to British officers is one of fear and awe, a response which, Roberts asserts, is shared by British private soldiers. For example, the 'masterly manner' of Chamberlain and his 'personal influence' over the natives (*FOY*, p. 70) is similar to Roberts's description of the influence Harry Tombs exerted over his own men:

> inspiring all men with confidence in his power and capacity. He was somewhat of a martinet, and was more feared than liked by his men until they realized what a grand leader he was, when they gave him their entire confidence, and were ready to follow him anywhere and everywhere.
>
> (*FOY*, p. 74)

Published during the Boer War it may be that these works are a response to criticisms of leadership and the officer class during the war. Any concessions to the need for post-Mutiny reconciliation insist upon what is seen as a necessary detachment of officers from natives in order that the mystique of leadership be maintained. An interesting incident occurs at the end of *A Hero of the Mutiny*, which underlines the 'manbap' consciousness of the officers. After the mutiny has been suppressed, the hero, Dick Tracey, returns to England with one of his former private soldiers, Joe, whom he will employ as a servant; Dick also allows Alma, an Indian ayah, to accompany him, as she is devoted to his small son, Harold, and will act as his nurse. It is implied that Joe and Alma will marry, a symbolic reconciliation, perhaps, but one which would not be countenanced between an officer and an Indian woman. This union of the lower orders, both in a servant capacity, in fact affirms Dick's authority as master and peacemaker. Also, Joe's response to Alma justifies the attraction in purely sensual terms which confirm rather than displace racial distinctions:

> Lor Love me, Mr Tracey, you know 'ow I 'ates a Pandy. Funny the men is so 'orrible, and some 'o the gals is so nice ... And, after all, you know, she ain't really so dark; not for a nig – I mean, native. And such eyes and teeth!
>
> (*AHM*, p. 405)

I would argue that one significant reason for an authorial insistence upon the primacy of an officer class is that the majority of the soldiers who fought for the British in 1857 were, in fact, Indians.[30] If the novels were to acknowledge this, to any great extent, it would also mean having to acknowledge that the suppression of the Mutiny was largely due to those sepoys who 'remained true to their salt'. This would then necessitate a revision of the Mutiny in terms of racial complexity. The recognition of loyalty among Indians is usually credited to the charismatic authority of the officers, as I have already said, and this allows for the Mutiny to still be seen in terms of race against race, in order to reaffirm the importance of racial purity for the empire.

In order to justify a more authoritarian rule over India after the Mutiny, blame for it is often placed upon a softening of British authority, an assertion that is imaged in terms of hero figures. Close associations between the East India Company and British officers, prior to the Mutiny, afforded considerable material privileges to officers, who then emulated Company servants and 'extorted large presents from each new puppet [Indian Monarch]' (*52S*, p. 15). Roberts attributes the uprising to 'fatal indecision and timidity' and regrets Sir High Wheeler's 'misplaced belief in the loyalty of the Sepoys' and his trust in the Nana (*FOY*, p. 161). In *The Touchstone of Peril*, by Dudley H. Thomas, we have a Colonel Monk whom the author creates in order to rebuff the old paternalism: 'His knowledge of the manners and customs of the people was to prove a snare and a delusion.'[31] The young officers who distinguish themselves during the Mutiny represent the new order, which defines itself in terms of strength rather than empathy. Knowledge is perceived as more of a hindrance than a help.

The political implications of these attitudes embodied in the hero figures of such 'popular fiction' have been noted by Mark Naidis: 'Since imperial India in late Victorian times was usually made by an inner circle which came exclusively from the public schools, Henty's idea of India fell on fertile soil'. The devotion of Henty and others to the 'gentleman' soldier, adventurer, man of action, and a devotion to the public-school ethos, could well appeal, as Naidis argues, to a generation 'brought up on "Crimea" and "Mutiny" tales.'[32] Henty's novels were clearly intended to drum up support for the imperial cause and there was a formidable Henty industry, his publishers encouraging teachers to present his books as Sunday school prizes.[33] As has been pointed out, Kipling's *Stalky and Co.* provided the daredevil reckless template characters for Henty, with one reviewer recognizing that Stalky and his band were 'the very men the empire wants'.[34] The model for Stalky was Major-General Lionel Dunstertville, who later led a band which tried to seize the Baku oilfields in 1918.

In contrast to the fictional laurels bestowed upon the officer class, many Boer War novels reflect a disenchantment with that class and seek to create a different type of military hero. Given that the Mutiny and Boer War novels were published contemporaneously, or within a few years of each other, their very differences in representing the soldier express an ambivalence towards the army in general and the officer class in particular.[35] The officer-hero is lionized in the Mutiny novels, yet often criticized in the Boer War novels. The Mutiny novels suggest a nostalgia for a past event that was, in any case, more complex than many of the novels suggest. They could nevertheless act as comfort reading during the Boer War, when civil and military worlds were not conveniently disassociated. They may well be a form of cultural nostalgia rather than a proclamation of power. And if the hero protagonist of the Mutiny novels was a conventional nineteenth-century figure, that of the Boer War novels anticipated the lone anti-hero of the twentieth.

7
The African Adventure Game: Reconstruction of the Hero

The limping Tommy looked askance at the fat geese which covered the dam by the roadside, but it was much as his life was worth to allow his fingers to close round those tempting white necks. On foul water and bully beef he tramped through a land of plenty.

Doyle, Arthur Conan, *The War in South Africa Its Cause and Conduct*, London, Smith, Elder & Co., 1902, p. 86

When Lord Roberts desired to sum up the characters of the soldiers he had led, he declared that they had behaved like gentlemen.

Ibid., p. 107

We did not see a single homestead that was not in ruins, and at some places lay hundreds of sheep clubbed to death or bayoneted by the English troops, in pursuance of their scheme of denuding the country of live-stock to starve out the Boers.

Denys Reitz, *Commando*, London,
Faber & Faber, 1983, p. 189

Africa was for adventurers. It promised gold, diamonds, danger and passion. This was the popular British mythology and, unsurprisingly, fiction about Africa reflects this. But by the end of the century the specificities of a new kind of war made it difficult for the novelist to foreground conventional stereotypes from military fiction. Romantic, public-school educated gentleman officer or the doggedly loyal common soldier did not fit, and novels of the Boer War had to create a protagonist hero who could both serve the army yet not been constrained by it. The soldier image needed modifying if it were to serve the interests of both popular fiction and those of colonial policy in South Africa. The hero figure in these novels is, I show, more strongly identified with the figure of the common soldier, but as an 'outsider', rather than with officers. Given the military blunders of the war, writers needed to imagine just what Britishness meant in this conflict with a handful of Dutch farmers. If the army couldn't provide conventional heroes then novelists would have to be more resourceful and create a protagonist who epitomized something English and worthy, but moved more alone, as an outsider, critical and recalcitrant, more as a maverick twentieth-century anti-hero.

Publishers' lists and contemporary reviews may indicate, but do not necessarily suggest reasons for, the popularity of certain texts and writers. Inevitably there is some need for speculation, based on critical and contextual reading and historical awareness to give some indication of the cultural context of these novels, the sphere of ideas from which writers take and shape images; beyond this, to suggest a reading of the novels that reveals some of the moral values clustered around the figure of the hero. D. Weinstock suggests that the value of identifying the representative function of the hero is: 'to help establish with some precision what stereotypes and other commonly-shared (and therefore influential) attitudes and opinions were in circulation'.[1]

The writer who wished to produce a pro-British novel faced considerable difficulties. First, the public rehearsals of pro-Boer and anti-war feeling meant that any novel had to accommodate such criticisms within its own endorsement of the war if the novel was to have any historical credibility. An increasingly literate public could be expected to be more aware of the issues at stake than at any earlier period. There was a vociferous minority against the war and, while it would be specious to claim significant support for dissident voices, arguments against the war and against British intrusions in South Africa were widely available in the Press, pamphlets and public meetings.[2] Consequently, there was some pressure on writers to indicate an awareness of pro-Boer or anti-war voices if they were to avoid the risk of over-simplistic representations for a readership which would, doubtless, at least be aware that such views existed. This sometimes affected the form of the novel. For example, Fergus Hume's *A Traitor in London* (1900) gives considerable space to constructing a refutation of pro-Boer feeling and includes a long dramatization of an anti-war meeting in Trafalgar Square. Although the soldier is still an important figure, the moral focus of this novel is on the gradual conversion of a liberal politician, who begins with an anti-war stance, but whom 'experience' teaches to support England unequivocally.[3] Catherine Radziwill's

The Resurrection of Peter. A Reply to Olive Schreiner (1900)[4] is constructed purely as a refutation of Schreiner's *Trooper Peter Halket of Mashonaland* (1896),[5] which indicts British presence in South Africa. Both texts use the image of the soldier to convey their own polemical views.

Secondly, the British army was considered, by some, to be outmoded in its methods, fighting the Boers according to strategic principles acquired in previous wars against mostly black indigenous peoples who were often poorly armed and disorganized.[6] The mythology of adventure fiction, derived from these wars and built around such images as the daring cavalry charge and the British 'square' – was inappropriate to the increased technology in warfare, especially rapid-fire rifles and artillery, plus the guerilla tactics employed by the Boers for much of the war. Denys Reitz's fascinating work, *Commando*, which records the experience of Boer guerillas, and is one of a growing body of works from the South African point of view, repeatedly suggests a British failure of military imagination to come to terms with changes in war practices. He quotes the *Times History* which includes Kitchener's critical proclamation against the Boers (most of whom never read it as they were on patrol) for employing tactics which give them the advantage: the 'proclamation ... was replete with unconscious humour. The fourth paragraph in particular where the Boers were informed that they were incapable of carrying on regular warfare was a strange tissue of perverted logic.'[7] For the pro-British novelist, the problem lay in how to create a hero figure who fought for the British army, yet was disassociated from its antediluvian practices.

Thirdly, the Boer War allowed no easy distinction between blacks and whites, being what Kipling called a 'Sahib's war', a conflict between white races who, however far back, shared a common European tradition. In fact, it is now clear that black Africans played a significant role in the war, particularly for the British, who used blacks in a number of engagements with the Boers. We now know that many more blacks than were formally acknowledged died in internment camps.[8] However, during the war, it was considered to be an important part of British credibility that the army was fighting, among other reasons, ostensibly against maltreatment of blacks, and that this was seen as an essentially white confrontation. Some of the novels persist, however, in representing the South African war in terms of black/white, primitive/civilized dichotomies.

Most of the novels insist upon the primacy of the hero as an individual, consequently assuming that the war was fought and won according to a principle of individual heroism. Given that this was a war in which the British army numbered nearly half a million men, mostly regulars, while the number of Boers never reached more than 45 000, usually fighting in small guerilla bands, any insistence upon the British hero facing a numerically superior army and surviving through his own resources is historically undermined. The text is therefore both related to and distanced from the events it purports to describe, and the war is 'written out' according to an ideological preference for the lone hero confronting overwhelming odds and difficulties. Ideology is thus transformed and given an expressive form based on certain illusions about the war. Representations of David Livingstone and Cecil Rhodes were included because such figures carried strong associations of individualism and allowed South Africa to be 'seen' through pre-existent images of the British hero as adventurer, entrepreneur and morally superior civilizer.

The Boer War could not lend itself to novelists in the same way as the Mutiny; its attendant problems for the British army, such as facing a white enemy, suffering humiliating setbacks, and a new awareness of the army as being part of the nation, rather than simply representing it, made different demands upon the writer. What we see in many of the Boer War novels is a contradictory attitude towards the army which is visible in the protagonist, a soldier hero who is either critical of or ambivalent towards the regular army. He is often an outsider, not part of the regular army hierarchy and although his actions are assumed to represent the British nation, he is no longer part of the nation and its army; his own history has led him to the borders of empire and his relations with the British nation are ambiguous, critical or absent. This marks an important change in military fiction concerned with real events in Britain's imperial history, and aligns the hero with outlaw figures, or the 'alienated' anti-hero in much twentieth century fiction and popular culture.

The novels I discuss do not constitute an exhaustive list. Weinstock's bibliography lists over three hundred titles, many of which were written during the first few years of the twentieth century.

A.G. Hales' novels, *Telegraph Dick. A London Lad's Adventures in Africa* (1907)[9] and *McGlusky; Being a Compilation from the Diary of Trooper McWiddy of Remington's Scouts* (1902)[10] adumbrate, respectively, the boy hero and the man of action. Both types are presented as recalcitrant, roguish characters who confront Africa and its peoples as a 'dark' adventure, which allies them with the typical hero in other novels specifically concerned with the war. Hales is distinctive in that he was one of the few novelists who wrote about the war to have direct experience of it. An Australian writer and journalist, he covered the war for a London newspaper and was wounded and captured by the Boers, for whom, Weinstock states, he came to have considerable respect, to the extent that one of his protagonists, Driscoll, despite working for the British in the novel *Driscoll,*

King of Scouts: A Romance of the South African War (1901), was, ironically, modelled on a Boer scout.[11] The novel is a scathing attack on the British military system and on British politicians assumed to be responsible for the war. Hales also edited the popular *The New Boys World* and wrote over sixty novels, many of these during the 1890s. Most are adventure stories in which a lone hero visits exotic and dangerous colonies and through his personal strength and integrity, embodies an heroic vision of empire. His works were still being published in the 1930s and include types, such as McGlusky and Driscoll, whose exploits continued over several novels – what could be termed continuity adventures, each of which displays a different aspect of the hero's multifarious talents.

Olive Schreiner's novel, *Trooper Peter Halket of Mashonaland* (1896) is included here because it focuses on the moral predicament of a British trooper in the service of the Chartered Company. It also highlights the contradictions inherent in British presence in South Africa and anticipates themes which occur in the war novels, such as the protagonist's desire for personal wealth and attitudes towards black Africans. Schreiner was a vociferous opponent of the war, calling it 'the moment of the greatest moral degradation which England had ever known',[12] a statement which is thematically anticipated in the novel. A further reason for including it here is because of the reaction it provoked, and which Schreiner anticipated. Halket, a working-class British trooper who dreams of becoming wealthy in South Africa, is separated from his troop and has to spend a night alone on the veld. He builds a fire and becomes increasingly frightened until a stranger (Christ) arrives and sits with him. The stranger refuses to be drawn into anecdotalizing about wealth or exploits with 'nigger' women and eventually succeeds in converting Halket by pointing out to him the contradictions in colonialist thinking. The next day, Halket rejoins his troop, saves the life of a black prisoner and is shot by his commanding officer, thereby realigning moral guilt with the British. An analysis of the image of the trooper is a useful means of gauging what prompted criticisms of the novel.

The objections to her novel are adequately represented in Catherine Radziwill's book, *The Resurrection of Peter. A Reply to Olive Schreiner* (1901). Radziwill came from a literary and titled family with Polish aristocratic connections; sometimes writing under the pseudonym of 'Count Paul Vasili', she had a strong predilection for defending the political authority of European aristocracies, as well as writing polemical works on what she perceived as pernicious attacks on the political status quo in Russia before the revolution. In 1918 she published a book about Rhodes, *Cecil Rhodes, Man and Empire Maker*.

Owen Rhoscomyl (pseudonym Owen Vaughan) wrote several war novels, as well as books on Welsh history. *Old Fireproof* (1906)[13] is, as Weinstock states, a 'legitimate war novel' in the sense that it tries to interrogate the nature and function of warfare.[14] It focuses on the experiences of an irregular unit during the war, led by the 'Captain', a man whose highly personalized ideas on warfare distance him from the practices of the regular army.

G.A. Henty's career has been well documented elsewhere.[15] *With Roberts to Pretoria*[16] has as its protagonist Yorke, a public schoolboy who goes to South Africa in search of wealth and adventure, which the war provides, and to escape the stifling academic pursuits he feels condemned to should he stay in England. Henty chooses, like other writers, to place his hero outside the regular army, for reasons I discuss below.

Fergus Hume's writing career was long and prolific. Still working in the 1920s, he produced over one hundred novels (romance, adventure, spy stories, thrillers), often going into two or three editions. *A Traitor in London* (1900) includes representations of anti-war feeling. Set against these dissident voices are the images of two soldiers whose unflinching loyalty and heroism rebukes the 'Marxist' madness which fosters unpatriotic feelings.

Arthur Conan Doyle's work, *The War in South Africa. Its Cause and Conduct* (1902)[17] is here because, as a commentator on the war (he had already written *The Great Boer War* (1901)) his historical 'style' incorporates a number of narrative devices (metaphor, dialogue, dramatized incidents) while still maintaining that this is authentic 'history'. As such, it has something in common with explicitly fictional representations of the war. This work was sold cheaply in order to increase circulation, and exported internationally to plead the British cause.

Given the difficulties of writing about the Boer War, one strategy is to 'primitivize' Africa, just as the Mutiny novels 'orientalized' the Orient. While the novel may declare itself as a fiction about a historical South Africa, it is in fact a European fable of primitivism. The novels use imaginative license to take textual possession of Africa and to speak 'for' it. They lend themselves to what Robert Scholes calls 'fabulations':

> Fables have traditionally lent themselves to preaching, either as exemplar in medieval sermons or directly through moral tags appended to the tales themselves – or both. This didactic quality is also characteristic of modern fabulation ... [which], like the ancient fabling of Aesop, tends away from direct representation of the surface of reality but returns toward actual human life by way of ethically controlled fantasy.[18]

This line of thought anticipates some of the concerns of Said's *Orientalism*, in which indigenous histories are subsumed to the discourse of the colonizer. The fabulative impulse is particularly significant when it appropriates historical events and represents them as 'ethically controlled fantasy', while insisting upon the historical authenticity of its own fictive perspective. Not only are perceptions of events shaped and controlled by a partisan view of them, but there is frequently an insistence upon making the actuality of events yield to this view. Scholes goes further:

> fabulation is not simply something that happens after events, distorting the truth of the historical record. Fabulation is there before, making and shaping not merely the record but also the events themselves.[19]

Contemporaneous with these novels was the ascendancy of academic fields of study which purveyed ideas about race and civilization, in turn giving intellectual support to the ethical and ethnocentric premises of novels about the South African war. For example, Imperial History had a creditable place in the organization of ways of seeing other cultures. As I have said, J.R. Seeley's 'romantic approach to history' was widely popular, especially after the publication of his *The Expansion of England* in the early 1880s.[20] A review of the work of late nineteenth century historians claims that owing to the work of practitioners, such as Seeley:

> It was unhistorical, now, to think or write of 'England' in isolation from its empire; it had become part of 'Greater Britain' and its whole history had to be reinterpreted, teleologically, in relation to that fact. On the other side of the relationship, the dependencies also lost their autonomy.[21]

Historical theories were counterpointed by racial ones. As has been argued by Milburg-Stean (in his book *European and African Stereotypes in Twentieth Century Fiction*) the polygenistic idea of endemic and fixed racial differences, reinforced in the late nineteenth century by free adaptations of Darwinian ideas on natural selection, were used as an argument for European racial superiority. These still had considerable currency at the time of the South African war. A desire for stability in the empire concurred with ideas on racial superiority to support the new imperialism. In particular, Robert Knox's theory of stasis provided a rationale for the belief in a 'frozen state of African civilization'.[22] Like others, Benita Parry argues that this belief in a fundamental dichotomy between mummified 'primitive' cultures and European civilization meant that European modes of thought and material progress legitimated, for many, the 'natural' expansion of the west:

> Fundamental to a construction defending imperialism's formal goals as ethical and its practices as globally beneficial, and one which was accepted by large numbers within the metropolitan society as an accurate apprehension of realities and conforming to sound principles, were the premises that civilization was defined by an expanding technology, progress by an increased domination of the material environment, culture by the tastes of the European bourgeoisie and morality by Christian doctrine.[23]

Consequently, it was thought by many that Africa needed British presence, and that since Britain could make its resources and knowledge 'globally beneficial', there were no ethical problems involved in exploiting the wealth of Africa. In *The Resurrection of Peter* Radziwill's Christ figure tells a bemused trooper Halket why God put so many riches in Africa: 'they were put there to be found and used by man, used for noble purposes, used for a high moral aim, for the good of the world and the glory of the Almighty' (*ROP*, p. 56); 'man' here means white men, particularly the British, who can then civilize blacks who live in 'idleness and superstition':

> Go and help them to shake off all this darkness; make civilized beings out of them; remember that they must be treated with kindness and gentleness, and that they are but too ready to acknowledge your superiority.
>
> (*ROP*, p. 44)

Imperialism is rationalized as bringer of light to the 'dark' continent and of form to a formless (because uncivilized) culture. The existence of riches in Africa, put there for the white man by a racially preferential God, suggests also what the novel conspires with, the creation of an Africa which exists solely for the purpose of British rule.

Given that the Boers were white adversaries, a dominant strategy in these works is to cast the Boers as primitives, part of the arcane and 'frozen' map of Africa. They often appear as representatives of an earlier phase of European civilization, forgotten by history; a people who inhabit an outmoded world of Old Testament values rather than the new gospel of progress. As such, they have a dual role; they share an affinity with 'superstitious' and primitive blacks, but are also poor white brothers, subsumed by the dark continent and in need of guidance back to the path of progress. For example, Conan Doyle calls the Boers 'the most conservative of Teutonic races' (*HBW*, p. 11) thereby claiming for them both distance from and relationship with European civilization. He quotes, from an unspecified source, supposed exchanges between Boers in the two Raads (Parliaments), in an attempt to indicate and ridicule their political and cultural philistinism; one high-ranking Boer objects to the introduction of pillar boxes on the grounds that they are 'extravagant and effeminate'; he also insists that locusts should not be harmed, despite the damage they cause to crops, because they constitute a 'special plague sent by God for their sinfulness' (*HBW*, p. 27). In Henty's *With Roberts to Pretoria* the narrator tells us that 'it cannot be denied that the Dutch hate changes of any kind and would like the world to stand still' (*WRP*, p. 35). In the satirical *A Burgher Quixote* (1903) by Douglas Blackburn, the narrator is himself a Boer, and his stupidity, cowardice and laziness act as a critique of Boer mentality, while those Boers who are astute, like Van Zwieten in *A Traitor in London*, are portrayed as cunning, self-seeking agitators – an ill-directed intelligence which needs curbing and re-educating.

Such images act as a self-reflecting device which antithetically suggests the more enlightened British. In *A Traitor in London*, the hero, Harold, and his brother, Wilfred, are reverse images of Van Zwieten; Wilfred in particular is motivated by 'patriotic emotions', adores England as he would love a woman and 'hated Van Zwieten who was working darkly for her ill' (*ATL*, p. 125). Similarly in *With Roberts to Pretoria* the war is frequently reduced to a conflict of personal 'pluck', couched in the vocabulary of a public school, familiar to Henty novels, between the hero, Yorke, and the Boer villain, Birck Jansen, of whom Yorke says to his uncle: 'He is a great deal stronger and bigger than I am, uncle; but I don't suppose that he has the slightest idea of boxing, and I can use my fists pretty well' (*WRP*, p. 36). Set against the image of the primitive Boer the British hero is the forerunner of an advanced civilization, there to punish, order and plunder.

Action men

The image of the hero in these novels crystallizes different elements from colonial thinking. Oliver Ransford, who has written extensively on the South African war, has argued cogently that David Livingstone provided both a new way of seeing Africa and, as a public figure, embodied an image of the adventurer, both of which may be seen to have long-term implications for British presence in South Africa. The lionizing of Livingstone was an apposite antidote to depression about the Crimean war; he symbolized to many the zealous adventurer motivated by both missionary fervour and scientific inquiry. Ransford claims that his programme for the moral redemption of black Africans was actually a form of redemption for the British:

> With him he carried an entirely new concept of the people of Central Africa, together with a practical formula for the redemption of their bodies and souls, which would permit a century's accumulation of guilt for her share in the trans-Atlantic slave trade.[24]

Also, he clearly played an important role in fostering an enduring anti-Boer feeling. He called them a 'brigade of Satan's own', and rejoiced that 'malaria is not an unmitigated evil since it swept off many Boers in 1852'.[25] Ransford states: 'Livingstone's criticism of the Boers also had a long-term effect, for it became one of the factors responsible for the outbreak of two Boer wars'.[26]

If the popular image of Livingstone helped to suggest a particular stereotype of adventurer and redeemer, then Cecil Rhodes gave it substance and opinions. Apparently untouched by the debacle of the Jameson raid, Rhodes sometimes appears in these novels to serve as an aspirant model for the fictional hero. In *With Roberts to Pretoria* Yorke observes him keenly:

> As he spoke Rhodes himself came up. Yorke looked with interest at the man who is the Napoleon of South Africa – a square-built man, with a smoothly shaven face except for a thick moustache, with hair waving back from a broad forehead, strong and determined chin and mouth, somewhat broad in the cheeks, giving his face the appearance of squareness, light eyes, keen but kindly, altogether a strong and pleasant face.
>
> (*WRP*, p. 178)

Yorke is pleased that Rhodes declares a sense of affinity with him: 'I am a hard worker myself, and I am only too glad to have men round me with clear heads, a capacity for hard work, and, in a pinch, plenty of pluck and decision' (*WRP*, p. 175). We then see Yorke fulfil these conditions in his fight against the Boers and his final reward is a huge share in a gold mine, whereby he signifies an extension, or surrogate version, of

Rhodes himself. The impulse here is to create a simple chain of cause and effect between specific character traits and material reward. In *The Resurrection of Peter*, Rhodes is also used as an image with which to tutor the soldier. Chastising trooper Halket for doubting the purity of Rhodes's motives, a fervently and alarmingly pro-British Christ figure makes the dubious claim that Rhodes is close to sainthood:

> Yes, it is far easier to die than to stand alone with a great work before one, that one feels bound to perform ... The man who for long years has gone on with his self-imposed task solely because he felt it had been undertaken for his country's welfare ... that man has certainly contributed largely towards the peace Christ came into this world to preach.
>
> (*RP*, p. 35)

Later, Halket learns of the mystical nature of Rhodes:

> 'You want to know what that man is?' He asked in a solemn voice. 'He is a Creator.' Peter Halket looked up into the stranger's eyes in silent bewilderment.
>
> (*RP*, p. 72)

Baden-Powell, Roberts, Kitchener and Churchill also make cameo appearances which serve as exemplary models of military virtue. For example, Roberts has a 'knack of making himself loved by all with whom he came into contact' and Kitchener, although a stern 'man of iron' is 'admired and respected' (*WRP*, p. 307).

Figures such as these constitute a code of honour and achievement both in and across the texts, through which the hero comes into being. Historically, the popular image of Livingstone helped to establish a prototype of the adventurer with a moral purpose, and, as Ransford suggests, also partly established a set of feelings towards the Boers. In the novels, Rhodes symbolizes the powerful and wealthy entrepreneur, a living example of the riches waiting to be had in Africa, and, according to Zangwill and others, he also embodies a quasi-religious impulse in empire building, a muscular Christianity based on 'tough' character traits rather than transcendent spirituality. Roberts and other military figures represent the man of action, the cream of the British army, fighters to be feared and respected. These qualities define the hero, who unites, dramatizes and perfects them in the narrative.

However, our hero is troubled, and the clouds that shadow him harbour storms for England at home and abroad.

The lone hero

Hitherto, in military and war fiction, it was often officers who were singled out for heroic status. They usually epitomized courage, leadership, acumen and a public-school virtue of enjoying war as gamesmanship.[27] Certainly, such fiction continued to be written during the Boer war, but there was a growing tendency to articulate criticisms of the officer class which were being expressed through other mediums, such as the journalistic writings and criticism of W.T. Stead[28] and the persistently critical voice of Captain William Elliott Cairnes, who wrote three books on the army during the war and a daily article about it for the *Westminster Gazette*.[29] Even an extremely pro-British novel like *A Traitor in London* concedes criticism of British generals; a Boer says derisively: ' "Your men are very brave – Oh yes; but your generals – ah well! the dear Lord has shown them what they should do – for the benefit of the burghers" ' (*ATL*, p. 279).

In an authorial commentary Henty offers guarded criticism of Kitchener, whose military experience had hitherto been limited to fighting 'barbarous tribes' (*WRP*, p. 319). The attempt to storm the Boers at Paardeberg is seen as folly:

> The effect was terrible, and men went down by the score before the hail of bullets … It would have been well if … the impossibility of success had been recognised, and the troops had been ordered to remain in the same position throughout the day, contenting themselves with returning the Boer fire. But no such order was given.
>
> (*WRP*, p. 319)

Tom Bevan's novel, *Dick Dale, the Colonial Scout: A Tale of the Transvaal War* (1900) suggests how British officers ignore the advice of the colonials and, 'true to the traditions of their rank, must needs court a danger it had been wiser to avoid'.[30] G.K. Chesterton's parable of the war, *The Napoleon of Notting Hill* (1904) offers a cynical parody of Kitchener's and Buller's 'theory' of war, that numbers determine duration and outcome; Buck, a dull-witted leader states that 'fighting, when we have the stronger force, is only a matter of arithmetic'.[31]

Criticisms of officers in authorial commentaries or from Boer characters do not constitute the major critical voice; this is often left to the protagonist himself. In *McGlusky*, after the narrator has condemned the mindless slaughter of wounded British soldiers and Boer prisoners, and blames this upon the 'folly of a British officer' who orders that no more

171

Figure 7.1 'The effect was terrible, and men went down before the hail of bullets.'

Source: Painting by R. Coton Woodville, reproduced by kind permission of the National Army Museum.

prisoners be taken, McGlusky, as the hero protagonist, is given a long speech which lampoons British officers and develops into a diatribe against the political machinery, epitomized by Chamberlain, which motivates such officers:

> A hated ta see gude fechtin men like the Breetish Tommies doin' deevils' work, burnin' farms ower tha heeds o' puir wummin an' bairns; an' A felt sick in ma wammle ta see the wummin an' bairns o' our eeneemies cooped up like coos in death camps. A'm na a poleetician, but, as ma soul leeveth, A'm theenkin' that when Joseph Chem'erlain stan's in that preesence o' God A'Michty, pleadin' for mercy for his soul's sak' he will hear tha voices o' hunners o' little children cryin' oot ta tha God o' the fatherless askin' for justice.
>
> (*M*, pp. 353–4)

There are frequent occasions when McGlusky rejects what Spiers calls the 'citadel mentality' of officers, who carefully maintain distinctions of rank and privilege between themselves and private soldiers, yet, as McGlusky says, he has never known 'any officer or gentleman [who] objected to their company in tha hoor o' battle' (*M*, p. 282).

In *Old Fireproof* the priest/narrator acquires a condemnatory attitude towards British officers through hard experience, first-hand observations and through his admiration for the hero figure, the Captain, who is himself a virulent critic of officers in the regular army. The narrator first joins the Captain and his band of irregulars after his disgust with the 'grey' colonel of a column of regular soldiers who refuses to face a Boer attack since this would contravene his immediate orders. The irregulars are a cross between Robin Hood's band and the Wild Bunch, and in contrast to a rigid adherence to regulations, impress him with their self-reliance:

> Truly, I had come into another air, where everything breathed of self-reliance and of virile independence of thought encompassing one great end, instead of the crimped and patterned results of the atrophied intelligence of those men of Ephraim retiring yonder.
>
> (*OF*, p. 16)

The Captain calls the British commandant of a prison camp 'Sewer-noser! You Aunt Nancy!' (*OF*, p. 266) in one of his frequent diatribes against British officers. Suggestions of effeteness occur throughout the novel and are endorsed by the narrator, who compares the demeanour of regular officers with the Captain's irregulars:

> Here were no society men perforce enduring the war till they could resume the life of Mayfair, as it is shared by the army. The picture of a dancer from the music-halls, or an actress in tights from the theatres, was not the greatest thing in the world to them ... As to their views on the rest of the army, their great admiration was divided between the artillery and the British private in close battle: their great contempt – nay, they had more than one, but I will not name them, lest I should be led too far from the story I have to tell.
>
> (*OF*, p. 102)

British officers constitute a displaced class, better suited to an idle life in London society than to the rigours of war. According to the Captain, commissions signify effeteness rather than ability or rank, as he tells one 'monocle-man' who seeks to impress him with superior rank: 'Even at home you are cheap enough, God knows, for every amateur strumpet and semi-detached wife in society has one or two like you to get commissions for, now that a commission is the shibboleth' (*OF*, p. 328).

A further criticism of officers is their inability to envisage the army as anything other than a rigid, mechanistic unit. This point is made repeatedly at the beginning of George Wilton's book, *Scapegoats of the Empire* (1902), in which the qualities required of colonial irregulars were the antithesis of privates in the regular army whom officers drilled into 'machines' until they 'could merely drill and move their arms and feet as though they were worked on wire'.[32] In Wilton's book, British officers represent the army as mechanism and are related to the underpinning theme of hypocrisy, in which the army cannot survive without using unorthodox strategies, as employed by the irregulars, yet condemns them to protect its own public image. In *Old Fireproof*, in an anticipation of the slaughter in France a few years away, the Captain admonishes and ridicules a British officer for reaping 'such a butcher's bill' by unnecessarily losing soldier's lives, then complaining because his major does not supply him with immediate replacements:

> 'And yet he used to be such a kind-hearted man, I'm sure that if only he'd thought of it, he'd have sent back to the shops and bought you a whole nice box of men, tin ones, made in Germany, each with a little tin gun on his shoulder. And if they got knocked over you could

always stick them up again, not like those on that waggon, or in these ambulances', and he pointed to them as they rolled slowly past us along the road to camp.

(*OF*, pp. 328–9)

The hero here, as in other novels, is the antithesis of the British officer. Passages such as this presage the First World War – in which, as most histories and narratives tell us, the common soldier has a purely utilitarian value to the war machine. The social and military gaps between officer and private are criticized rather than celebrated, and through these criticisms the hero is emphatically identified with the common soldier, who is himself seen as a victim of military bungling. This divisiveness and ineptitude is also part of the 'real' history of the war, as it was part of a deep anxiety about the army. The inadequate officer has also been categorized as a psychological type for whom the British have both affection and contempt. In *On the Psychology of Military Incompetence*, the problem, as Norman Dixon sees it, is as much a matter of how the military machinery operates as it is a matter of individual psychology. A soldier is promoted according to his competence at a particular level, which may be entirely unsuitable at another level. Moreover, the specific qualities which allow an officer to triumph at one level may be the direct cause of failure at another, and as such, it is the judgement and procedures of the authorities which are failing. Redvers Buller has thus been described as a 'superb major, a mediocre colonel and an abysmal general.'[33] It was precisely because he had been a heroic leader earlier in his career that he was a bad general. Initially, he preferred direct assault over cunning and feeling over thought. Rigorous thought rather than heroism was needed in a war such as that with the Boers, yet it was pluck and daring over thought which the novels of the time extolled. However, Buller is not so easily categorized. Pakenham argues that history has dealt harshly but also unfairly with Buller, that it was in fact he who initiated strategies for countering Boer tactics and never got the glory accorded to Roberts.[34] Julian Symons' final assessment of Buller is that he was an enigma 'far more intelligent and sensitive than history has allowed'.[35]

Individual reputations aside, clearly there was a problem in how best to conduct this war, in how to lead, and the British army was often found wanting. Having had attention drawn to them, officers frequently became the focal point for debate, drawing fire from reformist and radical voices, such as Cairnes, who maintained that officer elites had become redundant and for whom the army had become 'a mere organization for the purpose of providing an elegant employment for the leisure hours of the wealthy classes'.[36] A select committee concluded that there was considerable laziness and incompetence among young officers. Lord Roberts also advocated improved training to promote a greater independence of thought among officers.[37]

The army had long provided employment for the wealthier classes, who could earlier buy commissions and maintain a lifestyle appropriate to the image of an officer and a gentleman. This view was still prevalent during the Boer War. The two new factors here are the amount of criticism drawn by a hitherto largely respected social group and, secondly, the incorporation of such criticisms into fiction. The novels have an almost unanimous authorial commitment to the war, yet need to contain contradictions concerning it, such as persistent setbacks, a numerically inferior enemy, and a discontent with officers as suitable fictional heroes.

Textual strategies: the outsider

Given that the war did not provide a catalogue of outright British victories and the army did draw criticism, many of the novels distance the problems by creating a hero who is himself distanced from the confines of the regular army. He is a composite figure, combining the qualities conventionally associated with the archetypal officer in fiction (leadership, bravery, independence, decision-making) with those of the common soldier ('pluck', ambivalence towards authority, lack of privilege, endurance of privation, basically dependable and patriotic), yet who is outside the upper echelons of military hierarchies.

To create the common soldier as hero, as Kipling did, would still be to create a fiction of the army. As military structures within the army were drawing criticism, the hero was placed within a freer milieu in which his own resources and specific abilities could be foregrounded. However, the major point of identification with the regular army for these heroic types was through the figure of the common soldier. In *Old Fireproof* there are constant reminders of the physical privations, poor training and poor equipment of the British Tommies, whom the Captain and his band of irregulars greatly admire for their courage 'in close battle' while their contempt is reserved for British officers. The hero is allied, through sympathy and identification, with the regular soldier in the army without losing his highly individualized outsider status. To an extent, he is *déclassé*, belonging neither to an officer elite, nor to the controlled world of common soldiers, yet it is to the latter that his allegiances are made.

The typical hero moves within a pattern of narrative repetitions. Simply stated, he goes to Africa independently of the regular army, either because of a general commitment to British presence in South Africa or, more often, to fulfil a desire for adventure and/or personal gain. His relations with the regular army are often ambiguous; invariably he will act as a scout, which makes him a partial outsider. His consequent freedom of movement, denied to regular troops, allows the narrator to present a more panoramic view of the war to the reader and creates opportunities to engage his hero in a greater number of battles and skirmishes. In *Old Fireproof*, Rhoscomyl foregrounds the attractions of the irregulars. The narrator claims that since the war, he has often been 'beguiled by the ladies' into recounting memories of the war, and that their fascination is most exercised by stories of the irregulars. The reason for this, he claims, 'lies all packed up and rounded in the one word – Romance' (*OF*, p. 56).[38] He uses the term Romance in both its medieval sense of having specific narrative components and in a more modern sentimental sense (i.e. the romantic fascination of the 'ladies'), and while officers in the regular army have a limited narrative potential, in which there is the 'same old... olden-told and iterated story, ending with wedding-bells and blushing bliss, in stately homes or rose-embowered cottages', to 'ponder upon a confused regiment of irregulars', however, allows personal fantasy a greater freedom:

> while perchance they think a little askance of its officers, as being somewhat suspect of being respectable, they pass on with eagerness to loose their fluttering dreams upon the wild rank-and-file, straightway adumbrating each man of it as hero of some moving, separate, strange romance... Thus, while they think of the regular regiment of romance amongst them, they dream upon the other as being composed of five hundred separate entities; wrecks and seared tokens of five hundred separate tragedies and sorrows.
>
> (*OF*, p. 57)

In this passage, Rhoscomyl's narrator suggests three important points concerned with how the novel should be read, and, in so doing, draws attention to how other novels under discussion are constructed. First, the maintaining of reader interest, if it is to create and fulfil the conditions of 'Romance', depends upon a telescoping of events and time so that the hero engages frequently in fights, skirmishes and major battles. Also, the role of spy is more appropriate to the irregular, who is not hidebound by uniform and is more used to acting on his own initiative; this disguise, in which the hero, such as Yorke in Henty's novel, comes into close contact with the Boers, allows greater opportunities for conflict between individuals. In a war where the use of big guns and the hit-and-run guerilla tactics of the Boers meant that there were fewer hand-to-hand engagements, the roving irregular who sometimes enters Boer camps as a spy provides opportunities to show enemies meeting face to face; it also allows for descriptions of Boers, representations of their beliefs and speech (something which would rarely happen with a black adversary) without having to transfer the narrative point of view from the British to the Dutch. Thus, the need for constant military excitement and concomitant frequent shifts in time and location commit these novels to creating hero figures which function outside the perimeters of the regular army. This negative identification carries an implied criticism of the army, for the qualities the hero possesses and which are there to excite admiration are precisely those which are absent in the regular army.

Secondly, Rhoscomyl is insistent upon the 'feminine' appeal of Romance; it is the 'ladies' who are fascinated by stories of the hero. Such a type compounds the allure of mystery, the solidity of self reliance and, ultimately, the 'right' ideological commitments, despite the outsider status. This kind of hero figure can compound a sense of community (through identification with the type) with a commitment to individuality. In *Old Fireproof* both the narrator, and presumably the reader, fulfil these 'feminine' relations with the hero; the narrator because he stands in awe of the hero to the extent that he sometimes doubts his own 'manliness', and the reader because, Rhoscomyl assumes, he shares both the curiosity and the spectatorial role of the 'ladies'. The hero is distinctive, displays an 'uncommon' level of self-reliant virilism which distances him from ordinary conceptions of masculinity, but allows for different levels of identification between hero and reader. 'Manliness' acquires an almost transcendent status, hence the frequent references to the Captain as god-like, mysterious, endowed with extraordinarily uncompromising physical and moral powers.[39]

Thirdly, because of the sheer range of military encounters and the transcendent qualities of the hero, the reader is given considerable imaginative space for his own fantasies of war to germinate. The narrative free play of the hero becomes a signifier to which the reader may attach his own version of the war, can 'pass on with eagerness to loose ... fluttering dreams upon the wild rank and file', adapting the associative values of the hero (a god, an outsider, a mystery) to 'some moving, separate, strange romance'. For a reader, the hero as outsider may have had two further possible functions. First, the image of a hero who, to some extent, acts as a criticism of military orthodoxy, allows the reader to acknowledge setbacks, military blunders and the often inappropriate strategies of generals – we might call this a gesture towards historical realism, but without blaming the hero, who achieves great things despite the blunders. Second, this allows British 'character' to be vindicated and thus acts as a recuperative strategy. These texts contain an antithetical pattern in which uncertainty or criticism of the regular army is mitigated by the heroism of the irregular; since it is the adventures of the latter which are foregrounded then the predominant message is that while systems may blunder and fall into disrepute, the individual (if he is British) can still win a war.

Outsiders and metonyms

Crucial to the image of the hero as a figure of romance, supplemented, according to Rhoscomyl, by the fantasies of the reader, is that he moves through an 'adventure' narrative, a series of events designed to test and display his combative and moral powers. As Spiers has argued, war correspondents were often responsible for swelling the myth of war as adventure, and, as the career of Henty demonstrates, the rhetoric of war correspondents is often indistinguishable from that of the writer of military fiction. Clearly, there was a large audience for stylistic embellishments in representations of war:

> War correspondents followed the army around the globe. Vivid and lyrical despatches were telegraphed home. Minor reverses were described in apocalyptic terms; minor victories were hailed with paeans of praise ... writers of military fiction found an apparently insatiable market for romantic and idealistic accounts of martial adventure in distant parts of the Empire.[40]

Fiction has to compete with the immediacy of '[v]ivid and lyrical' despatches, and history subsumed to 'romantic and idealistic' accounts, if a large readership, by now familiar with journalistic flourish, was to be captured.[41] Vivid prose also demanded vivid hero figures. In *With Roberts to Pretoria*, Yorke welcomes the possibility of war because it offers escape from the dreary pursuit of his studies: 'If I had not been out here I should be slaving at Greek and mathematics at home, whereas now, if war breaks out, which seems almost certain, I shall have a most exciting time of it' (*WR*, p. 55–6). The hero of *Telegraph Dick* meets an adventurer and hunter, Monsieur Le Vine, in London, and the tales of the intrepid traveller fire his own imagination; 'Dick felt his blood tingling in his

Figure 7.2 '...romantic and idealistic accounts of martial adventure.'

Source: Drawing by R. Coton Woodville in *South Africa and the Transvaal War.*

veins, for he was an adventurer born, the spirit of daring and romance was in every fibre of his being' (*TD*, p. 11). Once in South Africa, Dick meets 'Old Industry', a Devonshire man in whose image the soldier and the adventurer are welded:

> He was the man who rode alone through the ranks of the Basutos when ... [they] had sworn to wipe out every man, woman and child in South Africa who spoke the English tongue ... Look at him: six feet seven in his stockings, and yet so narrow and spare ... he could hurl a boulder of granite farther than any man, black or white, in all Africa ..., his face was the face of a woman, so beautiful in its chiselling, every feature seemed as if it might have been cut out of a piece of marble; and his complexion was dead white; neither wind nor rain, sun nor storm had been able to tan his skin, and not a hair grew on his face below his eyebrows.
>
> (*TD*, pp. 92–3)

The hyperbolic and theatrical presentation of 'Old Industry' is imperative to a fabulation which invests so much in the symbolic value of its heroes. The reader is invited to marvel at not only his bravery but also his genetic capacity to retain a classical racial purity, his 'marble' features and 'dead white' complexion which resist even the African sun and are therefore impervious to change.

For such types, war is a heightened form of adventure, welcomed for its cathartic capacity to excite extreme emotions and sensations. It is the Great Game. In *Telegraph Dick* we are told of Dick's 'lust for battle'. In *A Traitor in London*, Brenda, the hero's fiancé revels in the sensations of war; she and Harold are in a farmhouse, besieged by a party of Boers, one of whom (Van Ziewen) has sworn to claim Brenda for himself, thus adding a sexual excitement to the conflict:

> Had their leader been killed, he [Van Ziewen] imagined that the soldiers would have surrendered, quite forgetting that it was not the custom of Englishmen to yield to anything but death ... By all the gods he swore that Brenda should be his ... Far from being afraid, the girl, much to her own surprise, was filled with the terrible joy of battle; indeed, she was in the highest spirits ... As the bullets sang, and the smell of powder became stronger, Brenda could hardly contain her excitement.
>
> (*ATL*, p. 270)

Brenda and Harold, like the Captain and Old Industry, act as metonyms, signifying an assumed essentially 'British' set of values and characteristics and organizing a way of perceiving the war as a testing ground for 'character'.[42] The role of the narrator is to present events through his enthusiasm for the heroine's own excitement and courage, as suggested in the above passage. The South African War is then itself subsumed to a typical narrative pattern which romanticizes it as a welcome diversion for the adventurous spirit in particular, and as a wider opportunity to make enemies bow to what one military commentator, Colonel C. Caldwell, called the 'forces of civilization'.[43]

Tribal reprobates

As I said, there existed a reluctant, but expedient, admiration for the hooligan type, such as Young Alf. This type was seen, by some, as prime material for the army; his self-reliance, self-assertion and violent propensities which constituted a social threat on the streets of London, could, in a colonial context, prove a useful source of belligerence. Henley's obvious admiration for his version of a Byronic hero and Kipling's creation of Tommy Atkins are also variations of the hero as part outlaw, part patriot. Similarly, in the novels under discussion, we can see how a significant part of the hero's attraction is an element of volatility unsuited to the disciplined ranks of the regular army.

He may have a fatal flaw which, in another context, would designate him as a social reprobate. McGlusky, for example, is an adventurer, a 'barbarian' who has a weakness for drink and an ensuing weakness to indulge in a 'drunken frenzy of fighting' (*M*, p. 106). In *Telegraph Dick* Danny Develin is a 'lion' in battle who glories in the 'song of the sword', but is also an ex-hussar, cashiered from the army for bouts of drunkenness, during which he would become an 'unresponsible white savage' (*TD*, p. 54). The army apparently cannot accommodate these weaknesses, but, these novels assure us, the empire can, for they single out the hero and are a counterpoint to conventional heroism. The hero not only faces constant external dangers, but also has to contend with his own moral failings; the recovery or proving of his own innate integrity thus becomes a second reason for admiring him. Kipling's *Stalky and Co.* present similar types: anti-authority, resourceful, independent minded.

A further sign of his outlaw status is an anti-authoritarian stance. I have discussed the Captain's antagonism in *Old Fireproof*, in which he favours 'natural' qualities over the economic and class determinants which create officers in the regular army. McGlusky is a hater of Baal, and '[b]y Baal he meant anything or anyone who might happen to be in power' (*M*, p. 8). Both these heroes admire Cromwell, McGlusky because of his 'grim religion and soldierly sides' (*M*, p. 8) and the Captain because, for him, Cromwell embodied a coherent vision of the soldier which had the power to rouse a whole nation and take on the powers that be at home. Both are nostalgic for an imagined age of noble warfare in which personal morality and vision transcend political and military vicissitudes. This nostalgia becomes a means of implicitly criticizing not empire itself, but the forms of empire; both McGlusky and the Captain are placed outside and critical of an administration headed by lacklustre politicians and officers who command a military machine rather than a band of soldiers.

Despite the relative independence and isolation of the hero, he is nevertheless part of a group, a sub-set of the army. The group usually bears signs of tribalism, which links it to but differentiates it from the army. Tribalism becomes a totem, in which a group of men similarly unsuited to the sublimating influences of the regular army, recognize the hero's unique abilities and promote him to leadership. The group is not dissimilar to the street gang on the streets of London or Manchester, discussed in Chapter 4. Such a group acquires the mystique we are familiar with in popular culture, such as Robin Hood's band of outlaws, in which the group is uniquely defined from within. In *Old Fireproof*, the Captain's squadron is organized according to the 'old Welsh laws' (the Captain is Welsh) and the acceptability of the narrator to the group allows him 'privilege of kin with D Squadron', entitling him to the 'clan's help in all his feuds'. Even before he meets them, he hears of them, for they are a product of 'common repute' which casts them as 'men reckless and headlong, fearing neither God nor man' (*OF*, p. 7). When he does encounter them they signify, for him, the 'real world', unlike the 'grey' columns of regulars he has just left. What immediately distinguishes them is the exteriorizing of individual personality into surface effects, such as clothes and the idiosyncratic wearing of bandoliers. At first sight, they look like 'lazy tramps at home' but this is the contrived and casual surface of a band of 'iron' men:

> Of many guises, too, they were. Each man seemed to wear what bandoliers he thought fittest for his strength and habit of body, as, for instance, two crossed upon the chest, or two, one above the other, round his hips and waist. Others, again, wore one over the chest and one round the hips, just whatever way seemed good to them ... It needed but a word, a glance at an enemy seen, and this line would be grim iron again – a line of death.
>
> (*OF*, pp. 15–16)

This could easily be a description of a band of Boer guerillas. The novel borrows the more attractive and individuating image of a group of Boer soldiers with their hit-and-run tactics, ability to outmanoeuvre and out-think a numerically superior enemy. They embody a code of difference rather than uniformity. The formulation of a group's own internal laws is apparent in *Telegraph Dick* in which the former London messenger boy, considered to be a reprobate by his family at home, draws up his own code of behaviour in South Africa, a secular ten commandments which he and his companion swear to uphold 'by the lights o' London, that never go out'. In *McGlusky*, the hero gathers around him a group of black Africans, whose 'tribal' instincts recognize in him a warrior worthy of being made a prophet and a king. He fulfils the white colonial dream of being apotheosized by natives:

> The warriors did not understand one half of what was said to them, but they understood enough to know that this new prophet held out a prospect of much war, and war to those wild fighters was the only game for a man – war and women and hunting meant bliss untrammelled to them.

> (*M*, p. 71)

Similarly, in *With Roberts to Pretoria*, Yorke commandeers a group of Kaffirs into joining his band of scouts to work for the British army. In both Yorke's and McGlusky's case, they are white men writ large, and in each case, the tribal element is crucial in differentiating the hero from the regular army. They are warriors, not Yes men or bureaucrats.

What the hero confronts here is the 'dark continent' or geographical adversary (ironically appropriate since the Boers made inventive use of the terrain), or the enemy may be concentrated into images of the black African population, animals or strange life forms. As such, the hero confronts a largely preformed vocabulary of images of savagery and danger which are, as Hugh Ridley, in *Images of Imperial Rule* states, already recorded in European life and 'waiting merely for actual faces and landscape to take up pre-ordained roles'.[44] These novels are not 'literary' in either intention or effect, but they are tangentially related to more metaphysically searching works, notably Conrad's *Heart of Darkness*, and to the adventure fantasies of Rider Haggard.

In *Telegraph Dick*, Dick and Sim set off for 'the great Dark Continent' where every enemy they encounter is a manifestation of a 'dark' force and in which 'evil' blacks and dangerous creatures are often conflated. The numerous adversaries they encounter include pariah dogs, adders, a shark, an ostrich, apes and an elephant with 'cruel, malignant eyes' similar to those of black Africans they confront, such as 'the tribe of noseless men, the big, ugly men who eat human beings' (*TD*, p. 233). The adventurer, Old Industry, explains to them that blacks are invariably 'outlaw' savages and 'a savage has animal instincts' (*TD*, p. 148). Their chief enemy is a Hottentot witch doctor, a 'mad dog' whose appearance momentarily checks the hero: 'Dick recoiled when he first saw the prisoner, for the fellow had not the face of a man; it was the face of a devil' (*TD*, p. 187), and Danny Develin affirms the implications of having a black skin: 'You've got a dark skin, and you may have dark knowledge' (*TD*, p. 200).

It is this 'dark knowledge' which the hero confronts as he battles with its various manifestations, each of which reinforces the European myth of Africa as not only a physical but also a psychically hostile force. His fight against it then becomes a fight on behalf of light and white civilization. In this novel, the penultimate enemy is a 'thing' which embodies the image of Africa for the white hero:

> It was a vast head, with strange hair falling all round it – hair that might have been human, or it might have formed part of a lion's mane. It was black as night, and matted and tangled, and full of grass ends and thorns and leaves... Then came the great gaping mouth, full of big, fierce-looking, yellow teeth. It was not a human face, neither was it the face of an ape.
>
> (*TD*, p. 214)

The map of Africa is textually redrawn into a prevalent colonial myth, that of the few, lone white men facing hostile, often subhuman enemies, and it is this myth which underpins much of the fiction specifically concerned with representing the Boer War. Such a myth also had the intellectual support of racial theorists, historians and polemical works, such as Conan Doyle's, in which he argued that Africa needs 'to be drawn into the settled order of civilized rule' because of the barbaric qualities of its indigenous peoples, such as 'the dwarf bushmen, the hideous aborigines, lowest of the human race' (*HBW*, p. 15). Henty's *With Buller in Natal*, nostalgic for an earlier campaign, was deliberately brought out in the Christmas rush in 1900, and represented Britain as a civilizing power against an enemy 'without even the basic elements of civilization, ignorant and brutal beyond any existing white community'.[45]

This way of seeing Africa permeated British culture to the extent that, to some, during the war, African culture could be 'read' in the light of the myth outlined above. For example, Trevor R. Griffiths argues that Herbert Tree's production of *The Tempest* invited analogies to be made between the production and the war. Journalist and writer, W.T. Stead, who attended the performance, clearly saw the whole play as an extended metaphor for South Africa: Caliban's protest at Prospero's usurpation of his island is, Stead argues, a reminder of Dr. Jameson's treatment of the Matabale; Trinculo is a thinly disguised version of Lord Roseberry; Stephano's deception of Caliban is Chamberlain's deception of the British electorate, who are the dupes of political chicanery:

> we see the pitiful tragedy of the Jingo fever and the South African war. Both political parties combine to pass the bottle to the poor monster ... despite the Roseberian gibes and sneers, the poor, scurvy, monster kisses the foot of the Jingo party, and finally the scene ends with a deliberately drunken dance ... As the curtain fell amid roars of laughter, I remembered I had seen it all before on a much larger scale. It was Mafeking night all over again.[46]

Stead also identifies Caliban with the plight of the Boers, in which they are being usurped of territory by the British. His idiosyncratic reading of the performance was, Griffiths argues, a response to 'a quite obvious invitation from the production's treatment of Caliban' but he goes on to argue that the real invitation was to identify Caliban with the indigenous peoples of South Africa in a way which suggested a need for British colonial, rather than Boer, rule.[47] The final image of the play was of Caliban alone on a rock, implying that he is 'lost without the civilising influence exerted upon him by Prospero and his companions; the islander needs the Europeans, the slave needs the master as much as the master needs the slave'.[48]

Certainly, the hero in the novels is often presented as a Prospero figure in that he embodies western civilized values and, more importantly, is a worker of magic among the black Africans. Griffiths's argument implies a further point, which is relevant to those novels which represent Africa as an arcane, barbaric and hostile place to the English mind.[49] There is an implied role for the Boers; as fellow Europeans, albeit primitive ones, they are subliminally appealed to through the image of a hostile Africa. They should engage with the British in subduing the dark continent and enfranchise fellow Europeans, or remain as primitives themselves who fail to recognize the civilizing mission of the British and therefore suffer the consequences. As Parry says, even those who criticize the assumptions of colonialism, as Stead did, are still prone to a use of imagery which conspires with colonial perspectives: 'customary ways of seeing together with constellations of images congenial to the dominant consciousness, coalesce in producing a view of the world that conforms to colonialist theology'.[50] All well and good, but how else can one see, save for the language of one's own time?

Conflicting heroes

Olive Schreiner's *Trooper Peter Halket* offers the most concise and eloquent analysis of the political and economic realities underlying British presence in South Africa and goes further in examining conventional notions of heroism; that she does this by employing the idea of Christian conversion is an undermining of those who subscribed to a theological dimension in colonial activity. It is also of interest because of the counter text it provoked, *The Resurrection of Peter*, by Catherine Radziwill.

The frontispiece of the first American edition of Schreiner's book has a photograph of three black Africans hanging from a tree, watched by a group of whites, presumably their murderers and members of the Chartered Company, since the book is primarily concerned with attitudes towards race and Africa as epitomized by the Company. The book clearly prompted controversy, as the photograph was suppressed in the English edition.[51]

British practices which are barely mentioned in other novels are a predicate in this text and, collectively, present an image of empire as it is 'lived' rather than imagined: the keeping and discarding of black mistresses; random murders of black Africans; the destruction of kraals and granaries as a pugilistic form of control of the black population. Halket explains to the stranger that Cecil Rhodes is the model for this behaviour and, in Halket's eyes, is vindicated by his vast wealth:

> 'Now he's death on niggers,' said Peter Halket, warming his hands by the fire; 'they say when he was Prime Minister down in the colony, he tried to pass a law that would give masters and mistresses the right to have their servants flogged whenever they did anything they didn't like ... ' 'I prefer land to niggers,' he says. They say he's going to parcel them out, and make them work on our lands whether they like it or not – just as good as having slaves, you know ... Now, there I'm with Rhodes ... We don't come out here to work; it's all very well in England; but we've come here to make money, and how are we to make it, unless you get niggers to work for you, or start a syndicate? He's death on niggers, is Rhodes!
>
> (*TPH*, pp. 35–7)

The British in Africa are gold-hunting 'vultures' in whom the desire to dominate is both pragmatic and vindictive, the stranger tells Halket. The Company that employs him functions by creating expectations of wealth in its employees (troopers). The irony of this fantasy is made explicit; Halket imagines that '[a]ll men made money when they came to South Africa', yet the only examples he can cite are Rhodes and Barnato. Halket is himself merely a small link in the labour chain created by a few wealthy entrepreneurs. He too is a victim of colonial myth-making, an ill-paid trooper employed to manage the black African population for the benefits of a few mine owners.

The stranger's re-educating of Halket is both personal and political; he points out underlying contradictions, particularly in a self-aggrandizing notion of a civilizing 'mission' which is actually based on a desire for personal gain and a denial of all rights to indigenous peoples. Halket's conversion serves to highlight the misanthropic behaviour of both his officer, who shoots him for being a 'traitor' and the Chartered Company, which endorses the officer.

Radziwill's *The Resurrection of Peter* takes the form of a long moral tract. Whereas Schreiner portrays Halket as a problematic identity, confused by the oppositional desires for personal wealth, a racial hatred fostered by the Chartered Company, and the emotive and logical arguments of the stranger, Radziwill simply makes him the dumb audience to the rhetoric of her own Christ figure, whose image is, to some extent, conflated with that of Rhodes. He explains to Halket that the issue of black labour is largely irrelevant – they are paid to work, so work they must – the real issue is, he states, to appreciate the divine qualities of Rhodes, who is a 'creator', a philanthropist, a ruler who 'has certainly contributed largely towards the peace Christ came into this world to preach' (*RP*, p. 35) and a man who so loves England 'that he felt he must give her something and he gave her a whole continent' (*RP*, p. 66). The stranger aligns a Christian mission with British imperialism, and instructs Halket:

> take my message to England. Go to that great people and cry aloud to it … keep up your old renown of chivalry, to protect those amongst your children who, far away on foreign soil and in strange lands, are fighting for the glory of the English name, for that individual freedom England has always been so jealous of … English civilization, English laws, and England's sense of knowledge and duty.
>
> (*RP*, pp. 39–40)

188 *Nationalism, Imperialism, Identity in Victorian Culture*

The hectoring tone continues, until Halket has learnt the 'truth' about the British in South Africa, whereupon he is allowed to die and be uplifted by angels.

These two novels illustrate a polemical debate on both the war and British presence in South Africa. The other novels I have discussed anticipate a modernity in the lone soldier hero whose integrity can only survive outside the army, or tangentially related to it. He is a patriot fighting all sides, where pluck, loyalty and a sense of daring may run against the tide of military bungling.[52] Naively portrayed, he nevertheless has more in common with Hemingway's soldier characters or Rambo than with Kitchener or Buller. Moreover, the hero's outlook and style of fighting aligned him closer to the Boers he was fighting than with his own side. Their Calvinistic determination and rugged individualism, their hit-and-run tactics, are prototypes for a new kind of guerilla fighter. This, plus technological advances, the industrializing of death in camps, and the rapid use of communications to both mediate and create 'truth' became signposts of twentieth-century life. The Boer War triggered absolutely fundamental questions about patriotism and national character. If culture is essentially the story a people tell about themselves to themselves, the Boer War stretched an old narrative to the limits and the cracks in it reached through an Edwardian twilight to 1914.

Conclusion

I have a photograph of Queen Victoria. She is elderly, seated at a table outside, engrossed in writing a letter. A fringed canopy protects her from above and a screen at her back stops whatever breeze there might be. She wears a formal decorated black bonnet, her customary black skirts and shawl and has a striped blanket to warm her knees. On the table before her are boxes of papers, and more to the side on a chair, along with an umbrella. Nothing has been forgotten. She and the table are on a carpet which has been laid across the grass. Standing in front and a little to the right is an Indian man in formal dress, wearing a turban. Only the shiny brogue shoes look incongruous. He holds a walking stick, presumably the Queen's, for when she has finished her labours. On the back of the photograph it simply says 'QUEEN VICTORIA AND SERVANT'. The man is looking at her. Perhaps he is honoured to be her servant, to be this close, and part of this story, but there is something in his demeanour, the fact that he stands on the royal carpet and not the grass, his watchfulness, that is not subservient. She is only engrossed in her immediate task, he seems to be alert to the whole situation, all that is happening and perhaps about to happen. It is a moment when the world is held still, framed, but could be about to change.

The imperial sensibility found it difficult to accommodate change over which it had no control. By the end of the nineteenth century the Boer War and the mountains of texts and images accompanying it were reshaping England's sense of itself, as a nation, a people and an imperial power. There were assurances that after the war it would be business as usual, but these were not universal. The sources in this book suggest something of the contemporary certainties and uncertainties, assertions and counter assertions, the sheer difficulty of knowing what a nation is, and how it shapes itself for a future it can only imagine. The voices, ideas and forces that drive patriotism, nationalism and imperialism are diverse and often contradictory.

Edward Said's critics see him as the clever lawyer who suppresses those facts which do not support his case. Keith Windschuttle's diatribe against Said in *The Criterion* (Jan 1999) dismantles *Orientalism* as vacuous scholarship and Marxist clichés. He bemoans the fact that Michael Bentley (editor) devotes a whole chapter to Said in the *Companion to Historiography*, giving him as much space as the whole corpus of ancient Greek historians. Windschuttle claims that *Orientalism's* prevalent essentialism derived from the then latest (1960s/1970s) Parisian versions of Freudian and Marxist theory and Foucault's notion of all discourse as power; from this position Said assumes that all Oriental Studies have been part of an imperialist discourse but without ever establishing a plausible connection between the two. Less vituperative critics, such as Robert Young and Dennis Porter have shown how preferential Said is in his choice of representations to prove his case; he adopts, as Ismail Talib says: 'on the one hand, a Nietzschean anti-realism or constructivism that says there are only ever representations and no realities, while, on the other, retains the authority to show up the deficiencies or falsehoods' of those representations he wishes to condemn.[1]

Yet the very fact that Said's work has generated such a mass of engaged, argumentative scholarship and popular debate, is itself a vindication of it. Discourse, as it has informed the work of this book, is a useful but flawed conceptual tool. It can be explored and tested against a variety of texts. Works may be put together in order to be usefully differentiated, may be combined to be individuated. Many texts about the Boer War both conform to and rebel against a dominant ideology.

The centenary of the war generated significant new media interest and research activities. Web sites proliferated and grow daily. New materials are emerging, especially in the form of unpublished stories, letters and autobiographies. These all need reading, investigating, properly cataloguing, and will be part of the continuing story of South Africa, Britain, and the colonies from which troops were drawn. Recently a few enterprising Australians started a forum for those who had relatives in the Boer War, and within which information and stories could be exchanged. It has been inundated with requests. A similar enterprise will probably begin for New Zealanders and Canadians. In South Africa there are archives treasures held by the Van Riebeeck Society in Cape Town, the South African National War Museum, private collections in Cape Town and Pretoria, and Clarke's Bookshop in Cape Town. These amount to thousands of memoirs, stories and autobiographies which conventional historical research and more discursive approaches could usefully feed on.

Part of working on this book inevitably generated an awareness of other areas for further research: in music hall more sustained work on the content of acts in relation to the dynamics of performance, and specific biographies which are contextually informed rather than nostalgically whimsical; more work on texts written by Boer commandos; more work is called for on the role of black Africans during the war. The role of women in the Boer War has been largely neglected. Unpublished siege diaries of the time would make a useful collection. Other images and representations could be explored. The examination of specific images is invariably telling and revealing and in this book images of the soldier suggest how civil and military relations at any time are a shifting, troubled and often complex sphere.

Notes

Introduction

1. W.B. Pemberton, *Battles of the Boer War* (London, Batsford, 1964), p. 32.
2. Quoted in N. Dixon, *On the Psychology of Military Incompetence* (London, Jonathan Cape, 1976), p. 55.
3. Ibid., pp. 62–3.
4. T. Pakenham, *The Boer War* (London, Weidenfeld & Nicolson, 1979). The fact that this book has gone into numerous reprints and is substantially quoted by many historians suggest its significance to scholarship.
5. Ibid., p. 456.
6. Ibid., p. 311.
7. The background to the war is complex. In a sense it was the culmination of a long imperial struggle which began during the Napoleonic wars. The Dutch had established a port of call for their shipping at the Cape of Good Hope in 1652. Napoleon compelled them to join the economic blockade on British shipping until the British gained control of the Cape for the second time in 1806. A process of settling and annexing then began, some 4 000 British settlers arriving at the Cape in 1820. Resisting the abolition of slavery by the British, many Boers trekked across the Vaal River in 1836 to establish homes beyond British jurisdiction. Natal was annexed as a colony in 1843 by the British, and Transorangia annexed as Orange River Sovereignty in 1848. The British recognized the right to self-government for the Transvaal in 1852 and for the Orange Free State in 1854. The next thirty years saw clashes between native tribes, mostly the Zulu, invading from the north, and the Boers. In 1871 Kimberley was annexed to Cape Colony, now self-governing. The British assumed the role of restraining the Kaffirs (as the black natives were called) and the Transvaal was annexed as a British Crown Colony by Britain in 1877. British forces invaded Zululand in 1879 and annexed it in 1887, to be incorporated in Natal. The dates in the 1870s are important, as interest in South Africa had increased, as a result of the diamond rush to Kimberley in 1870–71, joined by the eighteen-year-old Cecil Rhodes. An unsuccessful British attempt was made to federate the whole of South Africa; British rule became threatening for the Boers and Paul Kruger led them in the First Boer War (alias 'First War of Independence') in a bid for independence. After British defeat in small actions at Laing's Nek and Majuba, Gladstone called a halt to military operations and at the Convention of Pretoria in 1881 the Dutch obtained limited independence for the Transvaal Republic, while recognizing British suzerainty. In 1884 the key precipitous event in the Second Boer War was the discovery of gold in the Transvaal. Two years later came the gold rush to Witwatersrand and an influx of people – mostly British. To protect their own interests the Dutch imposed many restrictions on 'Uitlanders', a policy bitterly resented by the newcomers. During this period Rhodes had built a successful business empire with a significant amount of political power; he obtained a

British Royal Charter for his British South Africa Company, the Chartered Company, with its own police force, and became Prime Minister at the Cape. From 1890 onwards Rhodes' expansionist ambitions were plain. In 1890 his Chartered Company sent pioneers to occupy Lobengula's country, renamed Rhodesia. In 1895, relying on a rising by discontented Uitlanders, Dr. Jameson launched his doomed raid into the Transvaal with five hundred Chartered Company police. A British enquiry into the raid did not satisfy the Boers and after the British Cabinet decided to send 10 000 troops to defend Natal, Kruger called up the Transvaal burghers and persuaded Steyn to follow suit in the Free State. As the British army increasingly mobilized, Kruger issued an ultimatum and war began on 11 October 1899.

8. H. Arendt, *The Origins of Totalitarianism* (San Diego, Harvest/HBJ, 1979), p. 17.
9. B. Anderson, *Imagined Communities: Reflections on the Origin and Spread of Nationalism* (London, Verso, 1983), p. 40.
10. Ibid., p. 49.
11. R. Samuel (ed.), *Patriotism: The Making and Unmaking of British National Identity* (London, Routledge, 1989), vol. 1, p. xi.
12. J.M. Mackenzie, *Propaganda and Empire: The Manipulation of British Public Opinion 1880–1960* (Manchester University Press, 1984), p. 7.
13. J.H. Grainger, *Patriotisms. Britain 1900–1939* (London, Routledge & Kegan Paul, 1986), ch. 4.
14. Ibid., p. 11.
15. A. Bullock and S. Trombley (eds), *The New Fontana Dictionary of Modern Thought* (London, HarperCollins, 3rd edn, 1999).
16. See, for example, S. Friedrichsmeyer (ed.), *The Imperialist Imagination* (University of Michigan Press, 1999); S. Smith, *British Imperialism* (Cambridge University Press 1998; T. Lloyd, *Empire* (Hambleden & London Ltd., 2001); R. Griffiths, *Patriotism Perverted* (Constable, 1998); F. Barker (ed.), *Colonial Discourse/Postcolonial Theory* (Manchester University Press, 1996).
17. H. Arendt, *The Origins of Totalitarianism*, p. 125.
18. Ibid., p. 231.
19. B. Anderson, *Imagined Communities*, p. 15.
20. Ibid., p. 17.
21. E.J. Hobsbawm, *Nations and Nationalism since 1780* (Cambridge University Press, 1990), p. 108.
22. S.G. Millin, *Rhodes* (London, Macmillan, 1933), p. 138.
23. H. Arendt, *The Origins of Totalitarianism*, p. 126.
24. Ibid., p. 125.
25. Ibid., p. 126.
26. Ibid., p. 128.
27. Ibid., p. 125.
28. P. Cain and A. Hopkins, *British Imperialism: Innovation and Expansion 1688–1914*, and *British Imperialism: Crisis and Deconstruction* (London, Longman, 1993).
29. Quoted in J.S. Marais, *The Fall of Kruger's Republic* (Oxford University Press, 1961), p. 172.
30. H.F. Wyatt, 'War as the Supreme Test of National Value', in *The Nineteenth Century*, vol. LXV, 1899, pp. 216–25, 220.
31. T. Hodgkin, 'The Fall of the Roman Empire and its Lesson for Us', in *The Contemporary Review*, vol. 73, 1898, pp. 51–70, 70.

32. E. Said, *Orientalism* (London, RKP, 1978), p. 1; see also: E. Said, 'Orientalism Reconsidered', in *Europe and its Others, Vol. 1: Proceedings of the Essex Conference on the Sociology of Literature*, July 1984, (Colchester, University of Essex, 1985), pp. 23–4; E. Said, *Culture and Imperialism* (London, Chatto & Windus, 1993). There is, of course, a vast body of work on literature, imperialism and colonialism. Good overviews appear in collected papers in *Cultural Studies*, vol. 14, no. 3/4, July/October 2000; *World Literature Written in English*, vol. 36, no. 2, 1997; P. Lalu 'The Grammar of Domination and the Subjection of Agency: Colonial Texts and Modes of Existence', in *History and Theory, Studies in the Philosophy of History*, vol. 39, no. 4, December 2000. See also D. Bivona, *Desire and Contradiction: Imperial Visions and Domestic Debates in Victorian Literature* (Manchester University Press, 1990); A. White, *Joseph Conrad and the Adventure Tradition: Constructing and Deconstructing the Imperial Subject* (Cambridge University Press, 1993); E. Boehmer, *Colonial and Postcolonial Literature: Migrant Metaphors* (Oxford University Press, 1995); H.K. Bhabha (ed.), *Nation and Narration* (London, Routledge, 1990).
33. E. Said, *Orientalism*, p. 3.
34. B. Parry, 'Problems in Current Theories of Colonial Discourse', in *Oxford Literary Review*, vol. 9, nos. 1–2, 1987, pp. 27–58, p. 40.
35. E. Said, *Orientalism*, p. 5.
36. See P. Warwick (ed.), *The South African War: The Anglo-Boer War 1899–1902* (Essex, Longman, 1980); B. Farwell, *The Great Boer War* (New York, Harper & Row, 1975/London, Allen Lane, 1977); D. Hall, *The Hall Handbook of the Anglo-Boer War* (Pietermaritzburg, University of Natal 1998); I. Knight, *The Boer Wars 1898–1902* (London, Osprey, 1997); I. Smith, *The Origins of the South African War, 1899–1902* (Essex, Longman, 1992), and the more populist T. Jackson, *The Boer War* (Channel 4 Books, 1999).
37. See P. Bailey (ed.), *Popular Culture and Performance in the Victorian City* (Cambridge University Press, 1998; D. Kift, *The Victorian Music Hall: Culture, Class and Conflict* (Cambridge University Press, 1996); J.S. Bratton *et al.* (eds), *Acts of Supremacy: The British Empire and the Stage 1790–1930* (Manchester University Press, 1991). Other sources are cited in Chapter 1.
38. T. Pakenham, *The Boer War*, Introduction. Given that the war included a number of South African races as well as Boers and the British, there is an argument for calling it the South African War. However, given that both contemporary sources and later historical works refer to the 'Boer War' I prefer to adhere to this convention.
39. For a good account of Kipling's activities during the Boer War see H. Ricketts, *The Unforgiving Minute: A Life of Rudyard Kipling* (London, Chatto & Windus, 1999), pp. 260–70.
40. See C. Kent, 'Victorian Social History: post Thompson, post Foucault, post Modern', in *Victorian Studies*, 40, Autumn 1996, pp. 97–133; P. Joyce, *Democratic Subjects: The Self and the Social in Nineteenth Century England* (Cambridge, 1994); C. Steedman, *The Radical Soldier's Tale* (London, Routledge, 1988).

1   The Music Hall

1. J.B. Booth, quoted in C. Pulling, *They Were Singing* (London, G. Harrap, 1952), p. 78.

2. W. MacQueen-Pope, *The Melodies Linger On* (London, W.H. Allen, 1950), p. 185.
3. R. Kipling, quoted in D.H. Simpson, 'Variations on an Imperial Theme', *R.C.S. Library Notes*, April 1965.
4. J. Hobson, *Imperialism: A Study* (London, Nisbet, 1902).
5. L. Senelick, 'Politics as Entertainment: Victorian Music Hall Songs', in *Victorian Studies*, vol. 19, 1975, pp. 84–98.
6. See, for example, H. Scott, *The Early Doors: Origins of the Music Hall* (London, 1946); L. Senelick, 'Politics as Entertainment: Victorian Music Hall Songs', op. cit.; J.M. Mackenzie, *Propaganda and Empire: The Manipulation of British Public Opinion 1880–1960* (Manchester University Press, 1984).
7. L. Senelick, 'Politics as Entertainment', p. 87.
8. P. Joyce, *Visions of the People: Industrial England and Questions of Class 1848–1915* (Cambridge University Press, 1991); P. Joyce, *Democratic Subjects: The Self and the Social in Nineteenth Century England* (Cambridge University Press, 1994).
9. D. Kift, (trans. R. Kift), *The Victorian Music Hall, Culture, Class and Conflict* (Cambridge University Press, 1996), p. 7.
10. P. Bailey (ed.), *Music Hall: The Business of Pleasure* (Oxford University Press, 1986), p. xv. Bailey's book offers localized information on the composition of audiences in a few music halls in the North of England. This is not specifically useful to my discussion, but does suggest the need for more comprehensive information on audiences, although such information is scanty, given that many records have been lost, destroyed, or were poorly kept.
11. C. Kent, 'Victorian Social History: post Thompson, post Foucault, post Modern', in *Victorian Studies*, 40 (Autumn 1996), pp. 97–133.
12. Titterton is also mentioned in M. Booth and J.H. Kaplan (eds), *The Edwardian Theatre: Essays on Performance and the Stage* (Cambridge University Press, 1996).
13. J. Hobson, *Imperialism*, op. cit. p. 7.
14. L. Senelick, 'Politics as Entertainment', op. cit., p. 87.
15. H. Cunningham, 'The Language of Patriotism, 1750–1914', in *History Workshop*, vol. 12, 1981, pp. 8–33, 10.
16. P. Summerfield, 'The Effingham Arms and the Empire: Deliberate Selection and the Evolution of the Music Hall in London', in S. and E. Yeo (eds), *Popular Culture and Class Conflict, 1590–1914* (Sussex, 1981).
17. D. Farson, *Marie Lloyd and Music Hall* (London, Tom Stacey Ltd, 1972), pp. 11–29.
18. Quoted in R. Mander and J. Mitchenson, *British Music Hall* (London, Gentry Books, 1974), p. 51.
19. J.B. Booth, *Old Pink 'Un Days* (London, Grant Richards, 1924), p. 336.
20. P. Summerfield, 'Patriotism and Empire in Music Hall Entertainment, 1870–1914', in *Imperialism and Popular Culture*, ed. J. Mackenzie (Manchester University Press, 1986), p. 29.
21. R. Price, *An Imperial War and the British Working Class: Working Class Attitudes and Reactions to the Boer War 1899–1902* (London, RKP, 1972), p. 176.
22. Quoted in R. Mander and J. Mitchenson, *British Music Hall*, p. 52.
23. See P. Davison, *Songs of the British Music Hall* (London, Oak Publications, 1971), Introduction. Of course, cities other than London had their own

strong music hall culture, but London had the most halls and it was here that most new acts and big stars reflected patterns of taste.

24. E.R. Pennell, 'The Pedigree of the Music Hall', in *The Contemporary Review*, vol. 63, April 1893, pp. 575–83.
25. Ibid., p. 582.
26. Ibid.
27. W.R. Titterton, *From Theatre to Music Hall*, (London, 1912), p. 41.
28. *The Era*, 28/12/95, p. 4.
29. P. Bailey (ed.), *Popular Culture and Performance in the Victorian City* (Cambridge University Press, 1998), p. 137. Bailey points out that the term 'knowingness' was first used in eighteenth century racing talk, describing one who knew the turf, who was 'in the know.'
30. Bailey admits that his own essay is 'largely speculative and impressionistic', *Popular Culture and Performance in the Victorian City*, op. cit., p. 131.
31. P. Bailey, *Leisure and Class in Victorian England: Rational Recreation and the Contest for Control 1830–1885* (London, RKP, 1978), p. 154.
32. *The Era*, 28/12/95, p. 4.
33. Ibid., 13/04/95, p. 11.
34. Ibid., 09/09/99, p. 11.
35. *The Theatre*, vol. xxvi, 01/10/95.
36. For further discussion, see J.S. Bratton (ed.), *Music Hall: Performance and Style* (Milton Keynes: Open University Press, 1986).
37. R. Low and R. Manvell, *The History of the British Film 1896–1906* (London, 1948), pp. 66–8. Rachael Low and Roger Manvell's book provides useful information on the newsreels and Boer War films produced by British companies during the war.
38. I have interviewed three people who remember early film showings as part of a music hall programme. Although only one person could remember a Boer War film, all three said that it did not occur to them at the time that 'documentary' films could be fabricated. Interviews took place on: 23/09/83 with Mrs C. Warby; 09/10/83 with J. Lambert; 12/11/83 with F. Warby.
39. C. Pulling, *They Were Singing*, pp. 20–1.
40. M. Vicinus, *The Industrial Muse* (London, Croom Helm, 1974), p. 1.
41. I. Watson, *Song and Democratic Culture in Britain* (London, Croom Helm, 1983), p. 45.
42. H. Cunningham, 'The Language of Patriotism', in *Patriotism: The Making and Unmaking of British National Identity*, vol. 1, ed. R. Samuel (London, Routledge, 1989), p. 79.
43. L. Senelick, 'Politics as Entertainment', op. cit. See also J. Mackenzie, *Propaganda and Empire* (Manchester University Press, 1984), p. 172.
44. Written by G.W. Hunt, published in *Music Hall Songster* (London, W.S. Fortey, 1893).
45. In J. Mackenzie, *Propaganda and Empire*, p. 172.
46. Written by Henry Pettit, quoted in P. Davison, 'A Briton True: A Short Account of Patriotic Songs and Verse as Popular Entertainment', in *Alta, University of Birmingham Review*, Spring, 1970, pp. 209–23, 216.
47. P. Bailey, *Popular Culture and Performance*, op. cit., p. 133.
48. Published by Francis & Day.
49. Published by Francis & Day.

50. C. Macinnes, *Sweet Saturday Night* (London, MacGibbon and Kee, 1967), p. 80.
51. *Francis and Day's Album of Famous Old Songs*, Day & Hunter (bound edn, Birmingham Public Library, 1970).
52. Ibid.
53. C. Pulling, *They Were Singing*, p. 79.
54. H. Cunningham, 'The Language of Patriotism', p. 80.
55. Ibid., p. 79.
56. G. Stedman Jones, 'Working Class Culture and Working Class Politics in London 1870–1900', *Journal of Social History*, 7, 1974, pp. 460–508, 491.
57. D. Kift, *The Victorian Music Hall*, op. cit., p. 43.
58. C. Pulling, *They Were Singing*, p. 186.
59. In *The Lyric Songster* and *The Mogul Songster*, collected together in *The Music Hall Songster* (London, W.S. Fortey, 1893).
60. W.H. Auden, C. Kallman and N. Greenberg (eds), *An Elizabethan Song Book* (New York, Doubleday, 1956), pp. xvi–xvii.
61. Quoted in J.B. Booth, *Old Pink 'Un Days*, p. 397.
62. H.C. Newton, *Idols of the Halls* (Wakefield, E.P. Publishing Co., 1975), p. 113.
63. P. Davison, 'A Briton True', p. 219.
64. Ibid.
65. See C. Pulling, *They Were Singing*, op. cit., chs II and VII; see *From Theatre to Music Hall*, op. cit., p. 26, where Titterton argues that music hall acted as a substitute for revolutionary zeal.
66. *The Music Hall Songster*.
67. Ibid.
68. Ibid.
69. P. Fitzgerald, *Music Hall Land* (London, Ward and Downey, 1890), p. 33.
70. Ibid.
71. N. Jacobs, *Our Marie* (London, Hutchinson, 1936), p. 52. See also R.A. Baker, *Marie Lloyd: Queen of the Music Halls* (London, Robert Hale, 1990).
72. Ibid.
73. Lady De Frece, *Recollections of Vesta Tilley* (London, Hutchinson, 1934), p. 146.
74. Ibid., pp. 141–4. See also S. Maitland, *Vesta Tilley* (London, Virgo Press, 1986).
75. J.B. Booth, *A Pink 'Un Remembers*, p. 113.
76. W.R. Titterton, *From Theatre to Music Hall*, p. 146.
77. Ibid., p. 147.
78. Ibid., p. 149.
79. Ibid., p. 148.
80. Ibid., pp. 148–9.
81. Lady De Frece, *Recollections of Vesta Tilley*, p. 142.
82. C. Beg, *Tommy Atkins at Home* (London, Gale & Polden, 1901), pp. 5, 81.
83. Ibid., p. 7.
84. J. Milne, *The Epistles of Atkins* (London, Dent & Sons, 1900), p. 117.
85. Ibid., p. 156.
86. C. Pulling, *They Were Singing*, pp. 79–80.
87. Quoted in J.B. Booth, *A Pink 'Un Remembers*, p. 123.
88. See C. Macinnes, *Sweet Saturday Night*. Macinnes argues that music hall songs and acts reflected a growing disenchantment with the Boer War.

2 The Image of the Common Soldier in Contemporary Accounts of the Boer War

1. H. James, 'The British Soldier', in *Lippincott's Magazine*, vol. XXII, Aug. 1878, p. 214.
2. B. Anderson, *Imagined Communities*, p. 16.
3. See G. Harries-Jenkins, *The Army in Victorian Society* (London, RKP, 1977), ch. I.
4. See, for example, *The Soldier's Life, from Enlistment to his Return Home, Exhibiting the Trials and Hardships of Battle* (London, W.S. Fortey, 1900); W.H.G. Kingston, *Our Soldiers* (London, n.p., 1902); H.E. Maxwell, *British Soldiers in the Field* (London, n.p., 1902).
5. T. Pakenham, *The Boer War*, p. 247.
6. L. James, *The Rise and Fall of the British Empire*, p. 212.
7. For a discussion of juvenile literature during this period, see J. Bristow, *Empire Boys: Adventures in a Man's World* (London, HarperCollins, 1991). For a discussion of the role of the school textbook, see J. Mackenzie, *Propaganda and Empire*, ch. 7.
8. T. Pakenham, *The Boer War*, p. 87.
9. L. James, *The Rise and Fall of the British Empire*, p. 203.
10. See 'W.T. Stead and the Boer War', in *Canadian Historical Review*, vol. 40 (1959), pp. 304–14.
11. T. Pakenham, *The Boer War*, p. 109.
12. *Reynolds News*, 19/11/99, p. 6; 26/11/99, p. 2.
13. See T. Reese, *The History of the Royal Commonwealth Society* (London, 1968), for a full discussion of the school textbook and politics.
14. J. Cowham, *A New School Method* (London, n.p., 1900).
15. See P. Burroughs, 'John R. Seeley and British Imperial History', in *Journal of Imperial and Commonwealth History*, vol. 1, 1972–73, p. 192.
16. L. James, *The Rise and Fall of the British Empire*, p. 205.
17. F.E. Huggett, *Cartoonists at War* (London, Guild, 1981), p. 108.
18. J. Bristow, *Empire Boys*, p. 45.
19. J. Mackenzie, *Propaganda and Empire*, p. 205.
20. C. Beg, *Tommy Atkins at Home* (London, Gale & Polden, 1901). Hereafter, any quotations from this book in the chapter will be followed by *TAH*, then the page number. Titles such as these and the two below were discovered in the British Library Catalogue, contemporary publishers lists and in the advertisement pages of newspapers published during the war.
21. R. MacCarthy and R. O'Moore, *The Romance of the Boer War (Humours and Chivalry of the Campaign)* (London, Elliot Stock, 1901). Hereafter, any quotations from this book in the chapter will be followed by *RBW*, then the page number. I refer to MacCarthy because the book in fact only had a single author.
22. J. Milne, *The Epistles of Atkins* (London, Dent & Sons, 1901). Hereafter, any quotations from this book in the chapter will be followed by *EA*, then the page number.
23. For example, R. Blatchford, *Tommy Atkins of the Rumchowders* (London, Edward Arnold, 1895); A. Shirley and B. Landeck, *Tommy Atkins*, a play performed at the Pavilion Theatre in September 1895 and at the Duke of York's, December 1895.

24. W.E. Henley and J.S. Farmer, *A Dictionary of Slang and Colloquial English* (London, Routledge, 1905). The full entry is: Tommy Atkins (Mr Atkins, or Tommy (1) A soldier (of privates only); and (2) among soldiers themselves, a private's pocket account book). [On attestation forms and other documents occurs the sample name Thomas Atkins. 'I, Thomas Atkins, swear to do so-and-so'. The same bogus name appears in the Mutiny Act; it is, in fact, a tradition of a century, and was popularized by Rudyard Kipling in *Barrack Room Ballads*.] (Also Tom-Noddy – a fool or Tom-fool.)

25. R. Barthes, *Mythologies* (London, Granada, 1973), p. 91.

26. P. Fussell, *The Great War and Modern Memory* (London, Oxford University Press, 1975).

27. P.J. Keating, *The Working Classes in Victorian Fiction* (London, RKP, 1971), p. 247.

28. *Reynolds News*, 15/10/99, p. 4.

29. H. Arendt, *The Origins of Totalitarianism*, pp. 124–34.

30. R. Baden-Powell, *Scouting for Boys*, 2nd edn (London, 1908), p. 283. Baden-Powell had written in similar vein in *Reconnaissance and Scouting*, published in 1884.

31. Ibid, p. 17.

32. Quoted in G. Arnold, *Hold Fast for England: G.A. Henty, Imperialist Boys Writer* (London, Hamish Hamilton, 1980), p. 63.

33. *The Spear*, vol. 1, no. 12, 04/11/1900. See also *Black and White Budget*, which began weekly publications on 7 October 1899 and was registered as a newspaper. It was strongly patriotic and tended to ignore setbacks for the British army during the war.

34. *The Sketch*, vol. 30, no. 383, 30/05/1900.

35. T. Pakenham, *The Boer War*, pp. 372–5.

36. Ibid., p. 408.

37. L. James, *The Rise and Fall of the British Empire*, p. 203.

38. A Soldier, *True Stories of South Africa* (London, Thomas Burleigh, 1899), p. 3.

39. H. Knollys, 'English Officers and Soldiers – as They Will Be', in *Blackwoods*, February 1896, pp. 199–211, 206.

40. Ibid.

41. Ibid., p. 210. See also H. Knollys, *The Recruiting Question* (London, Kegan Paul & Co., 1891).

42. J.A. Hobson, *Imperialism: A Study* (London, George Allen & Unwin, 1902), p. 212.

43. Ibid., p. 213.

44. Ibid., p. 214.

45. See, for example, R. MacCarthy and R. O'Moore, *The Romance of the Boer War*, pp. 22–4.

46. L. James, *The Rise and Fall of the British Empire*, p. 207.

47. A. Porter, 'The South African War (1899–1902): Context and Motive reconsidered', in *Journal of African History*, 31, 1990.

48. H.F. Wyatt, 'War as the Supreme Test of National Value', in *The Nineteenth Century*, vol. XLV, January–June 1899, pp. 215–25, 221. See also A.T. Mahan, 'The Peace Conference and the Moral Aspect of War', in *North American Review*, no. DXV, October 1899, pp. 433–7.

49. J. Hobson, *Imperialism*, p. 213.

50. H. Knollys, 'English Officers and Soldiers', pp. 205–6.

51. T. Pakenham, *The Boer War*, p. xv.
52. Ibid., p. xvii.
53. See, for example, L.S. Amery (ed.), *The Times History of the War in South Africa*, 7 vols (London, Sampson & Low, 1900–1909). In vol. II, p. 40, the British army which fought in South Africa is criticized as a 'sham'. All volumes constitute a criticism of the army, with a design to implement reforms. Amery was also Roberts's man, who helped orchestrate a damning view of Buller.
54. F.E. Huggett, *Cartoonists at War* (London, Guild, 1981), p. 116.
55. E. Sandow, *Sandow's Magazine*, 27 September 1906, p. 386.
56. Ibid.

3 Rudyard Kipling's Barrack Room Ballads: The Soldier as Hooligan or Hero

1. R. Kipling, *Barrack Room Ballads and Other Verses* (London, Methuen, 1892). Hereafter referred to as *BRB*, followed by the page number, when quoted from, and referred to as the *Ballads* in the discussion. The *Ballads* had run to 25 editions by 1908, an indication of their popularity.
2. R. Buchanan, 'The Voice of the Hooligan', in *Contemporary Review*, vol. LXXVI, December 1899, pp. 774–89. Published with Walter Besant's reply and Buchanan's final reply to this by Tucker Publishing Co., New York, 1900. The article is reprinted in *Rudyard Kipling: The Critical Heritage*, ed. R.L. Green (London, RKP, 1971), pp. 233–49, and page numbers refer to this edition.
3. See Chapter 4, for an extended discussion of the term 'hooligan'.
4. See, for example, *The Times*, 4/10/1898, p. 12; 26/9/1898. p. 11.
5. W. Besant, 'Is it the Voice of the Hooligan?', in *The Critical Heritage*, op. cit., pp. 250–9. First appeared in *Contemporary Review*, vol. LXXVII, January 1900, pp. 27–39.
6. See P.J. Keating, *The Working Classes in Victorian Fiction* (London, RKP, 1971).
7. J.M. Barrie (pseudonym Gavin Ogilvy), 'The Man from Nowhere', in the *British Weekly*, 02/05/1890. Reprinted in *Critical Heritage*, p. 17.
8. See P. Keating, *The Working Classes in Victorian Fiction*; R. Kipling, *Something of Myself* (London, Macmillan, 1964), pp. 47, 53, 205, 213–14.
9. See C. Norton, 'The Poetry of Mr. Rudyard Kipling', in *Atlantic Monthly*, vol. LXXIX, January 1897, pp. 111–15, 115.
10. See, for discussion of the 'New Imperialism', E.J. Hobsbawn, *The Age of Empire 1875–1914* (London, Weidenfeld & Nicolson, 1987), ch. 3.
11. R. Kipling, op. cit. Hereafter referred to as *SOM* in the text, followed by the page number, when quoted from.
12. P.J. Keating, *The Working Classes in Victorian Fiction*, p. 159.
13. H. Ricketts, *The Unforgiving Minute. A Life of Rudyard Kipling* (London, Chatto & Windus, 1999), p. 163.
14. R. Buchanan, 'The Voice of the Hooligan', p. 239. See G. Stedman Jones, ' "The Cockney" and the Nation, 1780–1988', in D. Feldman and G. Stedman Jones (eds), *Metropolis London: Histories and Representations since 1800* (London, Routledge, 1989).
15. See note 4.

16. *The Times*, 26/09/98, p. 11.
17. M. Arnold, *Culture and Anarchy* (Harmondsworth, Penguin, 1971), p. 56.
18. Ibid., p. 65.
19. Henley first published the *Barrack Room Ballads* in the *Scots Observer*, though not as a collection. See also *SOM*, p. 82.
20. Rudyard Kipling: *The Critical Heritage*, p. 49.
21. Op. cit., p. 86.
22. See *SOM*, pp. 84–7.
23. Oscar Wilde, *The Times*, 25/09/91.
24. C. Whibley, 'Good Stuff and Bad', in *Scots Observer*, 20/09/1890. Reprinted in *Rudyard Kipling: The Critical Heritage*, p. 61.
25. Anon., in *Athenaeum*, no. 3261, 26/04/1890, p. 528.
26. R.L. Stevenson, in *Rudyard Kipling: The Critical Heritage*, p. 60.
27. H. James, in Ibid., p. 68.
28. Ibid., p. 69.
29. C.E. Norton, in *Atlantic Monthly*, vol. LXXIX, January 1987, pp. 111–15, 113.
30. L. Strachey, in *Rudyard Kipling: The Critical Heritage*, p. 42.
31. Ibid.
32. H. Ward (?), 'Mr Kipling's writings', in *The Times*, 25/03/1890.
33. R. Kipling, *Rudyard Kipling's Verse. Definitive Edition* (London, Hodder & Stoughton, 1948), p. 445.
34. See P. Davison, *Songs of the British Music Hall* (London, Oak Publications, 1971). See also *Popular Culture* (The Open University Press, 1981), block 2, unit 5.
35. R. Buchanan, 'The Voice of the Hooligan', p. 234.
36. Ibid.
37. Ibid., p. 235.
38. Ibid., pp. 235–8.
39. Ibid., p. 236
40. Ibid., p. 237.
41. Ibid., pp. 248–9.
42. E. Wallace, *Writ in Barracks* (London, Methuen & Co., 1900).
43. T. Pakenham, *The Boer War*, pp. 375–6. See also J. Ralph, *War's Brighter Side: The Story of 'The Friend' Newspaper Edited by the Correspondents with Lord Robert's Forces, March–April 1900* (London, C. Arthur Pearson, 1901); J. Ralph, *At Pretoria* (London, C. Arthur Pearson, 1901).
44. M. Smith, *Drummer Hodge*, ch. 4.
45. J. Ralph, *War's Brighter Side*.
46. Coldstreamer (Harry Graham), *Ballads of the Boer War* (London, Grant Richards, 1902).
47. T.W.H. Crosland, *The Five Notions* (London, Grant Richards, 1903).
48. Ibid., p. 34.
49. R. Kipling, 'Once upon a Time There was a Man', in *Rudyard Kipling's Verse: Definitive Edition* (London, Hodder & Stoughton, 1940), pp. 210–11. Subsequent references to the poems will be to this edition and will be followed by page numbers.
50. Kipling's autobiography suggests that the Boer War was a watershed in his thinking about the British Empire, and left him with a sense of 'unease'. See R. Kipling, *SOM*, p. 147.

4   Empire of the Hooligan

1. Particularly useful here is the unpublished work by H.D. Blanch, 'The Boer War and British Society', in the National Army Museum Archives, accession no. 7904–109.
2. A. Davey, *The British Pro-Boers 1877–1902* (Cape Town, Tafelburg Publishers, 1978), pp. 123–7.
3. Ibid.
4. R. Price, *An Imperial War and the British Working Class: Working Class Attitudes and Reactions to the Boer War 1899–1902* (London, RKP, 1972).
5. A. Davey, *The British Pro-Boers*.
6. See P. Warwick (ed.), *The South Africa War: The Anglo-Boer War 1899–1902* (London, 1980).
7. See G. Pearson, *Hooligan: A History of Respectable Fears* (London, Macmillan, 1983), for a socio-historical discussion of the history of the hooligan. See also B. Schwartz, 'Night Battles: Hooligan and Citizen', in M. Nava and A. O'Shea (eds), *Modern Times: Reflections on a Century of Modernity* (London, Routledge, 1996).
8. C. Rook, *The Hooligan Nights* (London, Oxford University Press, 1979), pp. 14–15.
9. Ibid.
10. E. Hobsbawm, *Industry and Empire* (Harmondsworth, Penguin, 1969), p. 164.
11. See, for example, G. Pearson, *Hooligan*; *Minority Report of the Poor Law Commission 1909*, S. Webb and B. Webb (eds) (London, Kelley, 1974), part II; J. Whitehouse (ed.), *Problems of Boy Life* (London, King, 1912), p. 263.
12. See R. Blatchford, *Dismal England* (London, Walter Scott, 1899), p. 37.
13. C.F.G. Masterman, *From the Abyss: Its Inhabitants* (London, 1902). The edition to which I refer is published by Garland Publishing Co., New York, 1980, pp. 67–9.
14. *The Times*, 30 October 1900, p. 7.
15. Ibid., 6 December 1900, p. 13.
16. K. Pearson, *National Life and Character: A Forecast* (London, Dent, 1894), p. 257.
17. See T. Hodgkin, 'The Fall of the Roman Empire and Its Lesson for Us', in *Contemporary Review*, vol. 73, (January 1898), pp. 65–90, 70.
18. C.F.G. Masterman, *From the Abyss*. This conflation of class and race is a theme in Masterman's book, one which he often presents ironically.
19. *The Times*, 30 October 1900, p. 7.
20. Quoted in G. Pearson, *Hooligan*, p. 109.
21. C.F.G. Masterman, *From the Abyss*, p. 71.
22. C.F.G. Masterman, *Heart of the Empire* (1901) (Brighton, Harvester, 1973), pp. 7–8.
23. See, for example, T.A. Joyce, 'Negro' in *Encyclopaedia Britannica*, 11th edition, 1910–11.
24. C. Rook, *Hooligan Nights*, pp. 16–18.
25. *The Times*, 4 December 1900, p. 7.
26. Ibid., 30 October 1900, p. 7.
27. Ibid.
28. *Daily Chronicle*, 9 July 1902.

29. R. Bray, *The Town Child* (London, Fisher & Unwin, 1907), pp. 145–6.
30. C.F.G. Masterman, *From the Abyss*, p. 1.
31. Ibid., pp. 2–3.
32. *Punch*, 23 July 1892, p. 33.
33. Ibid., 18 June 1892, p. 292.
34. Ibid., 16 July 1892, p. 33; 31 December 1892, p. 310.
35. Ibid., 23 April 1898, p. 187; 13 September 1899, p. 123; 16 August 1899, p. 81.
36. W. Besant, *East London*, quoted in G. Pearson, *Hooligan*, p. 176.
37. C. Rook, *Hooligan Nights*, p. 16.
38. See G. Pearson, *Hooligan*, chs 2, 3 and 4.
39. W. Besant, quoted in ibid., p. 177.
40. C. Rook, *Hooligan Nights*, p. 18.
41. C.F.G. Masterman, *From the Abyss*, p. 2.
42. Ibid.
43. *The Times*, 28 September 1898, p. 5.
44. Ibid., 6 December 1900, p. 13; 10 December 1900, p. 12; 18 December 1900, p. 12.
45. Ibid., 6 December 1900, p. 13.
46. Ibid., 1 November 1900, p. 10.
47. R. Baden-Powell, 'Boy Scouts', in *National Defence*, vol. 4 (August 1910), p. 446.
48. *The Times*, 6 December 1900, p. 13.
49. C.F.G. Masterman, *From the Abyss*, p. 64.
50. *Justice*, 17 February 1900, p. 2.
51. Quoted in ibid.
52. Ibid., 17 February 1900, p. 1.
53. Ibid.
54. Ibid., 17 March 1900, p. 1.
55. Ibid.
56. Ibid.
57. Ibid.
58. Ibid.
59. Ibid., 17 February 1900, p. 1.

5 Popular Poetry of the Boer War

1. M. Van Wyk Smith, *Drummer Hodge: The Poetry of the Anglo-Boer War (1899–1902)*, (Oxford, Clarendon Press, 1978), p. 43.
2. Ibid., p. 5.
3. Ibid., p. 8.
4. W. Watson, *For England* (London, John Lane: The Bodley Head, 1904), p. 22.
5. For further discussion of specifically socialist criticisms of the war, see B. Semmel, *Imperialism and Social Reform* (Cambridge, Mass, 1976).
6. *Truth*, 12/04/00. (No author given.)
7. G.K. Chesterton, *Heretics* (London, 1905), pp. 288–9.
8. G.K. Chesterton, 'The National Anthem', in D. Collins (ed.), *The Glass Walking Stick* (London, 1955), pp. 71–2.
9. G.K. Chesterton, *Autobiography* (London, 1937), p. 270.

10. H. Bate, *The Transvaal War* (London, George Stoneman, 1900), p. 3.
11. A. Austin, 'Spartan Mothers', in the *Graphic*, 06/01/00.
12. *The Owl*, 19/10/00. (No author given.)
13. In H. Newbolt, *The Sailing of the Long Ships* (London, John Murray, 1902).
14. H.C. Macdowall, in the *Spectator*, 15/12/00.
15. H. Newbolt, 'Minora Sidera', in *The Sailing of the Long Ships*.
16. H. Newbolt, 'Vitai Lampada', ibid.
17. N. Bennett, *The Little Bugler and Other War Lyrics* (London, Elliot Stock, 1900), p. 9.
18. See, for example: H. Bate, *The Transvaal War*; H. Begbie, *The Handyman and Other Verses* (London, Grant Richards, 1900); *The London Reciter and Popular Reader* (London, W.S. Fortey, 1899); *Black and White Budget*, 1900–01; *Black and White*, 1899–1901.
19. M. Wyk Smith, *Drummer Hodge*, p. 4.
20. M. Wyk Smith, *Drummer Hodge*, p. 5.
21. See T. Pakenham, *The Boer War*, p. 375.
22. See R. Auberton, *The Nineteen Hundreds* (London, Allen & Unwin, 1922), for a full description of fabricated accounts. Also, *The Morning Leader*, 11/06/01, which complained that journalists at the front 'invent for us victories that have no foundation in fact'.
23. M. Wyk Smith, *Drummer Hodge*, p. 162.
24. J. Smith, *Ballads of the Boer War* (London, n.p., 1902).
25. Smith, (Private), 'The Battle of Magersfontein', written December 1899, in National Army Museum (no acc. no.).
26. National Army Museum, acc. no. 7203–42-1.
27. Ibid.
28. P.T. Ross, 'The Ballad of the Bayonet', privately printed, 1900.
29. For example, the *Daily Mail* received over 700 poems written a month of the outbreak of war.
30. W.E. Henley, in C. De Thiery, *Imperialism* (London, Duckworth & Co., 1898), p. ix.
31. W.E. Henley, 'Concerning Atkins', in *Pall Mall Magazine*, xvi, 1900, p. 283.
32. See A. Guillaume, *William Ernest Henley et Son Groupe*, Librairie (C. Klincksieck, 1973), ch. XI. See also J.H. Buckley, *William Ernest Henley. A Study in the 'Counter-Decadence' of the 'Nineties* (NJ, Princeton University Press, 1945), Preface, p. vii.
33. These 'Hospital Sketches', first published collectively by H.B. Donkin (ed.), in *Voluntaries for an East London Hospital*, 1887, were included in *Poems* (London, David Nutt, 1898). Unless otherwise indicated, I refer to this latter edition whenever quoting from poems, indicated by the title of the poem and page no., in brackets immediately following the quotation, or where frequent reference is made to the same poem, just the page number.
34. See J.H. Buckley, *William Ernest Henley*, ch. 3, pp. 42–55 for a biographical account of Henley's illness.
35. C. De Thiery, *Imperialism* (London, Duckworth & Co., 1898), with an introduction by Henley, p. xii.
36. Ibid.
37. Ibid., p. 59.
38. Ibid., p. 26.

39. W.E. Henley, 'A Note on Romanticism', in *Views and Reviews. Essays in Appreciation*, vol. 2 (London, David Nutt, 1902), p. 28. Hereafter, references from this work will be included in the text, indicated by *VR* for vol. 2, *ER* for vol. 1, followed by the page number, in brackets immediately following the quotation.

40. C. De Thiery, *Imperialism*, p. ix.

41. W.E. Henley, 'Ex Libris – Concerning Atkins', in *Pall Mall Magazine*, p. xxi, 1900, p. 283.

42. Henley's fear and dislike of Socialism was based on a fear of uniformity, and a suppression of individuality, which would, he thought, denigrate both humanity and Art. His arguments are not unlike those of D.H. Lawrence some twenty years later. See W.E. Henley, 'Socialism in Excelsis', *Scots Observer*, 1, 1889, p. 377.

43. W.E. Henley, 'The Man in the Street', in *For England's Sake* (London, David Nutt, 1900), p. 4. All future references to this collection included in the text, are indicated by *F'S* and the page number, in brackets, immediately following the quotation.

44. C. De Thiery, *Imperialism*, p. ix.

45. Ibid., p. viii.

46. Ibid., p. xi.

47. W.E. Henley, 'Ex Libris – Concerning Atkins', p. 283.

48. 'Socialism in Excelsis', in *Scots Observer*, 1, 1889, p. 377.

49. A. Guillaume, *William Ernest Henley*, ch. xi.

50. W.E. Henley, *National Review*, p. xxu, 1893, pp. 268–71.

51. J.H. Buckley, *William Ernest Henley*, Preface.

52. W.E. Henley, *National Review*, p. 270.

53. J.H. Buckley, *William Ernest Henley*, chs 9 and 10.

54. W.E. Henley, 'Ex Libris – Concerning Atkins', p. 283.

55. J. Bailey, *The Poetry of Thomas Hardy* (Chapel Hill, University of North Carolina Press, 1970). See also R.T. Hopkins, *Thomas Hardy's Dorset* (London, Cecil Palmer, 1922).

56. R. Williams, 'Thomas Hardy', in *Critical Quarterly*, vol. vi, 1964, pp. 341–51.

57. Ibid., p. 345.

58. T. Hardy, 'The Dorsetshire Labourer', in T. Hardy, *Life and Art* (NY, Haskell House, 1966), pp. 20–47. (First published in *Longman's Magazine*, July 1883, pp. 252–69.)

59. Ibid., p. 23.

60. Ibid., p. 24.

61. Ibid., p. 25.

62. Ibid., p. 21.

63. The poems were written and published very quickly, while events were still fresh in the public mind. Hardy also chose to use 'popular' newspapers which would have a wide readership, such as the *Daily Chronicle* and the *Graphic*. See F.E. Hardy, *The Life of Thomas Hardy* (London, Macmillan, 1962), pp. 84–5.

64. H. Orel, *The Final Years of Thomas Hardy* (London, Macmillan, 1976), ch. 8. See also K.R. King and W. Morgan, 'Hardy and the Boer War: The Public Poet in Spite of Himself', in *Victorian Poetry*, vol. 17, pp. 66–84.

65. K.R. King and W. Morgan, 'Hardy and the Boer War'.

66. T. Hardy, *The Complete Poems*, ed. J. Gibson (London, Macmillan, 1976), p. 86. Hereafter, any quotation from this edition will be followed by the abbreviation *CP* and the page number.
67. K.R. King and W. Morgan, 'Hardy and the Boer War'.
68. J. Hazen, 'Hardy's War Poetry', an internally printed collection of papers (University of Nevada, 1980), p. 85.
69. Letter to Florence Henniker (24/12/1900) in *Collected Letters of Thomas Hardy*, vol. 2, R.T. Purdy and M. Millgate (eds) (Oxford University Press, 1980), p. 277.
70. Ibid., p. 235.
71. Ibid., p. 277.
72. Quoted in K.R. King and W. Morgan, 'Hardy and the Boer War', p. 72.

6   Disoriented Fictions: Indian Mutiny Novels

1. B. Gupta, *India in English Fiction 1800–1970: An Annotated Bibliography* (New Jersey, Scarecrow Press, 1973). Primary sources were also found in the London Library catalogue. The novels in this chapter were first discussed in *Encounter*. See S. Attridge, 'Dis-Oriented Fictions', in *Encounter*, vol. LXVI no. 2., February 1986, pp. 438–61.
2. E.W. Said, *Orientalism* (London, RKP, 1978), p. 1. See also, P. Brantlinger, *Rule of Darkness: British Literature and Imperialism 1830–1914* (Ithica, NY, Cornell University Press, 1988); I.S. Talib, 'In Celebration of Said's Orientalism: Twenty years', in *World Literature Written in English*, vol. 36, no. 2 (1997).
3. For an extended discussion of this, see, for example, R. Shannon, *The Crisis of Imperialism 1865–1915* (London, Granada Publishing Ltd, 1975).
4. J.E. Ruddock, *The Great White Hand* (London, Hutchinson & Co., 1896), p. XI. Hereafter, any quotation from this text will be followed by the letters *GWH*, followed by the page number.
5. R.H. Hutton, 'Mr Arnold and his Creed', in *Contemporary Review*, vol. XIV, June 1870, pp. 329–41.
6. F.A. Steel, *On the Face of the Waters* (London, Heinemann, 1897), p. 240. Hereafter, any quotation from this text will be followed by the letters *OFW*, followed by the page number.
7. E. Lynn, *A Hero of the Mutiny* (London, W. & R. Chambers Ltd, 1913), p. v. Hereafter, any quotation from this text will be followed by the letters *AHM*, followed by the page number.
8. A.H. Miles and J. Paltte (eds), *52 Stories of the Indian Mutiny* (London, Hutchinson, 1895), p. 20. Hereafter, any quotation from this text will be followed by *52S*, followed by the page number.
9. See H. John Field, *Towards a Programme of Imperial Life. The British Empire at the Turn of the Century* (Oxford, Clio Press, 1982).
10. 'The Indian Mutiny in Fiction', in *Blackwood's Edinburgh Magazine*, vol. CLXI, February 1897, pp. 218–31, 219.
11. J.E. Ruddock, *The Great White Hand*, p. 6.
12. H.S. Merriman, *Flotsam* (London, Longman's, Green & Co., 1896), p. 42. Hereafter, any quotation from this text will be followed by the letter *F*, followed by the page number.

13. Lord Roberts, *Forty One Years in India* (London, Macmillan & Co., 1901), p. ix. Hereafter, any quotation from this text will be followed by *FOY*, followed by the page number.
14. J.R. Seeley, *The Expansion of England*, ed. John Gross (Chicago, 1971), p. 161.
15. David Fieldhouse, 'Can Humpty-Dumpty be Put Together Again? Imperial History in the 1980s', in *The Journal of Imperial and Commonwealth History*, vol. xii, January 1984, no. 2, pp. 9–23, 9. See also Deborah Wormell, *Sir John Seeley and the Uses of History* (Cambridge University Press, 1980), pp. 1–10.
16. For example, G.A. Henty, who wrote nine adventure novels set in India, enjoyed a circulation of 150000 to 250000 a year by 1898. (R.S. Kennedy and B.J. Farmer, *Bibliography of G.A. Henty and Hentyana*, London, 1955, p. 21.) There is still a Henty newsletter.
17. Edward Farley Oaten, *A Sketch of Anglo Indian Literature* (London, Kegan Paul, 1908), p. 14.
18. Rev. Caesar Caine (ed.), *Barracks and Battlefields in India* (York, John Sampson, 1891), p. 116.
19. F.S. Brereton, *A Hero of Lucknow* (London, Blackie & Son, 1905), p. 82. Hereafter, any quotation from this text will be followed by *AHL*, followed by the page number.
20. Charlotte Despard, *The Rajah's Heir* (London, 1890), vol. 11, p. 6.
21. P. Wentworth, *The Devil's Wind* (London, Andrew Melrose, 1912). Hereafter, any quotation from this text will be followed by *DW*, followed by the page number.
22. Quoted in B. Gardner, *The East India Company* (London, Hart Davis, 1971), p. 81.
23. K.R. Iyengar, Srinivasa, *The Indian Mutiny in English* (London, Asian Publishing House, 1962), p. 7.
24. For a further discussion, see Allan, J. Greenberger, *The British Image of India* (London, Oxford University Press, 1969), pp. 11–12.
25. Lucy Taylor, *Sahib and Sepoy* (London, 1897), p. 239.
26. T.B. Strange, *Gunner Jingo's Jubilee* (London, Remington & Co., 1893), p. 138. Hereafter, any quotation from this text will be followed by *GJJ*, followed by the page number.
27. Philip Meadows Taylor, *Confessions of a Thug*, 3 vols (London, Richard Bentley, 1840), pp. 60–1.
28. G.A. Henty, *On the Irrawaddy* (NY, Charles Scribner & Sons, 1914), p. 186. See also Mark, Naidis, 'G.A. Henty's Idea of India', in *Victorian Studies*, September 1964, vol. viii, no. 1, pp. 49–58.
29. Edward J. Thompson, *The Other Side of the Medal* (London, Hogarth Press, 1925), p. 6. See also F. Metcalf and R. Thomas, *The Aftermath of Revolt: India 1857–1870* (Princetown, 1965), p. 310.
30. A.T. Embree discusses the role of sepoys who fought with the British in his review of historical works on the Mutiny, in *Victorian Studies*, vol. iii, no. 3, March 1965, pp. 288–90.
31. D.H. Thomas, *The Touchstone of Peril*, 2 vols (n.p., 1886), p. 17.
32. M. Naidis, 'G.A. Henty's Idea of India', p. 49.
33. R.H. James, *The Rise and Fall of the British Empire* (London, Abacus, 1997), p. 209.
34 R.H. Macdonald, 'Reproducing the Middle-Class Boy: From Purity to Patriotism in the Boys' Magazines, 1892–1914', in *Journal of Contemporary History*, 24, 1989.

35. Other novels surveyed are cited below, and are included in the general bibliography:

   Cotes, E., *Story of Sony Sahib* (London, n.p., 1894).
   Croker, B., *Beyond the Pale* (London, Chatto & Windus, 1897).
   Croker, B., *Village Tales and Jungle Tragedies* (London, Chatto & Windus, 1895).
   Fenn, C., *For the Old Flag* (London, Harrap & Co., 1899).
   Hume, N., *The Queen's Desire* (London, n.p., 1901).
   Jackson, A., *Brave Girl, A True Story of the Indian Mutiny* (London, n.p., 1899).
   Kipling, R., *Kim* (London, Macmillan, 1901).
   Lillie, A., *An Indian Wizard* (London, Chatto & Windus, 1887).
   Steel, F.A., *The Hosts of the Lord* (London, Heinemann, 1900).
   Taylor, P.M., *Confessions of a Thug*, 3 vols (London, Richard Bentley, 1840).

7   The African Adventure Game: Reconstruction of the Hero

1. D. Weinstock, 'The Boer War in the Novel in English, 1884–1966: A Descriptive and Critical Bibliography', PhD, University of California, 1968, University of Microfilms, p. 16.
2. See S. Koss (ed.), *The Pro-Boers: The Anatomy of an Anti-War Movement* (University of Chicago Press, 1973).
3. F. Hume, *A Traitor in London* (London, John Long, 1900). Hereafter, any quotation from this text will be followed by the letters *ATL*, followed by the page number.
4. C. Radziwill, *The Resurrection of Peter. A Reply to Olive Schreiner* (London, Hurst Blackett Ltd, 1900). Hereafter, any quotation from this text will be followed by the letters *RP*, followed by the page number.
5. O. Schreiner, *Trooper Peter Halket of Mashonaland* (Boston MA, Robert Bros., 1897). Hereafter, any quotation from this text will be followed by the Letters *TPH*, followed by the page number.
6. See, for example, W.E. Cairnes, *The Absent-Minded War* (London, Milne, 1900). For a later discussion, see Edward M. Spiers, *The Army and Society 1815–1914* (London, Longman, 1980).
7. D. Reitz, *Commando, A Boer Journal of the Boer War* (London, Faber & Faber, 1983), p. 221. The journal was written in 1903 and first published in 1929. Other works include: *The Memoirs of General Ben Bouwer*, as written by P.J. Le Riche, cloth bound (1980); *The War Memoirs of Commandant Ludwig Krause 1899–1900*, ed. J. Taitz, Van Riebeeck Society, Second series no. 26, (Cape Town, 1996).
8. See, for example, T. Pakenham, *The Boer War* (London, Weidenfield & Nicolson, 1979), ch. 33. See also I. Jones, 'The Boer War', in *History Today*, vol. 34, May 1984, pp. 46–9.
9. A.G. Hales, *Telegraph Dick. A London Lad's Adventures in Africa* (London, Cassell & Co., 1907). Hereafter, any quotation from this text will be followed by the letters *TD*, followed by the page number.
10. A.G. Hales, *McGlusky: Being A Compilation from the Diary of Trooper McWiddy of Remington's Scouts* (London, Anthony Traherne & Co., 1902). Hereafter, any quotation from this text will be followed by the letter *M*, followed by the page number.

11. Ibid., p. 305.
12. From a speech given by Schreiner at a public meeting in Cape Town on 9 July 1900. See *The Letters of Olive Schreiner 1876–1920*, S.C. Cronwreight-Schreiner (ed.) (London, T. Fisher Unwin, 1924), p. 373.
13. O. Rhoscomyl, *Old Fireproof* (London, Duckworth & Co., 1906). Hereafter, any quotation from this text will be followed by the letters *OF*, followed by the page number.
14. Ibid., pp. 18–19.
15. See, for example, G.M. Fenn, *George Alfred Henty: The Story of an Active Life* (London, Blackie & Son, 1907).
16. G.A. Henty, *With Roberts to Pretoria (A Tale of the South African War)* (London, Blackie & Son, 1902). Hereafter, any quotation from this text will be followed by the letters *WRP*, followed by the page number.
17. A. Conan Doyle, *The War in South Africa. Its Cause and Conduct* (London, Smith, Elder & Co., 1902). This book was written as a response to critics of Britain's role in the war, as Doyle himself states in the Preface. His position as historical commentator is to say the least, ambiguous. He wishes to plead the British cause yet also remain an 'independent' commentator; he feels compelled by duty to 'lay the facts before the world', yet these 'facts' appear to be a product of 'national honour' rather than historical objectivity. Before the case is argued, it is taken as a premise that 'the British government has done its best to avoid war, and the British army to wage it with humanity'. Of further interest are Doyle's assumptions about the history of South Africa; for him, the 'beginning' of this history is when white settlers first arrive, and the history of indigenous people is apparently irrelevant. Also, his vocabulary creates place as commodity, a common feature of colonial thinking; words like 'purchase', 'bargain', 'estate' occur frequently to the extent that the value of South Africa to the British is as 'a house of call upon the way to India' (p. 10).
18. R. Scholes, *Fabulation and Metafiction* (Urbana, University of Illinois Press, 1979), p. 3.
19. Ibid., p. 208.
20. See D. Wormell, *Sir John Seeley and the Uses of History* (Cambridge University Press, 1980), pp. 1–10.
21. D. Fieldhouse, 'Can Humpty-Dumpty be Put Together Again? Imperial History in the 1980s', in *The Journal of Imperial and Commonwealth History*, vol. XII, January 1984, no. 2, pp. 9–23, 9.
22. S.L. Milburg-Stean, *European and African Stereotypes in Twentieth-Century Fiction* (London, Macmillan, 1980), esp. pp. 4–5.
23. B. Parry, *Conrad and Imperialism (Ideological Boundaries and Visionary Frontiers)* (London, Macmillan, 1983), p. 13. See also P. Brantlinger, *Rule of Darkness: British Literature and Imperialism 1830–1914* (Ithica, NY, Cornell University Press, 1988); P. Lalu, 'The Grammar of Domination and the Subjection of Agency: Colonial Texts and Modes of Evidence', in *History and Theory, Studies in the Philosophy of History*, vol. 39, no. 4, December 2000; for an article on developments during the 1990s in thinking about theory and colonialism see R. Wilson, 'Afterword' in *Cultural Studies*, vol. 14 no. 3/4, July/October 2000, pp 593–605.
24. O. Ransford and David Livingstone, *The Dark Interior* (London, John Murray, 1978), p. 118. Ransford has written three books on the South African War: *The Battle of Majuba Hill*, *The Battle of Spion Kop*, *The Great Trek*.

25. Ibid., p. 74.
26. Ibid.
27. See, for example, P. Howarth, *Play Up and Play the Game. Heroes of Popular Fiction* (London, Eyre-Methuen, 1973).
28. As editor of the *Pall Mall Gazette*, W.T. Stead had been a strident, imperialist and his capitulation was equally impassioned; his *Review of Reviews* was extremely pro-Boer and he wrote and campaigned against the British position both during and after the war. He was clearly able to antagonize others into responding. In *The War in South Africa. Its Cause and Conduct*, Stead is one of the few critical voices Doyle names and seeks to refute. Stead's view of *The Tempest* as an allegory of the war, which I discuss in this chapter, irritated the *Era* into satirically responding to Stead's ideological reading of the play (*Era*, 22 October 1904). See also Raymond L. Schultz, *Crusader in Babylon. W.T. Stead and the Pall Mall Gazette* (Lincoln, University of Nebraska Press, 1974).
29. For a discussion of Cairnes' criticisms, see Spiers, *The Army and Society*, ch. 9.
30. T. Bevan, *Dick Dale, the Colonial Scout: A Tale of the Transvaal War of 1899–1900* (London, S.W. Partridge, 1900), p. 189.
31. G.K. Chesterton, *The Napoleon of Notting Hill* (London, John Lane, 1904), p. 196.
32. G. Wilton, *Scapegoats of the Empire* (London, Angus & Robertson, 1982), p. 2 (first published in 1902). This novel has been dramatized as a film, *Breaker Morant*.
33. N. Dixon, *On the Psychology of Military Incompetence* (London, Jonathan Cape, 1976), p. 220.
34. T. Pakenham, *The Boer War*, op. cit., p. 457. Pakenham shows that even early in the twentieth century Buller's reputation was being reclaimed and defended by eminent military commentators. Buller was a victim of the fierce hostilities between the 'Indians' and the 'Africans' in the War Department (see my Introduction). He was made a scapegoat for military blunders by Leo Amery, a lackey of Roberts, and whose polemical *The Times History of the War in South Africa* (7 vols, 1900–09) is both impressive and impressively partisan.
35. J. Symons, *Buller's Campaign* (London, The Cresset Press, 1963), p. 293. See also P. Trew, *The Boer War Generals* (Sutton Publishing, 1999).
36. W.E. Cairnes, *The Absent-Minded War* (London, Milne, 1900), p. 146.
37. E.M. Spiers, *The Army and Society*, p. 246.
38. 'Romance' is a notoriously difficult term. I have tried throughout to gauge what each writer intends – Henley's concept of character, history and imperial mission, for example, and here, in *Old Fireproof*, to denote adventure and enchantment, a more medieval idea of the picturesque and Promethean. In its relation to Romanticism, the term is both international and national, and can have nationalistic assumptions, as in Henley's work. See S. Curran (ed.), *The Cambridge Companion to Romanticism* (Cambridge University Press, 1993); I. Berlin, *The Roots of Romanticism* (Pimlico Books, 2000); D.B. Brown, *Romanticism* (London, Phaidon Press, 2001); D. Wu (ed.), *Romanticism* (Blackwell, 1995).
39. See M. Roper and J. Tosh, *Manful Assertions. Masculinities in Britain since 1800* (London, Routledge, 1991), esp. ch. 6. Also, G. Dawson, *Soldier Heroes: British Adventure, Empire and the Imagining of Masculinities* (London,

Routledge, 1994), although this work tends towards autobiographical self-indulgence in later parts, amounting to little more than the realization that playing soldiers as a little boy has something to do with masculinity.

40. Ibid., p. 207.
41. See R. Greenwall, *Artists and Illustrators of the Anglo-Boer War* (Fernwood Press, 1994).
42. The concept of 'character' has only relatively recently received serious attention from historians. See, for example, H.J. Field, *Towards a Programme of Imperial Life: The British Empire at the Turn of the Century* (Oxford, Clio Press, 1982).
43. C.E. Caldwell, *Small Wars: Their Principle and Practice* (London, HMSO, 1896), pp. 75–6.
44. H. Ridley, *Images of Imperial Rule* (London, Croom Helm, 1983).
45. G. Henty, *With Buller in Natal*, op. cit., p. 15.
46. T.R. Griffiths, 'Caliban and Colonialism', in *Yearbook of English Studies*, vol. 13, 1983, p. 171.
47. Ibid.
48. Ibid., p. 171.
49. See, for example, D. Bivona, *Desire and Contradiction: Imperial Visions and Domestic Debates in Victorian Literature* (Manchester University Press, 1990).
50. B. Parry, *Conrad and Imperialism*, p. 21.
51. In a letter to J.T. Lloyd, Schreiner stated: 'The book I have written (Peter Halket) has cost me more than anything I ever wrote, and I am broadening my back already for the Chartered Company attacks. I do not think I feel anything so much as the attacks from members of my own family'. Written December 1896. *The Letters of Olive Schreiner 1876–1920*, p. 233.
52. I base this conclusion on a systematic study of Boer War novels and accounts which cite novels; those not already discussed in the chapter are cited below for easy reference and are also included in the concluding bibliography:

Aitken, W.F., *Baden-Powell: The Hero of Mafeking* (London, S.W. Partridge & Co., 1900).

Arthur, R., 'The Death of a Coward', in *Pall Mall Magazine*, vol. 20, 1900, pp. 273–7.

Arthur, R., *Our Heroes of the South African War*, parts 1–4 (London, George Newnes Ltd, 1900).

Blackburn, D., *A Burgher Quixote* (Edinburgh, Blackwood & Sons, 1900).

Blatchford, R., *Dismal England* (London, Walter Scott, 1899).

Blatchford, R., *My Life in the Army* (London, Clarion Press, 1904).

Blore, H., *An Imperial Light Horseman* (London, C. Arthur Pearson, 1900).

Bowen, H.C., *Descriptive Catalogue of Historical Novels and Tales* (London, Edward Stanford, 1905).

Cossins, G., *A Boer of To-Day: A Story of the Transvaal* (London, George Allen, 1900).

Gallagher, M., *Mick Gallagher at the Front* (Liverpool, n.p., 1900).

Hayens, H., *Scouting for Buller* (London, T. Nelson & Co., 1901).

Jay, E., *The Queen's Own Traitors: Being an Account of the Desperate Enterprise of Billy, Lord Wrackington* (London, Hutchinson, 1904).

Kestell, J.D., *Through Shot and Flame: The Adventures of J.D. Kestell* (London, Methuen, 1903). [1902]

Lloyd, J.B., *1,000 miles with the C.I.V.* (London, Methuen, 1901).
Merriman, H., *Barlasch of the Guard* (London, Smith, Elder & Co., 1903).
Mitford, B., *Aletta* (London, Blackie & Son, 1900).
Moor, C., *Marina De La Rey* (London, T. Nelson & Co., 1900).
Neilly, J.E., *Besieged with B-P, Siege of Mafeking* (London, C.A. Pearson, 1900).
Nicholson, L., 'A Boer Love Story', in *Pall Mall Magazine*, vol.7, 1899–1900, pp. 723–35.
Nisbet, F., *The Empire Makers* (London, F.W. White & Co., 1900).
Robertson, J.M., *Wrecking the Empire* (London, Grant Richards, 1901).
Steevens, G.W., *From Capetown to Ladysmith* (London, Blackwood, 1900).
Wilson, H.W., *With the Flat to Pretoria. A History of the Boer War of 1899–1902* (London, n.p., 1900–02).

Conclusion

1. I.S. Talib, 'In Celebration of Said's Orientalism: Twenty Years', in *World Literature Written in English*, vol. 36, no. 2 (1997), p. 4.

Bibliography

I. Primary Sources

Aitken, W.F., *Baden Powell: The Hero of Mafeking* (London, S.W. Partridge & Co., 1900).

Arthur, R., *Our Heroes of the South African War*, parts 1–4 (London, George Newnes Ltd, 1900).

Baden-Powell, R., *Scouting for Boys*, 2nd edn (London, 1908).

Bate, H., *The Transvaal War* (London, George Stoneman, 1900), p. 3.

Beg, C., *Tommy Atkins at Home* (London, Gale & Polden, 1901).

Begbie, H., *The Handyman and Other Verses* (London, Grant Richards, 1900).

Bennett, N., *The Little Bugler and Other War Lyrics* (London, Elliot Stock, 1900).

Bevan, T., *Dick Dale, the Colonial Scout: A Tale of the Transvaal War of 1899–1900* (London, S.W. Partridge, 1900).

Blackburn, D., *A Burgher Quixote* (Edinburgh, Blackwood & Sons, 1900).

Blatchford, R., *Tommy Atkins of the Rumchowders* (London, Edward Arnold, 1895).

——*Dismal England* (London, Walter Scott, 1899).

——*My Life in the Army* (London, Clarion Press, 1904).

Blore, H., *An Imperial Light Horseman* (London, C. Arthur Pearson, 1900).

Boehmer, E., *Colonial and Postcolonial Literature: Migrant Metaphors* (Oxford University Press, 1995).

Bouwer, B., *The Memoirs of General Ben Bouwer*, as written by P.J. Le Riche, cloth bound (Cape Town, 1980).

Bowen, H.C., *Descriptive Catalogue of Historical Novels and Tales* (London, Edward Stanford, 1905).

Bray, R., *The Town Child* (London, Fisher & Unwin, 1907).

Brereton, F.S., *A Hero of Lucknow* (London, Blackie & Son, 1905).

British Library Manuscripts Collection: Lord Chamberlain's Plays.

Caine, Rev. Caesar (ed.), *Barracks and Battlefields in India* (York, John Sampson, 1891).

Callwell, C.E., *Small Wars: Their Principle and Practice* (London, HMSO, 1896).

Chesterton, G.K., *The Napoleon of Notting Hill* (London, John Lane, 1904).

——*Heretics* (London, John Lane, 1905), pp. 288–9.

Coldstreamer (Harry Graham), *Ballads of the Boer War* (London, Grant Richards, 1902).

Cossins, G., *A Boer of To-Day: A Story of the Transvaal* (London, George Allen, 1900).

Cotes, E., *Story of Sony Sahib* (London, n.p., 1894).

Croker, B., *Village Tales and Jungle Tragedies* (London, Chatto & Windus, 1895).

——*Beyond the Pale* (London, Chatto & Windus, 1897).

Crosland, T.W.H., *The Five Notions* (London, Grant Richards, 1903).

Despard, Charlotte, *The Rajah's Heir* (London, n.p., 1890).

Fenn, C., *For the Old Flag* (London, Harrap & Co., 1899).

Francis and Day's Album of Famous Old Songs, Francis, Day & Hunter (bound, Birmingham Public Library, 1970).

Gallagher, M., *Mick Gallagher at the Front* (Liverpool, privately printed, 1900).
Hales, A.G., *McGlusky: Being a Compilation from the Diary of Trooper McWiddy of Remington's Scouts* (London, Anthony Traherne & Co., 1902).
Hardy, T., *Collected Poems* (London, Macmillan, 1962).
—— *Life and Art* (New York, Haskell House, 1966).
—— *The Complete Poems*, Gibson, J. (ed.) (London, Macmillan, 1976).
Hayens, H., *Scouting for Buller* (London, T. Nelson & Co., 1902) [1901].
Henley, W.E., *Poems* (London, David Nutt, 1898).
—— *For England's Sake* (London, David Nutt, 1900).
—— *Views and Reviews. Essays in Appreciation* (London, David Nutt, 1902).
Henty, G., *With Buller in Natal* (London, Blackie & Son, 1900).
—— *With Roberts to Pretoria* (London, Blackie & Son, 1902).
—— *On the Irrawaddy* (New York, Charles Scribner & Sons, 1914).
Hume, F., *A Traitor in London* (London, John Long, 1900).
—— *The Queen's Desire* (London, n.p., 1901).
Jackson, A., *Brave Girl, A True Story of the Indian Mutiny* (London, n.p., 1899).
Jay, E., *The Queen's Own Traitors: Being an Account of the Desperate Enterprise of Billy, Lord Wrackington* (London, Hutchinson, 1904).
Kestell, J.D., *Through Shot and Flame: The Adventures of J.D. Kestell* (London, Methuen, 1903) [1902].
Kingston, W.H.G., *Our Soldiers* (London, n.p., 1902).
Kipling, R., *Barrack Room Ballads and Other Verses* (London, Methuen, 1892).
—— *Kim* (London, Macmillan, 1901).
—— *Rudyard Kipling's Verse. Definitive Edition* (London, Hodder & Stoughton, 1948).
—— *Something of Myself* (London, Macmillan, 1964).
Krause, L., *The War Memoirs of Commandant Ludwig Krause 1899–1900*, Taitz, J. (ed.), Van Riebeeck Society, Second series no. 26 (Cape Town, privately printed, 1996).
Lillie, A., *An Indian Wizard* (London, Chatto & Windus, 1887).
Lloyd, J.B., *1,000 Miles with the C.I.V.* (London, Methuen, 1901).
The London Reciter and Popular Reader (London, W.S. Fortey, 1891).
Lynn, E., *A Hero of the Mutiny* (London, W. & R. Chambers Ltd. 1913).
MacCarthy, R. and O'Moore, R., *The Romance of the Boer War (Humours and Chivalry of the Campaign)* (London, Elliot Stock, 1901).
Masterman, C.F.G., *From the Abyss* (London, T. Fisher Unwin, 1895).
—— *Heart of the Empire* (London, Harvester Press, 1973. First published 1901).
Maxwell, H.E., *British Soldiers in the Field* (London, n.p., 1902).
Merriman, H., *Barlasch of the Guard* (London, Smith, Elder & Co., 1903).
Merriman, H.S., *Flotsam* (London, Longman's, Green & Co., 1896).
Miles, A.H. and Paltte, J. (eds), *52 Stories of the Indian Mutiny* (London, Hutchinson, 1895).
Milne, J., *The Epistles of Atkins* (London, Dent & Sons, 1900).
Mitford, B., *Aletta* (London, Blackie & Son, 1900).
Moor, C., *Marina De La Rey* (London, T. Nelson & Co., 1900).
Music Hall Songster (London, W.S. Fortey, 1893).
National Army Museum Archives.
Neilly, J.E., *Besieged with B-P, Siege of Mafeking* (London, C.A. Pearson, 1900).
Newbolt, H., *The Sailing of the Long Ships* (London, John Murray, 1902).
Nisbet, F., *The Empire Makers, A romance of adventure and war in South Africa* (London, F.W. White & Co., 1900).

Radziwill, C., *The Resurrection of Peter. A Reply to Olive Schreiner* (London, Hurst & Blackett Ltd, 1900).
Ralph, J., *War's Brighter Side: The Story of 'The Friend' Newspaper Edited by the Correspondents with Lord Robert's Forces, March–April 1900* (London, C. Arthur Pearson, 1901).
Ralph, J., *At Pretoria* (London, C. Arthur Pearson, 1901).
Reitz, D., *Commando* (London, Faber & Faber, 1983).
Rhoscomyl, O., *Old Fireproof* (London, Duckworth & Co., 1906).
Roberts, Lord, *Forty One Years in India* (London, Macmillan, 1901).
Robertson, J.M., *Wrecking the Empire* (London, Grant Richards, 1901).
Rook, C., *The Hooligan Nights* (London, Oxford University Press, 1979).
Ross, P.T., 'The Ballad of the Bayonet', privately printed, 1900.
Ruddock, J.E., *The Great White Hand* (London, Hutchinson & Co., 1896).
Schreiner, O., *Trooper Peter Halket of Mashonaland* (Boston, MA, Robert Bros., 1897).
Smith, J., *Ballads of the Boer War* (London, n.p., 1902).
A Soldier, *True Stories of South Africa* (London, T. Burleigh, 1899).
The Soldier's Life, from Enlistment to his Return Home, Exhibiting the Trials and Hardships of Battle (London, W.S. Fortey, 1900).
Steel, F.A., *On the Face of the Waters* (London, Heinemann, 1897).
—— *The Hosts of the Lord* (London, Heinemann, 1900).
Steevens, G.W., *From Capetown to Ladysmith* (London, Blackwood, 1900).
Strange, T.B., *Gunner Jingo's Jubilee* (London, Remington & Co., 1893).
Taylor, Lucy, *Sahib and Sepoy* (London, J.F. Shaw & Co., 1897).
Taylor, Philip Meadows, *Confessions of a Thug*, 3 vols (London, Richard Bentley, 1840).
Thomas, D.H., pseud. [i.e. Forrest, R.E.T.] *The Touchstone of Peril*, (2 vols) (London, T. Fisher Unwin, 1886).
Wallace, E., *Writ in Barracks* (London, Methuen & Co., 1900).
Watson, W., *For England* (London, John Lane: The Bodley Head, 1904).
Wentworth, P., *The Devil's Wind* (London, Andrew Melrose, 1912).
Whitehouse, J. (ed.), *Problems of Boy Life* (London, King, 1912).
Wilson, H.W., *With the Flat to Pretoria. A History of the Boer War of 1899–1902* (London, n.p., 1900–02).

Articles, journals and newspapers

Anon., *Athenaeum*, No. 3261, 26/04/1890.
Arthur, R., 'The Death of a Coward', in *Pall Mall Magazine*, vol. 20, 1900, pp. 273–7.
Athenaeum
Black and White Budget
Daily Chronicle
The Era
Graphic
James, H., 'The British Soldier', in *Lippincott's Magazine*, XXII, August 1878, pp. 214–21.
Justice
Longman's Magazine
Morning Leader

Nicholson, L., 'A Boer Love Story', in *Pall Mall Magazine*, vol. 7, 1899–1900, pp. 723–35.
Pennell, E.R., 'The Pedigree of the Music Hall', in *The Contemporary Review*, vol. 63, April 1893, pp. 101–15.
Wyatt, H.F., 'War as the Supreme Test of National Value', in *The Nineteenth Century*, vol. XLV, 1899, pp. 216–25.
Punch
Reynolds News
Sandow's Magazine
The Sketch
The Spear
The Spectator
The Theatre
The Times
Truth

II. Secondary Sources

Adams, J.E., *Dandies and Desert Saints: Styles of Victorian Manhood* (Ithica, NY, Cornell University Press, 1995).
Amery, L.S. (ed.), *The Times History of the War in South Africa*, 7 vols (London, Sampson & Low, 1900–09).
Anderson, B., *Imagined Communities: Reflections on the Origin and Spread of Nationalism* (London, Verso, 1983), p. 40.
Arendt, H., *The Origins of Totalitarianism* (San Diego, CA, Harvest/HBJ, 1979), p. 17.
Arnold, G. *Hold Fast for England: G.A. Henty, Imperialist Boys Writer* (London, Hamish Hamilton, 1980).
Arnold, M., *Culture and Anarchy* (Harmondsworth, Penguin, 1971. First published 1869).
Auberton, R., *The Nineteen Hundreds* (London, Allen & Unwin, 1922).
Auden, W.H., Kallman, C., Greenberg, N. (eds), *An Elizabethan Song Book* (New York, Doubleday, 1956).
Bailey, J., *The Poetry of Thomas Hardy* (Chapel Hill, University of North Carolina Press, 1970).
Bailey, P., *Leisure and Class in Victorian England: Rational Recreation and the Contest for Control 1830–1885* (London, RKP, 1978).
—— (ed.), *Music Hall: The Business of Pleasure* (Oxford University Press, 1986).
——*Popular Culture and Performance in the Victorian City* (Cambridge University Press, 1998).
Baker, R.A., *Marie Lloyd: Queen of the Music Halls* (London, Robert Hale, 1990).
Bakhtin, M., 'Discourse in the Novel', in *The Dialogic Imagination: Four Essays*, M. Holquist (ed.), trans. M. Holquist and C. Emerson (Austin, University of Texas Press, 1981).
Barker, F. (ed.), *Colonial Discourse/Postcolonial Theory* (Manchester University Press, 1996).
Barthes, R., *Mythologies* (London, Granada, 1973).
——*Image – Music – Text* (London, Fontana, 1977).
Belsey, C., *Critical Practice* (London, Methuen, 1980).
Bennett, T. (ed.), *Popular Culture and Social Relations* (Oxford University Press, 1986).

Berlin, I., *The Roots of Romanticism* (London, Chatto & Windus, 1999).

Bhabha, H. (ed.), *Nation and Narration* (London, Routledge, 1990).

Biel, R., *The New Imperialism* (London, Zed Books, 2000).

Bivona, D., *Desire and Contradiction: Imperial Visions and Domestic Debates in Victorian Literature* (Manchester University Press, 1990).

Blanch, H.D., 'The Boer War and British Society', National Army Museum Archives, accession no. 7904–109.

Boehmer, E., *Colonial and Postcolonial Literature: Migrant Metaphors* (Oxford University Press, 1995).

Booth, J.B., *Old Pink 'Un Days* (London, Grant Richards, 1924).

——*A Pink 'Un Remembers* (London, T. Werner Laurie, 1937).

——*Seventy Years of Song* (London, Hutchinson & Co., 1941).

Booth, M. and Kaplan, J.H. (eds), *The Edwardian Theatre: Essays on Performance and the Stage* (Cambridge University Press, 1996).

Brantlinger, P., *Rule of Darkness: British Literature and Imperialism 1830–1914* (Ithica, NY, Cornell University Press, 1988).

Bratton, J.S. (ed.), *Music Hall: Performance and Style* (Milton Keynes, Open University Press, 1986).

——*et al.* (eds), *Acts of Supremacy: The British Empire and the Stage 1790–1930* (Manchester University Press, 1991).

Bristow, J., *Empire Boys: Adventures in a Man's World* (London, HarperCollins, 1991).

Brown, D.B., *Romanticism* (London, Phaidon Press, 2001).

Buckley, J.H., *William Ernest Henley, A Study in the 'Counter-Decadence' of the 'Nineties* (New Jersey, Princeton University Press, 1945).

Bullock, A. and Trombley, S. (eds), *The New Fontana Dictionary of Modern Thought*, 3rd edn (London, HarperCollins, 1999).

Butler, L.J., *Britain and Empire* (London, I.B. Tauris, 2001).

Cain, P. and Hopkins, A., *British Imperialism: Crisis and Deconstruction* (London, Longman, 1993).

——*British Imperialism: Innovation and Expansion 1688–1914* (London, Longman, 1993).

Cairnes, W.E., *The Absent-Minded War* (London, Milne, 1900).

Chesterton, G.K., *Autobiography* (London, Hutchinson & Co., 1937).

Cohen, E.H., *The Henley–Stevenson Quarrel* (Gainesville, The University Presses of Florida, 1974).

Collins, D. (ed.), *The Glass Walking Stick* (London, Methuen & Co., 1955).

Colvin, S. (ed.), *The Letters of Robert Louis Stevenson*, 4 vols (New York, Charles Scribner, 1925).

Conan Doyle, A., *The War in South Africa. Its Cause and Conduct* (London, Smith Elder & Co., 1902).

Cowham, J., *A New School Method* (London, n.p., 1900).

Cronwreight-Schreiner, S.C. (ed.), *The Letters of Olive Schreiner 1876–1920* (London, T. Fisher Unwin, 1924).

Curran, S. (ed.), *The Cambridge Companion to Romanticism* (Cambridge University Press, 1993).

Dawson, G., *Soldier Heroes: British Adventure, Empire and the Imagining of Masculinities* (London, Routledge, 1994).

Davey, A., *The British Pro-Boers 1877–1902* (Capetown, Tafelburg Publishers, 1978).

Davison, P., *Songs of the British Music Hall* (London, Oak Publications, 1971).

De Frece, Lady (Vesta Tilley), *Recollections of Vesta Tilley* (London, Hutchinson, 1934).

De Thiery, C., *Imperialism* (London, Duckworth & Co., 1898).
Dean, S., *Hardy's Poetic Vision in the Dynasts* (Princeton, NJ, Princeton University Press, 1977).
Dixon, N., *On the Psychology of Military Incompetence* (London, Jonathan Cape, 1976).
Doyle, B., *English and Englishness* (London, Routledge, 1989).
Encyclopedia Brittanica, 11th edn (1910–11).
Farson, D., *Marie Lloyd and Music Hall* (London, Tom Stacey Ltd, 1972).
Farwell, B., *The Great Boer War* (London, Allen Lane, 1977. First published NY, Harper & Row, 1975).
Fenn, G.M., *George Alfred Henty: The Story of an Active Life* (London, Blackie and Son, 1907).
Field, H.J., *Towards a Programme of Imperial Life: The British Empire at the Turn of the Century* (Oxford, Clio Press, 1982).
Fieldhouse, D., 'Can Humpty-Dumpty be Put Together Again? Imperial History in the 1980's', in *The Journal of Imperial and Commonwealth History*, vol. XII, January 1984, no. 2, pp. 9–23.
Fitzgerald, P., *Music Hall Land* (London, Ward & Downey, 1901).
Friedrichsmeyer, S. (ed.), *The Imperialist Imagination* (University of Michigan Press, 1999).
Fussell, P., *The Great War and Modern Memory* (London, Oxford University Press, 1975).
Gardner, B., *The East India Company* (London, Hart Davis, 1971).
Grainger, J.H., *Patriotisms. Britain: 1900–1939* (London, Routledge & Kegan Paul, 1986).
Green, R.L. (ed.), *Rudyard Kipling: The Critical Heritage* (London, RKP, 1971).
Greenberger, Allan, J., *The British Image of India* (London, Oxford University Press, 1969).
Greenwall, R., *Artists and Illustrators of the Anglo-Boer War* (Johannesburg, Fernwood Press, 1992).
Griffiths, R., *Patriotism Perverted* (London, Constable, 1998).
Guillaume, A., *William Ernest Henley et Son Groupe* (Paris, Librairie C. Klincksieck, 1973).
Gupta, B., *India in English Fiction 1800–1970: An Annotated Bibliography* (New Jersey, Scarecrow Press, 1973).
Hall, D., *The Hall Handbook of the Anglo-Boer War* (Pietermaritzburg, University of Natal, 1998).
Hardy, F.E., *The Life of Thomas Hardy* (London, Macmillan, 1962).
Harries-Jenkins, G., *The Army in Victorian Society* (London, RKP, 1977).
Hazen, J., 'Hardy's War Poetry', in internally printed collection of papers (University of Nevada, 1980), p. 85.
Henley, W.E., *Views and Reviews. Essays in Appreciation*, Vols 1 and 2 (London, David Nutt, 1902).
——and Farmer, J.S. (eds), *A Dictionary of Slang and Colloquial English* (London, Routledge, 1905).
Hobsbawm, E.J., *Industry and Empire* (Harmondsworth, Penguin, 1969).
——*The Age of Empire 1875–1914* (London, Weidenfield & Nicolson, 1987).
——*Nations and Nationalism since 1780* (Cambridge University Press, 1990), p. 108.
Hobson, *Imperialism: A Study* (London, George Allen & Unwin, 1902).
Hoggart, R., *The Uses of Literacy* (London, Chatto & Windus, 1957).

Hopkins, R.T., *Thomas Hardy's Dorset* (London, Cecil Palmer, 1922).

Howarth, P., *Play Up and Play the Game. Heroes of Popular Fiction* (London, Eyre-Methuen, 1973).

Howe, I., *Thomas Hardy* (London, Weidenfield & Nicolson, 1968).

Huggett, F.E., *Cartoonists at War* (London, Guild, 1981).

Iyengar Srinivasa, K.R., *The Indian Mutiny in English* (London, Asian Publishing House, 1962).

Jackson. T., *The Boer War*, Channel 4 Books (London, 1999).

Jacobs, N., *Our Marie* (London, Hutchinson, 1936).

James, L., *Fiction for the Working Man, 1830–1850* (London, Oxford University Press, 1963).

——*The Rise and Fall of the British Empire* (London, Abacus, 1997. First published London, Little, Brown, 1994).

Jones, H. and Jones, M., *Gazetteer of the Anglo-Boer War 1899–1902* (Milton Keynes Military Press, 1999).

Joyce, P., *Visions of the People. Industrial England and Questions of Class 1848–1914* (Cambridge University Press, 1991).

——*Democratic Subjects: the Self and the Social in Nineteenth Century England* (Cambridge University Press, 1994).

Kane, M., *Modern Men: Mapping Sexuality in English and German Literature, 1880–1930* (London, Cassell, 1999).

Keating, P.J., *The Working Classes in Victorian Fiction* (London, RKP, 1971).

Kennedy, R.S. and Farmer, B.J., *Bibliography of G.A. Henty and Hentyana* (London, B.J. Farmer, 1955).

Kiernan, V.G., *Poets, Politics and the People* (London, Verso, 1989).

Kift, D., trans. Kift, R., *The Victorian Music Hall, Culture, Class and Conflict* (Cambridge University Press, 1996).

Kilgarriff, M., *Grace, Beauty and Banjos: Peculiar Lives and Strange Times of Music Hall and Variety Artists* (London, Oberon Books, 1998).

Kingston, W.H.G., *Our Soldiers* (London, n.p., 1902).

Knight, I., *The Boer Wars 1898–1902* (London, Osprey, 1997).

Koss, S. (ed.), *The Pro-Boers: The Anatomy of an Anti-War Movement* (University of Chicago Press, 1973).

Lee, E., *To the Bitter End: A Photographic History of the Boer War 1899–1902* (USA, Penguin, 1987).

Lewis, R., *Gendering Orientalism* (London, Routledge, 1995).

Lloyd, A.L., *Folk Song in England* (London, Lawrence & Wishart, 1967).

Lloyd, T., *Empire* (Hambleden & London Ltd, 2001).

Lodge, D. (ed.), *Modern Criticism and Theory. A Reader* (London, Longman, 1988).

Low, R. and Manvell, R., *The History of the British Film 1896–1906* (London, George Allen & Unwin, 1948), pp. 66–8.

Macinnes, C., *Sweet Saturday Night* (London, MacGibbon and Kee, 1967).

Mackenzie, J.M., *Propaganda and Empire: The Manipulation of British Public Opinion 1880–1960* (Manchester University Press, 1984).

——(ed.), *Imperialism and Popular Culture* (Manchester University Press, 1986).

Macqueen-Pope, W., *The Melodies Linger On* (London, W.H. Allen, 1950).

Maitland, S., *Vesta Tilley* (London, Virgo Press, 1986).

Mander, R. and Mitchenson, J., *British Music Hall* (London, Gentry Books, 1974).

Marais, J.S., *The Fall of Kruger's Republic* (Oxford University Press, 1961).

Marx, K., *Grundisse* (Harmondsworth, Penguin Books, 1973).
Masterman, C.F.G., *Condition of England* (London, Methuen, 1960. First published 1909).
Metcalf, F. and Thomas, R., *The Aftermath of Revolt: India 1857–1870* (Princeton, NJ, Princeton University Press, 1965).
Milburg-Stean, S.L., *European and African Stereotypes in Twentieth-Century Fiction* (London, Macmillan, 1980).
Millin, S.G., *Rhodes* (London, Macmillan, 1933), p. 138.
Moretti, F., *Signs Taken for Wonders* (London, Verso, 1988).
Naidis, Mark, 'G.A. Henty's Idea of India', in *Victorian Studies*, September 1964, vol. VIII, no. 1, pp. 49–58.
National Army Museum Archives
Nava, M. and O'Shea, A. (eds), *Modern Times: Reflections on a Century of Modernity* (London, Routledge, 1996).
Newton, H.C., *Idols of the Halls* (Wakefield, E.P. Publishing Co., 1975. First published 1928).
Oaten, Edward Farley, *A Sketch of Anglo Indian Literature* (London, Kegan Paul, 1908).
Orel, H., *Thomas Hardy's Personal Writings* (London, Macmillan, 1967).
—— *The Final Years of Thomas Hardy* (London, Macmillan, 1976).
Oxford English Dictionary
Pakenham, T., *The Boer War* (London, Weidenfield & Nicolson, 1979).
Palmer, A., *Boer War Casualty Roll 1899–1902* (Military Minded Paperback, 1999).
Palmer, R., *Poverty Knock* (Cambridge University Press, 1974).
Parry, B., *Conrad and Imperialism (Ideological Boundaries and Frontiers)* (London, Macmillan, 1983).
Pearson, G., *Hooligan: A History of Respectable Fears* (London, Macmillan, 1983).
Pearson, K., *National Life and Character: A Forecast* (London, Dent, 1894).
Pemberton, W.B., *Battles of the Boer War* (London, Batsford, 1964).
Popular Culture (The Open University Press, 1981), Block 2, Unit 5.
Price, R., *An Imperial War and the British Working Class: Working Class Attitudes and Reactions to the Boer War 1899–1902* (London, RKP, 1972).
Pulling, C., *They Were Singing* (London, George G. Harrap, 1952).
Purdy, R.L. and Millgate, M. (eds), *Collected Letters of Thomas Hardy*, vol. 2 (Oxford University Press, 1980).
Ransford, O. and David Livingstone, *The Dark Interior* (London, John Murray, 1978).
Reese, T., *The History of the Royal Commonwealth Society* (London, Oxford University Press, 1968).
Ricketts, H., *The Unforgiving Minute: A Life of Rudyard Kipling* (London, Chatto & Windus, 1999).
Ridley, H., *Images of Imperial Rule* (London, Croom Helm, 1983).
Roper, M. and Tosh, J., *Manful Assertions: Masculinities in Britain since 1800* (London, Routledge, 1991).
Said, E.W., *Orientalism* (London, RKP, 1978).
—— 'Orientalism Reconsidered', in *Europe and its Others*, Proceedings of the Essex Conference on the Sociology of Literature, July 1984 (Colchester, University of Essex, 1985).
—— *Culture and Imperialism* (London, Chatto & Windus, 1993).
Samuel, R. (ed.), *Patriotism: The Making and Unmaking of British National Identity*, vols 1–3 (London, Routledge, 1989).

Scholes, R., *Fabulation and Metafiction* (Urbana, University of Illinois Press, 1979).

Schultz, R.L., *Crusader in Babylon. W.T. Stead and the Pall Mall Gazette* (University of Nebraska Press, 1974).

Seeley, J.R., *The Expansion of England*, (Leipzig, Bernhard Tauchnitz, 1884).

Semmel, B., *Imperialism and Social Reform* (Cambridge, Mass., 1976).

Shannon, R., *The Crisis of Imperialism 1865–1915* (London, Granada Publishing Ltd, 1975).

Sharpe, J., *Allegories of Empire* (University of Minnesota Press, 1993).

Smith, I., *The Origins of the South African War, 1899–1902* (Essex, Longman, 1992).

Smith, S., *British Imperialism* (Cambridge University Press, 1998).

Smith, Van Wyck, *Drumme Hodge: The Poetry of the Angles–Boer War (1899–1902)* (Oxford: Clarendon Press, 1978).

Snyder, L.L. (ed.), *The Imperialism Reader* (Princeton, NJ, D. Van Nostrand Company Inc., 1962).

The Soldier's Life, from Enlistment to His Return Home, Exhibiting the Trials and Hardships of Battle (London, W.S. Fortey, 1900).

Spiers, E.M., *The Army and Society 1815–1914* (London, Longman, 1980).

Steedman, C., *The Radical Soldier's Tale* (London, Routledge, 1988).

Stokes, J., *In the Nineties* (Hemel Hempstead, Harvester Wheatsheaf, 1989).

——(ed.), *Fin de Siècle/Fin du Globe: Fears and Fantasies of the Late Nineteenth Century* (New York, St. Martin's Press, 1992).

Sullivan, Z.T., *Narratives of Empire (The Fictions of Rudyard Kipling)* (Cambridge University Press, 1993).

Summerfield, P., 'Patriotism and Empire in Music Hall Entertainment, 1870–1914', in *Imperialism and Popular Culture*, J. Mackenzie (ed.), (Manchester University Press, 1986), pp. 17–48.

Symons, J., *Buller's Campaign* (London, The Cresset Press, 1963).

Taylor, C., *Philosophical Papers, Vol. I, Human Agency and Language* (Cambridge University Press, 1985).

Thompson, E.P., *The Making of the English Working Class* (London, Gollancz, 1963).

——*Customs in Common* (London, Merlin, 1991).

Thompson, Edward J., *The Other Side of the Medal* (London, Hogarth Press, 1925).

Titterton, W.R., *From Theatre to Music Hall* (London, Stephen Swift & Co., 1912).

Trew, P., *The Boer War Generals* (Gloucestershire, Sutton Publishing, 1999).

Van Wyk Smith, M., *Drummer Hodge: The Poetry of the Anglo-Boer War (1899–1902)*, (Oxford, Clarendon Press, 1978).

Vicinus, M., *The Industrial Muse* (London, Croom Helm, 1974).

Warren, A., 'Citizens of the Empire', in *Imperialism and Popular Culture*, ed. J.M. Mackenzie (Manchester University Press, 1986), pp. 232–56.

Warwick, P. (ed.), *The South African War: The Anglo-Boer War 1899–1902* (Essex, Longman, 1980).

Watson, I., *Song and Democratic Culture in Britain* (London, Croom Helm, 1983).

Webb, S. and Webb, B. (eds), *Minority Report of the Poor Law Commission 1909* (London, Kelley, 1974).

Weinstock, D., 'The Boer War in the Novel in English, 1884–1966: A Descriptive and Critical Bibliography', PhD, University of California, 1968.

White, A., *Joseph Conrad and the Adventure Tradition: Constructing and Deconstructing the Imperial Subject* (Cambridge University Press, 1993).

Williams, R., *Culture and Society* (London, Chatto & Windus, 1957).
—— *Marxism and Literature* (Oxford University Press, 1977).
—— *Keywords* (London, Fontana, 1984).
—— *Writing in Society* (London, Verso, 1986).
Wilton, G., *Scapegoats of the Empire* (London, Angus & Robertson, 1982).
Wormell, D., *Sir John Seeley and the Uses of History* (Cambridge University Press, 1980).
Wu, D. (ed.), *Romanticism* (Oxford, Blackwell, 1995).
Yeo, S. and E. (eds), *Popular Culture and Class Conflict, 1590–1914* (Sussex, Harvester, 1981).

Articles, journals and newspapers

Attridge, S., 'Dis-Oriented Fictions', in *Encounter*, vol. LXVI No. 2, February 1986, pp. 60–70.
Baden-Powell, R., 'Boy Scouts', in *National Defence*, vol. 4, August 1910, pp. 438–61.
Bennett, T., 'Marxism and Popular Fiction', in *Literature and History*, vol. 7:2, Autumn 1981, pp. 138–65.
Buchanan, R., 'The Voice of the Hooligan', in *Contemporary Review*, vol. LXXVI, December 1899, pp. 774–89.
Burroughs, P., 'John R. Seeley and British Imperial History', in *Journal of Imperial and Commonwealth History*, vol. 1, 1972–73, p. 192.
Cole, S., 'Modernism, Male Intimacy and the Great War', in *ELH*, Johns Hopkins University Press, vol. 68, no. 2, Summer 2001, pp. 469–500.
Cultural Studies, vol. 14, nos 3–4, 2000. (A retrospective on Orientalism and papers on current state of Colonial studies and Post-Colonial thinking.)
Cunningham, H., 'The Language of Patriotism, 1750–1914', in *History Workshop*, vol. 12, 1981, pp. 8–33, p. 10.
Davison, P., 'A Briton True: A Short Account of Patriotic Songs and Verse as Popular Entertainment', in *Alta*, University of Birmingham Review, Spring 1970, pp. 209–23.
Fieldhouse, David, 'Can Humpty-Dumpty be Put Together Again? Imperial History in the 1980s', in *The Journal of Imperial and Commonwealth History*, vol. XII, January 1984, no. 2, pp. 9–23.
Griffiths, T.R., 'Caliban and Colonialism', in *Yearbook of English Studies*, vol. 13, 1983, pp. 159–80.
Hazen, J., 'Hardy's War Poetry', an internally printed collection of papers, University of Nevada, 1980.
Henley, W.E., 'Socialism in Excelsis', in *The Scots Observer*, 1, 1889, pp. 377–8.
—— 'Ex Libris – Concerning Atkins', in *Pall Mall Magazine*, 1900, pp. xxi, 283.
Hodgkin, T., 'The Fall of the Roman Empire and Its Lesson for Us', in *Contemporary Review*, vol. 73, January 1898, pp. 65–90.
Hutton, R.H., 'Mr Arnold and his Creed', in *Contemporary Review*, vol. XIV, June 1870, pp. 329–41.
Jones, I., 'The Boer War', in *History Today*, vol. 34, May 1984, pp. 46–9.
Joyce, P., 'The End of Social History?', in *Social History*, 20, Jan 1995, pp. 73–91.
Kent, C., 'Victorian Social History: post Thompson, post Foucault, post Modern', in *Victorian Studies*, 40, Autumn 1996, pp. 97–133.
King, K.R. and Morgan, W., 'Hardy and the Boer War: The Public Poet in Spite of Himself', in *Victorian Poetry*, vol. 17, pp. 66–84.

Kipling, R., quoted in Simpson, D.H., 'Variations on an Imperial Theme', *R.C.S. Library Notes*, April 1965.

Lalu, P., 'The Grammar of Domination and the Subjection of Agency: Colonial Texts and Modes of Evidence', in *History and Theory, Studies in the Philosophy of History*, vol. 39, no. 4, December 2000.

Macdonald, R.H., 'Reproducing the Middle-Class Boy: From Purity to Patriotism in the Boys' Magazines, 1892–1914', in *Journal of Contemporary History*, 24, 1989.

Norton, C., 'The Poetry of Mr. Rudyard Kipling', in *Atlantic Monthly*, vol. LXXIX, January 1897, pp. 111–15.

'Oxford English Limited', conference notes, 8 March 1986.

Parry, B., 'Problems in Current Theories of Colonial Discourse', in *Oxford Literary Review*, vol. 9, nos 1–2, 1987, pp. 27–58, 40.

Said, E., 'Orientalism Reconsidered', in *Europe and its Others, Vol. 1: Proceedings of the Essex Conference on the Sociology of Literature*, July 1984 (Colchester, University of Essex, 1985), pp. 23–4.

Sandow, E., *Sandow's Magazine*, vol. XIV, March 1905, no. 87.

Schwartz, B., 'Night Battles: Hooligan and Citizen', in M. Nava and A. O'Shea (eds), *Modern Times: Reflections on a Century of Modernity* (London, Routledge, 1996).

Senelick, L., 'Politics as Entertainment: Victorian Music Hall Songs', in *Victorian Studies*, vol. 19, 1975, pp. 84–98.

Stedman Jones, G., 'Working Class Culture and Working Class Politics in London, 1870–1900', in *Journal of Social History*, 7, 1974, pp. 460–508.

Talib, I.S., 'In Celebration of Said's Orientalism. Twenty Years', in *World Literature Written in English*, vol. 36, no. 2 (1997).

'The Indian Mutiny in Fiction', in *Blackwood's Edinburgh Magazine*, February 1897, pp. 218–31, 219.

Williams, R., 'Thomas Hardy', in *Critical Quarterly*, vol. VI, 1964, pp. 341–51.

Wilson, R., 'Afterword', in *Cultural Studies*, vol. 14, no. 3/4, July/October 2000, pp. 593–605.

World Literature Written in English, vol. 36, no. 2, 1997.

Index